UTOPIAN IDENTITIES
A COGNITIVE APPROACH TO LITERARY COMPETITIONS

LEGENDA

LEGENDA is the Modern Humanities Research Association's book imprint for new research in the Humanities. Founded in 1995 by Malcolm Bowie and others within the University of Oxford, Legenda has always been a collaborative publishing enterprise, directly governed by scholars. The Modern Humanities Research Association (MHRA) joined this collaboration in 1998, became half-owner in 2004, in partnership with Maney Publishing and then Routledge, and has since 2016 been sole owner. Titles range from medieval texts to contemporary cinema and form a widely comparative view of the modern humanities, including works on Arabic, Catalan, English, French, German, Greek, Italian, Portuguese, Russian, Spanish, and Yiddish literature. Editorial boards and committees of more than 60 leading academic specialists work in collaboration with bodies such as the Society for French Studies, the British Comparative Literature Association and the Association of Hispanists of Great Britain & Ireland.

The MHRA encourages and promotes advanced study and research in the field of the modern humanities, especially modern European languages and literature, including English, and also cinema. It aims to break down the barriers between scholars working in different disciplines and to maintain the unity of humanistic scholarship. The Association fulfils this purpose through the publication of journals, bibliographies, monographs, critical editions, and the MHRA Style Guide, and by making grants in support of research. Membership is open to all who work in the Humanities, whether independent or in a University post, and the participation of younger colleagues entering the field is especially welcomed.

ALSO PUBLISHED BY THE ASSOCIATION

Critical Texts
Tudor and Stuart Translations • *New Translations* • *European Translations*
MHRA Library of Medieval Welsh Literature

MHRA Bibliographies
Publications of the Modern Humanities Research Association

The Annual Bibliography of English Language & Literature
Austrian Studies
Modern Language Review
Portuguese Studies
The Slavonic and East European Review
Working Papers in the Humanities
The Yearbook of English Studies

www.mhra.org.uk
www.legendabooks.com

STUDIES IN COMPARATIVE LITERATURE

Editorial Committee
Chairs: Dr Emily Finer (University of St Andrews)
and Professor Wen-chin Ouyang (SOAS, London)

Dr Dorota Goluch (Cardiff University)
Dr Priyamvada Gopal (Churchill College Cambridge)
Professor Duncan Large (British Centre for Literary Translation,
University of East Anglia)
Professor Timothy Mathews (University College London)
Professor Elinor Shaffer (School of Advanced Study, London)

Studies in Comparative Literature are produced in close collaboration with the British Comparative Literature Association, and range widely across comparative and theoretical topics in literary and translation studies, accommodating research at the interface between different artistic media and between the humanities and the sciences.

ALSO PUBLISHED IN THIS SERIES

20. *Aestheticism and the Philosophy of Death: Walter Pater and Post-Hegelianism*, by Giles Whiteley
21. *Blake, Lavater and Physiognomy*, by Sibylle Erle
22. *Rethinking the Concept of the Grotesque: Crashaw, Baudelaire, Magritte*, by Shun-Liang Chao
23. *The Art of Comparison: How Novels and Critics Compare*, by Catherine Brown
24. *Borges and Joyce: An Infinite Conversation*, by Patricia Novillo-Corvalán
25. *Prometheus in the Nineteenth Century: From Myth to Symbol*, by Caroline Corbeau-Parsons
26. *Architecture, Travellers and Writers: Constructing Histories of Perception*, by Anne Hultzsch
27. *Comparative Literature in Britain: National Identities, Transnational Dynamics 1800-2000*, by Joep Leerssen with Elinor Shaffer
28. *The Realist Author and Sympathetic Imagination*, by Sotirios Paraschas
29. *Iris Murdoch and Elias Canetti: Intellectual Allies*, by Elaine Morley
30. *Likenesses: Translation, Illustration, Interpretation*, by Matthew Reynolds
31. *Exile and Nomadism in French and Hispanic Women's Writing*, by Kate Averis
32. *Samuel Butler against the Professionals: Rethinking Lamarckism 1860–1900*, by David Gillott
33. *Byron, Shelley, and Goethe's Faust: An Epic Connection*, by Ben Hewitt
34. *Leopardi and Shelley: Discovery, Translation and Reception*, by Daniela Cerimonia
35. *Oscar Wilde and the Simulacrum: The Truth of Masks*, by Giles Whiteley
36. *The Modern Culture of Reginald Farrer: Landscape, Literature and Buddhism*, by Michael Charlesworth
37. *Translating Myth*, edited by Ben Pestell, Pietra Palazzolo and Leon Burnett
38. *Encounters with Albion: Britain and the British in Texts by Jewish Refugees from Nazism*, by Anthony Grenville
39. *The Rhetoric of Exile: Duress and the Imagining of Force*, by Vladimir Zorić
40. *From Puppet to Cyborg: Pinocchio's Posthuman Journey*, by Georgia Panteli
41. *Utopian Identities: A Cognitive Approach to Literary Competitions*, by Clementina Osti
43. *Sublime Conclusions: Last Man Narratives from Apocalypse to Death of God*, by Robert K. Weninger
44. *Arthur Symons: Poet, Critic, Vagabond*, edited by Elisa Bizzotto and Stefano Evangelista
45. *Scenographies of Perception: Sensuousness in Hegel, Novalis, Rilke, and Proust*, by Christian Jany
46. *Reflections in the Library: Selected Literary Essays 1926–1944*, by Antal Szerb
47. *Depicting the Divine: Mikhail Bulgakov and Thomas Mann*, by Olga G. Voronina
48. *Samuel Butler and the Evolutionary Debate: Science, Literature and Unconscious Memory*, by Cristiano Turbil
49. *Death Sentences: Literature and State Killing*, edited by Birte Christ and Ève Morisi
50. *Words Like Fire: Prophecy and Apocalypse in Apollinaire, Marinetti and Pound*, by James P. Leveque

Utopian Identities

A Cognitive Approach to Literary Competitions

Clementina Osti

LEGENDA
Studies in Comparative Literature 41
Modern Humanities Research Association
2018

Published by Legenda
an imprint of the Modern Humanities Research Association
Salisbury House, Station Road, Cambridge CB1 2LA

ISBN 978-1-78188-693-9 (HB)
ISBN 978-1-78188-420-1 (PB)

First published 2018

All rights reserved. No part of this publication may be reproduced or disseminated or transmitted in any form or by any means, electronic, mechanical, photocopying, recording or otherwise, or stored in any retrieval system, or otherwise used in any manner whatsoever without written permission of the copyright owner, except in accordance with the provisions of the Copyright, Designs and Patents Act 1988, or under the terms of a licence permitting restricted copying issued in the UK by the Copyright Licensing Agency Ltd, Saffron House, 6–10 Kirby Street, London EC1N 8TS, *England, or in the USA by the Copyright Clearance Center, 222 Rosewood Drive, Danvers MA 01923. Application for the written permission of the copyright owner to reproduce any part of this publication must be made by email to legenda@mhra.org.uk.*

Disclaimer: Statements of fact and opinion contained in this book are those of the author and not of the editors or the Modern Humanities Research Association. The publisher makes no representation, express or implied, in respect of the accuracy of the material in this book and cannot accept any legal responsibility or liability for any errors or omissions that may be made.

Trademark notice: Product or corporate names may be trademarks or registered trademarks, and are used only for identification and explanation without intent to infringe.

© *Modern Humanities Research Association 2018*

Copy-Editor: Anna Davies

CONTENTS

	Acknowledgements	ix
	Author's Note	x
	Introduction	1
1	France 1900–1918: Utopian Society	26
2	Italy 1920–1945: Utopian Travels	56
3	Spain 1950–1975: Utopia and Dystopia	113
	Conclusion	148
	Bibliography	152
	Appendix	159
	Index	173

*This book is dedicated to my mother, to whom I owe everything,
and to my father and my grandparents, who would have been so proud.*

ACKNOWLEDGEMENTS

I am extremely grateful for the sponsorship provided by the Legenda Editorial Board and by the British Comparative Literature Association. Without their generosity and their belief in my project, this book would never have been completed. I would like to express my gratitude to Dr Graham Nelson, Managing Editor, and to Dr Dorota Goluch who guided me through the process of publication with unwavering patience and great kindness.

This book is derived from a PhD thesis in comparative literature, completed at the University of Cambridge. I am extremely grateful for the sponsorships offered by the Gates Cambridge Trust and by the Arts and Humanities Research Council. My gratitude goes to Professor Sarah Kay who believed in me and endorsed my application, to Dr Martin Crowley whose help and advice spurred me on throughout the first, challenging, months of research and — last but not least — to my supervisor, Dr Peter J. Collier, for his stimulating suggestions, patient corrections and steadfast belief in my project.

I am so very grateful to all those — and there have been many indeed — who, in the Italian Ministry of Foreign Affairs, supported me through hard personal times and helped me face the challenges of studying while working. In particular, my heartfelt gratitude goes to all the colleagues in the Policy Planning Unit and in the Embassies in Vienna and Berlin for their understanding, kindness and wonderful friendship.

v.o., Rome, May 2018

AUTHOR'S NOTE

All translations in the text are the author's own — unless otherwise stated — and are provided as a convenience for the reader. They are only aimed at paraphrasing the meaning and are not intended to substitute professional translations. Terms for which no literal translation seems appropriate are explained with notes in the text.

All illustrations are the author's own unless otherwise stated.

INTRODUCTION

Projet ou fiction, [l'utopie] compense une réalité jugée insatisfaisante, à travers l'exposition d'un microcosme homogène et stable...[1]

[Whether project or fiction, [utopia] compensates for a reality which is deemed unsatisfactory, through the display of a homogeneous and stable microcosm...]

I am arguing for cognitive linguistics to be more sociolinguistics, and the means of doing this is by being more critically aware of **ideology** in language. [...] Our cognition is embodied and experiential, but cognitive science has paid insufficient attention to the social and ideological roots of shared human conditions and experiences. [...] In adopting a more critically sophisticated approach, we would also necessarily make connections between microstructural matters of word and grammar choice and the macro-structural matters of global ideology and viewpoint. We would be forced to reconnect individual sentences with co-text and context, and we would have to address the natural occurrence of text in relation to the social conditions of its readership and projected world. [...] All that is missing is an element of critical theory to connect the reading process with wider social concerns.[2]

Literary Competitions Criticism — An Overview

Martin Page's opinion that 'un prix littéraire ne dit rien de la qualité d'un roman'[3] [a literary prize doesn't say anything about the quality of a novel] appears to be a popular one amongst academics and writers alike. Famous — more or less openly advertised — authorial refusals of literary prizes[4] can be read in parallel to the critic's observation that 'scholarly literature on the topic is surprisingly slim' regardless of 'how enormous the book-prize industry has become, how ubiquitous its rhetoric of competition, achievement, and reward'.

The economic dimension

Actually, one cannot help wondering if it is not precisely because of the industry-related nature of contemporary literary competitions that the body of works available on the topic is a relatively small one. So far, it is indeed the analysis of the economic dimension of literary prizes which, in academic publications having considered the phenomenon, appears to have been the most popular,[5] not to mention one of the most frequently referred to in journalistic, prize-season, chronicles.

Inscribed within the wider sociological paradigm which assesses the cultural sphere for its capacity of giving form to a market of both symbolic and non-symbolic goods,[6] such a critical approach reads the production of cultural objects through the lens of its economic and financial impact, emphasising how literary institutions — such as literary competitions — function as intermediaries regulating the exchanges between the author/producer, the publisher/distributor and the reader/customer. For instance, James English's *The Economy of Prestige. Prizes, Awards and the Circulation of Cultural Value*, explicitly seeks to address, through the study of 'the cultural prize in its contemporary form' the 'economic dimensions of culture, [...] the rules or logics of exchange for what has come to be called "cultural capital"'.[7]

Undoubtedly, the very nature of the institution of literary competitions brings to the forefront of any analytical procedure the issue of value in its monetary signification.[8] Not only are numerous prizes born out of the desire to ensure the financial support of would-be writers and/or the reward of established authors, but most of the major contemporary literary competitions are able to generate a financially significant number of sales. According to Giuliano Vigini, head of the Italian *Editrice Bibliografica* [TN: Italian publisher, specialised in bibliographic references], in Italy, one thousand six hundred literary prizes muster, each year, an economical turnover well in excess of ten million euro.[9] The same amount has been estimated by Guy Konopnicki to correspond to the sole turnover generated by a successful *Goncourt* prize.[10] Such potential is not unknown to aspiring — or even well-established — authors. Álvaro Pombo, 2006 *Planeta* winner with *La fortuna de Matilda Turpin* [Matilda Turpin's Fortune], in a good-humoured acknowledgement of the impact of the 601.000 euro prize on his lifestyle and potential readership, openly states: 'Si encima gano el Planeta, pueden leerme cientos de miles de personas y dispongo de dinero para gastar con alegría, ¡fenomenal! Cualquier escritor quiere muchos lectores' [If, on top of that, I win the *Planeta*, hundreds of thousands of readers can read me and, on top of that, I can also spend some money and have fun...That's great! Any writer would like to have many readers].[11]

Thus, accused of catering to the economic interests of a restricted range of influential publishers, allegedly set under the control of the literary market, literary competitions are often discounted as being little more than the financially advantageous stage on which potential bestsellers are presented to potential customers. Seen at best as marketing tools, to the extent — as stated — of being criticised by the winning authors themselves, literary competitions appear to be predominantly seen as embodiments of the increasingly powerful and all-encompassing alliance (so goes the argument) between art and the market. As the 'guarantee of sizeable paperback sales and considerable further spin-off in terms of global sales of books, future publishing contracts and film and television rights'[12] is set at the forefront of the analysis of literary competitions, the cultural and aesthetic criteria sustaining selection choices appear to be either wholly discounted or, though stated, rhetorically weakened by their being formulated in tantalizingly vague, perhaps deliberately all-encompassing, critical terms.[13]

As a result, as noted by James English, it is 'difficult to find anyone of any status in the world of arts and letters [...] and still more difficult to find books or articles' that, in their analysis of the literary prize phenomenon, 'do not strike the familiar chords of amused indifference, jocular condescension or outright disgust'.[14]

The historical/anecdotal/documentary dimension

When not openly challenged through the underlining of economic motivations, the justifications put forward for the selection of participants (and winners) appear to be at best considered as the rhetorical smoke-screen behind which highly subjective factors actually operate.[15] Thus, in an often-practiced referring to the personal (not to say unfathomable) nature of taste, sympathies and antagonisms, individual preferences and dislikes are seen as elements which strongly influence the judges' choices and, consequently, which determine *de facto* the attribution of literary prizes. It is what could be defined as the anecdotal perspective. For instance, the history of the Italian *Viareggio* has been assessed in the light of the influence, character and personal taste of founder Leonida Répaci, just as the choices of the *Strega* prize have been considered as expressive of the political positions and aesthetic preferences of literary sponsors and founders Maria and Goffredo Bellonci.

At the two opposite ends of such a trend, which seems to be particularly favoured by journalistic assessments, one can arguably set two distinct yet, in a sense, related approaches.

On the one hand, on the academic front, one notices a number of studies on the phenomenon of literary competitions relying on a historical/biographical perspective. The one hundred years of the *Prix Goncourt* have, for instance, provided the chronological cut at the basis of Olivier Boura's *Un siècle de Goncourt*[16] [A Century of *Goncourt*] as well as the thematic background for *Prix Goncourt, 1903–2003: essais critiques*[17] [*Goncourt* Prize, 1903–2003: Critical Essays] and for *Goncourt: Cent ans de littérature*[18] [*Goncourt*: One Hundred Years of Literature], both by multiple authors. A similar historical perspective emerges in Maria Bellonci's nostalgic *Il Premio Strega*[19] [The *Strega* Prize], in Marino Parenti's *Bagutta*[20] or in Antonia María Cabrera Santana's shorter *El Premio Eugenio Nadal y Carmen Laforet* [The *Eugenio Nadal* Prize and Carmen Laforet].[21]

On the other hand, ostensibly marked by the lack of authorial assessment or critical perspective, one should mention documentary catalogues and how-to guides listing the literary competitions organized yearly in each country.[22] As examples, one can refer to the Italian *A Catalogue of Literary Awards* (TN: original title in English),[23] listing the winners of all editions of the four major Italian literary prizes — *Viareggio, Strega, Campiello, Penna D'Oro* — as well as to the encyclopedic *Premiopoli*[24] or to the French *Les prix littéraires. Programmes, valeurs, dates, jurys, historique* [Literary Prizes. Programmes, Values, Dates, Juries and History].[25]

Such a clear distinction between historical analysis, anecdotal commentary and factual description is, however, not always easy to trace. To take the case provided by Olivier Boura's *Un siècle de Goncourt*, the text, flirting with the documentary precision of catalogues yet also characterized by a forcefully voiced personal opinion, such as generally displayed in journalistic assessments, hovers between objective description and subjective narration.

By extension, Boura's and other analytical attempts in the wide-ranging historical/anecdotal/documentary category, can possibly be seen as the textual background to Pierre Belfond's deeply satirical *La délibération*[26] [The Deliberation] which provides

— through a wholly fictional narrative construct — a biting critique of the literary prize phenomenon. Here, fiction overcomes documentary description and the judging process itself becomes an object of narration.

What such a variety of texts, running from the documentary to the fictive, appears to highlight is, overall, the difficulty of establishing an all-encompassing critical approach to a phenomenon characterized by an often significant chronological span and by the high number of factors — biographical elements, historical events, aesthetic values, stylistic and thematic choices, economic conditions — it calls into question.

The political view

Indeed, beyond economic motivations or idiosyncratic personal desires, no uniform explanation for the enacted selections has been put forward in the attempt to investigate the nature of winning literary works and, by extension, the socio-cultural function of the literary competitions directly responsible for the much discussed enhanced commercial visibility of such works.

With one notable exception. Literary prizes, so goes the argument, can be read as institutional embodiments of cultural politics. French studies of the *Prix Goncourt*, for instance, have repeatedly pointed to the strong links tying nationalism to the social role played by the literary competition.[27] Accordingly, the *Goncourt* has been seen as an instance of the ideology of *Frenchness* as it manifests itself in the cultural and, more specifically, in the literary sphere.

Significantly enough, such a view appears to have inspired the European Communities institutions' 1990 decision of promoting a European Literary Prize: the *Aristeion* Prize.[28] The competition was considered as a key tool within the framework of initiatives aimed at supporting the enhancement of a European consciousness.[29] Following the resolution of the Council of Culture Ministers of the European Community of 18 May 1989 on the promotion of books and reading, the *Aristeion* Prize was awarded each year from 1990 to 1999 to an 'important' work of contemporary European literature and to a literary translation of 'exceptional quality'. Two prizes of 20.000 ECU were therefore awarded yearly in a process which was aimed at setting a parallel between the idea of a European literature and the notion that such a literature represented the 'historical truth', 'the private history' of European nations[30] and, implicitly, of *the* European nation.

Yet, it is precisely the acknowledgement that the *Aristeion* prize — as opposed to the previously evoked *Goncourt* — was aimed at favouring the development of a trans-national, indeed, supra-national identity, which allows for a shift of perspective in the consideration of the social and cultural function of literary competitions. It is my contention that the focus of the analytical approach can go beyond the assessment of a territorially defined political/ideological dimension towards a more general consideration of the *identity-forming* potential of literary competitions.

Indeed, when studying the literary prizes phenomenon, one notices that structural/territorial frontiers hardly ever correspond to a given prize's symbolic impact area. Let us consider an example provided by the Italian literary competitions examined in this work. The *Bagutta* prize was founded on 11 November 1926 in Milan. According to the founders of the later (and rival) *Viareggio*, the *Bagutta* had only a local, sub-national, resonance.[31] In contrast with the allegedly parochial dimension of the *Bagutta*, Leonida Répaci, *Viareggio* founder, wanted a literary prize able to reach the whole of the Italian territory. However, Orio Vergani's ironic recalling of how, in the *trattoria Bagutta* [TN: *trattoria* indicates, in Italy, a small eating establishment, less formal than a restaurant], 'ci si riunisce alla milanese, si mangia alla toscana, si paga alla romana. Perfetta trinità della raggiunta unità d'Italia,[32] [people meet in the Milanese way, they eat in the Tuscan way and pay in the Roman way. Perfect trinity of the achieved Italian unification] significantly suggests the complex interaction between national and local identities occurring already, as in the case of the later *Viareggio* prize, in the context of the older literary competition. As for the *Viareggio* prize, in the mind of its founders, it was supposed to reach, in particular, those intellectual forces which had remained hostile to the rising Fascist power. It could thus be argued that the *Viareggio* too was born out of the desire to draw a new Italian state whose geography was based on political and cultural ideals rather than effective territorial consistency.[33]

The undermining of the link between *territory-based* identities and literary competitions leads to the consideration of the role played by the prizes in the articulation of *non-territory-based* identities. Indeed, such an aspect is particularly noticeable when one considers how distinct literary competitions, as mentioned in the Italian example, often seem to develop simultaneously on the cultural scene. To refer to the *Goncourt*, its hegemonic position in the early twentieth-century French cultural and literary landscape was very quickly — and radically — challenged. Thus, the 1926 *Renaudot* prize, created by ten critics who were impatiently awaiting the results of the *Goncourt* selection, was born with the avowed intention of correcting the 'unjust' choices of the older competition.[34] Similarly, the *Femina* prize, established in 1904 by the magazines *Femina* and *Vie Heureuse*, was avowedly aimed at celebrating literary works written by women, which, according to the organising members, would in all probability never have been acknowledged by the allegedly gender-biased *Goncourt* judging panel. Thus, the emphasis of readings — contemporary to the foundation of the prizes — appears to have significantly rested on the constitution of alternative, competing, authorial figures and reader figures on the social and cultural scene, in a perspective where the emphasis seems to have been on sub-national, often non-territorial, group-forming potential rather than on patriotic/nationalistic or territorially-bound ideological strategies.[35]

As a result, without discounting the specific nature of the identity that is called into question, it is the degree to which the phenomenon of literary competitions can be inserted within a more general process through which identity is formulated and articulated in the first place that is the object of the analysis that follows.

A New Approach

Let us therefore focus on the link tying literary prizes to a *general* identity-forming process. This study is indeed aimed at investigating the sustainability of such a link. It seeks to analyse why and how the functioning of literary competitions and the forming of identities can be considered as interrelated processes.

The purpose is to highlight the mechanisms through which literary competitions can be inscribed at the *theoretical* level within an identity-shaping matrix. Such a matrix is understood to embody the process which allows for *all* of the specific cases of identity-articulation occurring in the context of literary competitions. In order to understand the analytical framework illustrating the identity-shaping function of literary prizes, this study thus considers specific examples of identity-forming processes as illustrative instances only of a *general theory* of identity-formation through the social institution. Incidentally, it is my contention that the existence of a link between identity-forming dynamics and literary prizes is one of the main factors explaining their long-standing and ever-growing success.

In the light of the stated aims, it might seem somehow paradoxical to rely on a nation-based pattern of case studies, with each chapter of the current work corresponding indeed to the analysis of literary competitions in a specific country. Additionally, the temporal segments chosen for each specific country correspond to periods of political life in which identity-forming issues and political nationalism appear to have been tightly connected.

In that respect, it ought to be mentioned that this work does not seek to undermine the ideological potential which, indeed, can be attributed to literary competitions. As illustrated by the example of Olivier Boura's study of the *Goncourt*, literary prizes *can* and *do* perform as identity-forming mechanisms within specific ideological contexts. In Boura's text it is, significantly, through the very lens of cultural nationalism itself that the prize is considered: the critic frames the cultural production selected by the literary institution in a descriptive language whose patriotic sensuousness evokes the very ideal of *Frenchness* that the prize itself (he argues) celebrates.[36]

The country-based approach chosen in this study acknowledges and takes into consideration the nationalist potential of literary competitions in at least two perspectives.

First, literary competitions play a part in the arena of cultural politics. As such, they can be used to promote — or to attempt to promote — specific ideological frameworks and identity profiles. In the three countries and the literary prizes under examination, the influence of ideology — enforced, albeit not exclusively, through the use of censorship — cannot be underestimated. Although detailed analysis of the influence of political ideology in the literary competitions considered here goes beyond the scope of the current study — in particular as such influence is neither challenged nor discounted — the link between literary prizes and politics cannot go unmentioned.

To focus, for example, only on a very brief consideration of the Italian prizes (further analysed in chapter 2), the influence of Fascist cultural politics emerges in multiple instances. Both the *Viareggio* and the *Bagutta* prizes were born in 1926, well into the Fascist period and were part of a cultural scene where the regime's ideological framework intervened at multiple levels. One needs but to mention the selection of literary themes and styles dear to the Fascist worldview, the promotion of authors close to the government or the condemnation of works and authors deemed dangerous for the stability of the regime which took place on the Italian cultural scene as a whole: theatre, literature, cinema, architecture, art, music.[37] Thus, it is certainly no coincidence if the 1938 *Viareggio* winner Vittorio Rossi — with the novel *Oceano* [Ocean] — had signed the 1925 Fascist intellectuals' manifesto promoted by the philosopher Giovanni Gentile. Enrico Pea, the 1938 *Viareggio* winner — with *La maremmana* [TN: the *maremmana* is a breed of cattle reared in the Maremma, a marshland area between southern Tuscany and northern Lazio] — openly endorsed Fascist ideology, writing in notoriously pro-regime magazines such as *Il Selvaggio* and *Strapaese*, which supported nationalistic ideals. Giovanni Comisso, the 1928 *Bagutta* winner with *Gente di mare* [People of the Sea], remained a Fascist supporter throughout the regime years, up to the final period of the *Salò* Republic. A similar pathway can be traced for Enrico Sacchetti, 1935 *Bagutta* winner with *Vita d'artista* [An Artist's Life]. In short, did Italian literary prizes play a role in the regime's attempt to shape a new *type* of *Italian* citizen? They certainly did.

Moreover, if — and we refer here to the second perspective — we acknowledge that literary competitions can and do intervene in a *general* process of identity-formation, one can hardly argue that the selection of winning novels, and the related dynamics of identity-formation which we will illustrate, are not influenced, at least in part, by ideological or political attempts to alter the perceptions and processes whereby the individual establishes his/her belonging to determined social groups. This is naturally all the more true for regimes such as Fascism or Francoism, where dictatorship intervened with strength on the cognitive scene.

However, the very nature of the concept of identity should warn against a simplification of the relationship between literary competitions — no matter how exposed to ideological influences — and the construction of identity. Extensive research on identity by psychologists, sociologists, cultural and social theorists, and philosophers has indeed unveiled the degree to which any reflection on the topic must take into consideration the multiple — in a sense, combinatory — nature of identity development.[38] Joining the personal and the social dimensions, identity processes rely on the construction of an extremely articulated symbolic and cognitive hierarchy. The individual is framed within a multiplicity of interlocking and ever-evolving identities.[39]

To take the example of the social sphere, an extremely wide range of categories of belonging and self-definition have been identified by theorists: the family (son, daughter, mother, etc.), the social group (nationality, religious belonging, ethnic origin, etc.), the professional sphere (teacher, doctor, lawyer, etc.), the social status (member of parliament, CEO, etc.), the economic situation (homeless, millionaire, etc.) and so on. All concur as to the construction of an extremely complex pattern of categorisation, definition and transformation processes characterising the understanding of the self and of inter-personal and inter-group relations.

Incidentally, if this study uses the singular form of the term *identity*, it is purely with the purpose of ensuring textual clarity. In no way does the reference to *identity* wish to undermine — quite the opposite actually — the awareness that any process of identity construction entails a multiplicity of definitions and self-definitions. Thus, any enquiry on the topic of identity articulation needs to acknowledge multiple — often simultaneous — instances of identity formation.

What is the consequence of such an awareness for literary competitions? Let us turn back to the Italian example. We referred to the ways in which Fascist ideology could be said to have influenced literary competitions, seeking to add them to the ideological apparatus used to shape the *new* Italian identity articulated by the regime. If it can be argued that some authors or texts were indeed chosen — or favoured — for their compliance to Fascist ideology, the same argument does not apply to many other winners of those years. Corrado Tumiati won the *Viareggio* prize in 1931 with *Tetti rossi* [Red Roofs], a moving investigation of the world of mental illness and a remarkably provoking topic for a regime which associated mental illness — as well as any form of 'abnormal' conduct — with criminality.[40] Lorenzo Viani won the *Viareggio* prize in 1930 with *Ritorno alla patria* [A Return to the Homeland], a novel which undermines pro-war rhetoric by unveiling the tragic dimension of suffering and death in war. Significantly, when he won the *Viareggio* prize, Viani had already a history of anti-militarism, having criticized as early as 1912 the Italian occupation of Libya.[41] An even greater challenge to the Fascist vision of an idealized, ordered, society was posited by 1936 *Viareggio* winner — and *Bagutta* founder — Riccardo Bachelli. With his *Il rabdomante* [The Water Diviner], the author sketches an acid portrait of a society inherently undermined by greed, ignorance, corruption and foolishness. The satirical criticism of Riccardo Bachelli's texts was certainly not appreciated by the regime.[42] Indeed, several high-ranking officials asked Mussolini to intervene when, in 1941, Bacchelli won the *Premio Mussolini* for his novel *Il mulino del Po* [The Mill on the Po] — ex-aequo with Bruno Cicognani for the novel *L'età favolosa* [The Fabulous Age]. In answer to Mussolini's protests, however, Bruno Federzoni, the president of the *Accademia d'Italia*, who was responsible for the selection of the winning novels, judged that the attacks were unfounded as the literary value of the books having obtained the reward surpassed by far the work of any other candidate.[43] And similarly telling examples can only be multiplied, from Antonio Foschini's *L'avventura di Villon* [Villon's Adventure] (*Viareggio* prize 1932),[44] which challenged the Fascist emphasis on the Italianization of culture, to Maria Bellonci's *Lucrezia Borgia* (*Viareggio* winner 1939) which, in contrast with Fascist stereotypes of women, and on the basis of extremely accurate historical research, paints the infamous Lucrezia Borgia as an independent, cultivated and historically important character.[45] Finally, it might be worth remembering that, as Italy precipitated into war (between 1937 and 1946), the granting of the *Bagutta* prize was deliberately suspended by its own members to escape the influence of growing political pressures.

What this brief overview underlines is that an approach to the literary competitions/identity equation through the sole lens of cultural nationalism offers at best a limited, not to say biased, reading of a phenomenon which appears instead as a complex and, arguably, also as a contradictory one.

From a transnational perspective, the latter dimension is illustrated by the case of the 2007 pamphlet *Pour une littérature-monde en français*,[46] published by Le Monde and signed by forty-four French-speaking authors. The episode is chronologically set out of the framework of the current study — and certainly beyond the context of early nineteenth-century French nationalism — but is particularly expressive of the ambivalence characterising the connection between ideological drives, identity-building processes and literary competitions. The text opens with the observation that, in 2007, all the winners of the main French literary prizes, 'le Goncourt, le Grand Prix du roman de l'Académie française, le Renaudot, le Femina, le Goncourt des lycéens', were authors defined as 'des écrivains d'outre-France' [writers from beyond France]. This, it is argued, is the proof of a deep-seated transformation of the French literary world. Positing a parallel between the selection occurring in literary competitions and canon-building processes, the authors argue that the belief in a pre-eminence of Hexagon-based French authors over francophone 'external' writers is at best an outdated, vague, incorrect stereotype and at worst an expression of discrimination and racism. The authors refer therefore to the need for a new understanding of works written in French as the expression of a *constellation* without any pre-eminent centre, where the language and its related literary production are freed from any connection to territorial boundaries or to practices of cultural imperialism. Not only are the new boundaries of the French literary landscape extended to encompass the whole world; it is the world itself, 'le monde, le sujet, le sens, l'histoire' [the world, the subject, the meaning, the history], which is seen as the new object of literary attention and creation for French-speaking intellectuals everywhere.

On the one hand, the intention is that of undermining Hexagon-centric drives and sketching a new cultural and literary space which goes so far as to encompass the whole world. On the other hand, such a process entails, somewhat paradoxically, a re-construction of French cultural identity, based on the newly defined non-borders/world-borders of French literature and a new vision of French literary topics and literary style. French literary identity is undermined only to be reframed according to new criteria and new aesthetics. As a result, the link between identity and the selection process in competitions is reinforced as one definition of France and literary *Frenchness* replaces another, in a process which paradoxically appears to reinforce that which it intended to undermine.

Ultimately, no matter which specific identity is celebrated and which is condemned, the focus remains on the connection between identity and the process of selection. Widening the approach, this study proposes therefore a reading of literary competitions as prisms through which — at the cognitive level — perception of the world and perception of the self are negotiated in a much larger perspective.

Identity and literature

Before being able to speak of — and analyse — the constitution of identity through the socio-cultural phenomenon of literary prizes, let us explain why, in the first place, the mental processes at work in the dynamics of *identity-building* can be connected — at the theoretical level — to *literature*.

Integrating the position of identity theorists, who have demonstrated how processes of construction of the self are based on *perception*,[47] literary critics — in particular scholars influenced by the critical school of cognitive poetics — by considering the process of reading as part of the psychological processes defining human cognition,[48] have underlined how the perception of texts can be considered as a key element in the processes of articulation and definition of the self.[49]

Let us provide a brief example of how the traditional *ideological* reading of literary prizes, as previously evoked, can be transformed by the awareness of such cognitive mechanisms.

Any reference to processes of perception cannot escape the understanding that, cognitively, we live in a world defined by the notions of *time* and *space*. Indeed, if the Kantian[50] definition of 'intuition'[51] has perhaps evolved into the modern analysis of cognitive-sensory faculties, there remains the understanding that perception is, first and foremost, perception *within* and *of* space and time.[52]

We have seen how the analysis of literary competitions articulated in this book begins with an acknowledgement of their traditional nation-based *territorial* dimension. Let us now substitute this perspective by a *spatial* outlook. Now, environmental psychologists have argued that a person's self-identity is developed through an experience of physical space, incidentally coining in this context the neologism *place identity*.[53] Identity is here understood as being formed in relation to the environment. Space can, however, also be understood at a symbolic level. Lacanian psychoanalysis has unveiled how the highly symbolic space provided by an image reflected within a frame plays a crucial role in a process of identity definition.

Literary narrative is, in turn, marked by the notion of space at multiple levels: space can be perceived as the physical dimension in which the novel (as object) exists. It can also be the space — real, fictitious, symbolic — evoked through the narration or it can refer to the territory in which the novel is apprehended, etc. For each and every one of these aspects, a process of cognition of the spatial dimension — be it physical or symbolic — can indeed be traced and its corresponding or correlated dynamics of identity-formation identified.

This study applies aspects of such an approach to the field of literary competitions, when it considers not only the significance which the chosen text *embodies* for both its creator and its audience but also the processes of *embodiment* which derive from the act of reading as mediated by the literary competition institutional framework. The 'structures of the work of art',[54] including, in this case, the framework which presents such a cultural work *as* art, can be analyzed in relation to their 'psychological effects on the recipient'.[55] The psychological effects of the text — and, crucially, of the institution which promotes the visibility of the evoked text (a further physical and symbolic space) — are accordingly brought to light and analysed with a view to underlining the link between cultural object, aesthetic judgment and psychological causes and effects.

However, such an approach does not provide, if considered alone, a complete understanding of the historical, contextual and social roots of specific behaviours and experiences. As noted by Peter Stockwell, 'social negotiation [...] is the place where cultural models and cognitive models come from'[56] and the *cultural* dimension is not to be forfeited in the analysis of the literary prize phenomenon. In other words, identity and its articulation processes cannot be reduced to a psychological interaction between a brain and a book, or for that matter to the interaction of an isolated individual reader with the organisation which appraises, celebrates or criticises that self-same book. This study seeks therefore to analyse the dynamics of identity-formation, literary creation and social organisation via an inter-disciplinary approach, taking into consideration both the physical/psychological and the cultural elements operating in the context of literary competitions.

The understanding of human identity — not to mention human activities and behaviours — as deriving from the interaction of the *natural* and the *cultural* is certainly not a novelty. Considering only the specific field of literary criticism, the attempts at defining natural and cultural influences on artistic creation have spanned the twentieth century, ranging from the late nineteenth-century emphasis on the relationship between *Weltanschauung* [world view] and artistic creation, to modern feminist readings aimed at unveiling the cultural construction of gender identity.

In a somewhat cyclical perspective, *culture-oriented* and *nature-based* critical perspectives seem to alternate, though they also often overlap. In the last decades, while culture-oriented studies on the political, social and ideological aspects of literature have connected literary products to their economic and social contexts of production and reception, the cognitive approaches previously evoked appear to have derived predominantly from a nature-based perspective. As expressed above, this book seeks to combine both views, endorsing the opinion that 'it is not enough to emphasise the embodied nature of cognition and language, without also recognising the various discursive practices that structure both society and language inextricably'.[57]

Do the processes of embodiment which can be traced in literary texts influence the social behaviour of readers and critics? This study seeks to demonstrate that they do, in a complex pattern where processes of embodiment are projected from the individual sphere of the single reader on to the wider arena of shared aesthetic perception and social construction. As will be shown in the subsequent parts of this study, the institution of literary prizes itself can indeed be understood as being the result of a process of embodiment operating at the social level.

A sociological approach to literature emerges, in this context, as being particularly useful for the integration of the cognitive perspective. The reference is to Emile Durkheim's understanding of the blending between mental categorisation and social organisation. However, this study stops short of applying Durkheim's final conclusion on the chronological and factual descent of the former from the latter.[58] Indeed, cognitive processes and social processes are understood as being dynamically interconnected — neither being seen as preceding the other. Language, in particular literary language, mediates between the sphere of cognition and the social dimension. Literature is used as both an expression of and a tool for the pursuit of individual and collective interests. Such interests in turn amount to the constitution of psychological and social identity.

Social function, dynamics and limitations

If, however, literary competitions act as identity-articulating tools, what are, specifically, the *origins* of such a process? In other words, where does the input for the constitution of a literary competition come from, not simply from a historical perspective, but, specifically, at the theoretical level?

The point made by this work is that literary competitions are social embodiments of identity-forming *drives*. Such a reading is based on the awareness that the emergence of multiple and simultaneous instances of group-identity shaping attempts, through the means of literary competitions, in a specific socio-cultural and historical context, is not a casual event. In other words, the emergence of multiple literary prizes, in determined contextual circumstances and specific geo-political and historical settings, corresponds to a *need-answering process*. Such a process engages with requests for identity articulation, emerging at the communal level, in the social sphere, and encompasses both individual and group dimensions. In this view, the literary institution, seen as catering to an identity-articulating *need*, is understood to take shape in answer to a *cognitive and social necessity* and to interact with both micro and macro — individual and shared — aspects of identity articulation.

Once again, the starting point is seemingly provided by the context of cultural nationalism. In the Italian example previously evoked and — as will be seen further on in the book — in other instances of authoritarian regimes, literary competitions certainly flourished, suggesting a connection with determined cultural and political situations.

The reference to specific historical contexts posits, though, the problem of the lasting success and prolonged life of all of the studied literary institutions, opening the way for an assessment of the degree to which such phenomena, while arising from specific social needs, ultimately transcend the historical context in which they find their origins.

Such a view is related to a change in the analytical perspective, taking place in the second chapter: the approach moves from the consideration of the institution as an object of study arising from social needs, to its depiction as an active producer of determined behaviours, which in turn influence and transform the social scene itself.

If the need for the articulation of identity emerges from the contextual dimension and leads to the constitution of the literary prize, the prize, by acting as a producer of identity, as a mechanism through which identity is negotiated and reflected back on the social context, changes the very contextual dimension which has produced it and — by extension — changes its own role in accordance to the dynamism of the cycle. This analysis rests therefore on an understanding of the *evolving* nature of identity-shaping processes and seeks to answer the need to go beyond a *static* view of identity articulation. It does so in two steps.

On the one hand, this study offers a global assessment of the complexity of the identity shaping process, highlighting how it encompasses factors ranging from (to mention but a few) individual psyche to communal culture, aesthetic values to political drives, individual aspirations to group dynamics. On the other hand, it seeks to consider the specific ways in which the literary institution can *actually* function — through literary production and evaluation — as an identity construction tool. In particular, it focuses on how literary prizes embody, through their nature and functioning, the dynamic and ever-changing dimension which characterises identity formation.

The understanding of the identity-negotiating process in terms of its dynamic dimension leads to the analysis of the phenomenon of literary competitions in the light of its *evolutive, self-transforming, self-adapting* nature. By extension, the acknowledgement of the fundamentally problematic nature of the connection between social reality, aesthetic models and identity stabilisation ultimately leads this work to the assessment of the degree to which the identity-forming process promoted by literary institutions is subject to inherent *self-undermining* drives.

In particular, the interrelated network of individual, small group and large group identities emerging in the context of a literary competition is highlighted. The potential inner contradictions which such identities carry in themselves are underlined. The yearly renewal of the identity-negotiating process is stressed. The *time* factor, previously evoked — together with *space* — as one of the two elements at the basis of the processes of identity construction, takes here centre stage.

A three-step approach to the issue of identity articulation is accordingly displayed in the current study. First, this work acknowledges the identity-shaping and identity-stabilising role of literary competitions. Secondly, such an initial view is re-formulated to take into account the degree to which identity is also undermined and challenged in the context of literary competitions. Ultimately, it will be shown how it is the systematic questioning and destabilisation of identity which paradoxically ensures the lasting social and cognitive success of literary competitions. Thus, the analytical approach for the assessment of literary competitions and their identity-forming function which emerges in the current study rests on the recognition of the role played by three key factors: *necessity, dynamism* and *contradiction*.

The analytical model

This study represents the attempt at articulating such an approach through an integrated analysis. It considers the ways in which literary competitions enter the process of identity articulation, taking place at the cognitive level *via* the enactment of an aesthetic selection process at the social level. This work reads the social phenomenon of literary competitions in the light of the *three-fold* interaction it embodies between cognitive self-awareness and self-reflection, literary creation and social practices. In turn, all three factors are understood as being the drivers of the formulation of identity — *identity* being here intended as a *layered* sphere encompassing both individual and communal perspectives. The understanding of the inter-relation of these elements in the context of a dynamic articulation of identity ultimately provides the theoretical frame for the conception of literary competitions as instances of self-renewing, ever-changing and potentially self-undermining, identity-negotiating practices.

Within the specific field of the analysis of literary competitions, such an approach expresses a somewhat unorthodox assessment of the phenomenon in at least three instances.

This view entails, first of all, a re-definition of the notion of *value* such as it is considered in relation to the topic of literary competitions. We have previously evoked the frequent references to the notion of economic value occurring in criticism. Indeed, by negotiating the visibility of the winning text, sanctioning its rarity as *literary* product while simultaneously favouring its widespread circulation as literary *product*, the literary competition institutional framework certainly plays an important role in the economics of the cultural world. Simultaneously, however, literary competitions can be seen as the embodiment of a multifaceted axiological dimension. At its heart, the textual object plays a defining function with regard to the individual social figures — authors, publishers, critics, journalists, readers — involved in the functioning of the social institution itself. In this sense, the phenomenon of literary competitions not only rests on an exchange of monetary or economic value but gives origin to a semiotic system in which *value*, in a Saussurean perspective, is understood to express the reciprocal positions, inner relations — and, crucially, reciprocal identities — of the subjects involved with the institution. Specifically, the social resonance of the institution is given by its capacity to answer the communally formulated need for identity-articulation. Thus, when referring to *aesthetic value* and *cognitive value*, this work encloses within such terms their potential as identity-forming tools. The economic dimension, fuelling the material workings of the institutionalisation of literature, the constitution and social survival of literary competitions, is not undermined. It is, however, inscribed within a wider approach to the identity-forming sphere of interaction which is, in fact, understood to be the driving force *behind* the often evoked economic dimension.

Secondly, the current study seeks to recapture the *human, individual, factor* in the aesthetic selection process, without, however, narrowing the critical appraisal of aesthetic decisions to an anecdotal perspective. On the contrary, the evaluation of patterns of decision-making is driven by the awareness of the potentially fusional dynamics linking instances of individual cognition and instances of group cognition. This view is at the origin of the methodological decision underpinning the whole study, namely the choice to focus exclusively on prize winners. This approach does not seek to undermine or discount the importance of shortlisted texts or the role played by the controversies and contingent factors influencing the juries' choices. However, the methodological strategy is that of highlighting the common patterns and resounding echoes within the 'canon' built by literary prizes at a certain time, preferring a mid-distance view to what could arguably amount to a somewhat myopic approach. Thus, on the one hand, a decision has been made to take into consideration a wide-ranging temporal framework and an extended list of works. The type of analysis remains distinct from the technical assessment provided by distant reading methodology that the chosen number of texts is still compatible with a qualitative assessment. On the other hand, the emphasis on large chronological and geographical sections — nineteenth-century competitions in three European countries — suggests the usefulness of a critical approach which does not emphasise the microcosmic but seeks the wider common pattern across competitions and socio-cultural events. Thus, the study seeks to reach a balance between aggregating data from different authors, juries, countries and texts whilst also maintaining a focus on the thematic, stylistic, qualitative dimensions of the analysis. Ultimately, metaphorical schemes are used in order to tie the individual judge's choice critically to both authorial production and public taste, in a process which seeks to emphasise the common cognitive approaches within a determined social and historical pattern.

Finally, the *political* reading of literary competitions as instances of nationalism is reviewed in the light of the degree to which identity-building strategies transcend the specific instance of geo-political identity. The multi-layered, complex, identity-shaping potential emerging from the functioning of literary competitions is understood to resonate beyond the specifics of political ideology.

In this light — and as will be noted in the conclusion — such a view of the identity-forming process can arguably be extended to cultural phenomena distinct from the specific case of literary competitions. Arguably, the analytical model sketched in this text can offer a starting point for the assessment of the identity-forming function of cultural institutions and cultural expressions in a more general perspective, beyond the specifics of the world of literary prizes.

The Analytical Model

The analytical model used in the analysis of literary competitions can be summarised through the following scheme:

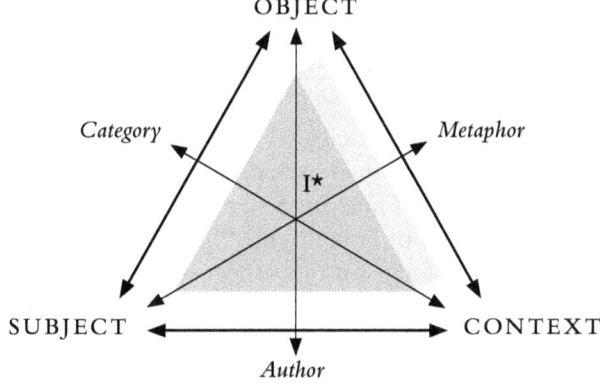

Fig. I.1. The analytical model (* Institution: Literary Prize)

The literary institution, here visually represented as a multi-dimensional form, is seen as the embodiment of the network of relations and interactions which originate from — and answer — an identity-forming need.[59]

Heading the scheme, the **OBJECT** is intended to refer to the novel selected in the context of the literary competition. At opposite ends of the institutional construct, the **SUBJECT** is aimed at expressing the subjective consciousness — for instance, the reader, the critic, etc. — engaging with the text and its contextual dimension. The **CONTEXT** is, in turn, understood to express the socio-historical and cultural factors directly influencing the constitution of the social institution as well as the cognition (creation and reception) of the selected aesthetic object.

Additionally, all three elements are understood to be connected by specific binary relations. Between **OBJECT** and **CONTEXT**, a *metaphorical* relation is understood to occur. Specifically, the text-object is seen as a metaphorical projection of the contextual dimension. Between **SUBJECT** and **CONTEXT**, the *author-figure* acts as the mediator of cognition and perception. The contextual dimension is filtered through the authorial figure before reaching the subject *via* the act of literary creation. Tying **OBJECT** and **SUBJECT**, there occurs a process of *categorisation* whereby the winning novel is attributed the label of *literature* or, in more general terms, is granted artistic value.

Additionally, each element of the scheme is directly related, in a tri-lateral network cutting across the above-mentioned links. Thus, the *metaphorical* relation tying **OBJECT** and **CONTEXT** is understood to influence the constitution of the **SUBJECT** directly. Logically, the *author-figure* at the heart of the interaction of **SUBJECT** and **CONTEXT** is the origin of the textual **OBJECT**. Additionally, the *categorisation* process at the basis of the relation between **OBJECT** and **SUBJECT** is understood to influence directly the social and historical contextual dimension.

Each trilateral relation, which can be isolated in the theoretical scheme, is at the basis of one chapter of this book. Each relation, schematically represented, in the following paragraphs, as a part — a third — of the above-illustrated scheme, represents a step in the progression of the critical argument and illustrates one aspect of the relation between literary competitions and the identity-building process.

Additionally, each chapter corresponds to the study of two particular literary competitions, during a specific historical moment, in a country-based perspective. Thus, the first chapter will consider the *Goncourt* and *Fémina* prizes in France in the 1900–1920 period. The second chapter will analyse the *Viareggio* and *Bagutta* prizes in Fascist Italy in the 1920–1940 period, while the third chapter will focus on the *Nadal* and *Planeta* prizes in Francoist Spain, in the period from the end of the Second World War to the end of Francoism.

Naturally, the decision to focus on one aspect of the critical framework in each chapter does not imply that all elements of the critical model do not apply to all competitions under examination. To take the case of the first chapter, the analysis focuses on French literary competitions and on the metaphorical dimension (see below). Such an approach does not intend to imply that the critical observations regarding the authorial role and the categorisation processes illustrated in the second and third chapter do not apply to the French case. The somewhat artificial distinction of one aspect of the critical framework from the others is only aimed at displaying for the reader a structured pathway in the critical scheme and at presenting — in a gradual progression — the critical elements within the framework in an orderly and detailed manner. The critical framework as a whole, and the observations derived from its application to literary competitions, are applicable to all the prizes considered in this work.

Chapter I: the metaphorical dimension — forming the subject

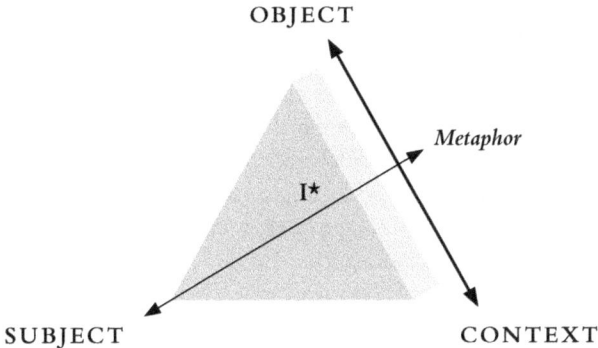

FIG. I.2. The metaphorical dimension (* Literary Prize)

Opening on the acknowledgement of the existence of a chronological and sociocultural connection between the birth of modern literary competitions in France and nationally diffused instances of cultural identity destabilisation, the analysis initially acknowledges and seeks to clarify the *identity-stabilising role* played by the institution of literary prizes at the social level. Such an identity-stabilising role, which can be derived from both the traditional view of literary competitions as potential nationalist tools and from the view of literary competitions as identity-forming tools at a more general theoretical level, is tied to the *utopian* potential which can be attributed to literary works and institutions when analysed in the light of Ernst Bloch's understanding of the social and cognitive function of art.

Such a utopian potential is fundamentally expressed, according to the philosopher, in the perception of art works as 'the means through which human beings *form* themselves' (my emphasis),[60] the means, in other words, through which humans reach — through the cognition of a stable and coherent structure (the art object) — the perception of a stabilised and coherent self. Indeed, such a potential appears to underscore the social motivation of the establishment of literary competitions at given historical moments, in particular (though not exclusively) when the problematisation of identity appears self-consciously to permeate the social discourse.

The argument for the identity-constructive-potential of art — and by extension of literary institutions which, with literary competitions, ensure the social visibility and circulation of artistic productions — rests on the assumption that the framing of identity, both at the individual and at the communal levels, emerges out of the establishment of a stabilised system of cognitive constructs acting as a Lacanian mirror in the context of identity definition and stabilisation. In the literary dimension, such cognitive constructs appear to be embodied in the fundamentally metaphorical nature of literary narratives. In other words, this book understands the metaphorical relation tying literary text to external context as a tool of cognitive stabilisation.

It does so by adopting the theoretical understanding of the literary text as embodiment of a conceptual metaphor and reads such a metaphor construction as a process of conceptual mapping through which properties from the external, contextual dimension are projected from one perceptive domain, the world domain, to the written, internal, sphere of literature. This is reflected, in the scheme drawn above, in the **OBJECT — CONTEXT** relation. The literary text is, in turn, seen as a schema provider, allowing for the cognitive structuring of the self, a relation illustrated in the **SUBJECT —** *Metaphor* binary relation, previously mentioned. A Lacanian reading of the metaphorical construct drives the integration of literary creation in the process of identity-shaping and assesses the metaphorical projection in terms of its *utopian* — in a Blochean perspective-*forming, structuring* — function, in the context of the subjective cognitive field.

Such a metaphorical mapping, running against the destabilisation of identity which can be evinced from the analysis of cultural and historical factors, is ultimately transferred — through the institutionalisation of the aesthetic choice — on the social group as a whole. Thus the cultural institution is seen as being at once the product and the producer of stabilisation tendencies in the process which provides the structure for both self-identity and group identity.

Chapter II: the authorial function — dynamism vs. objectification

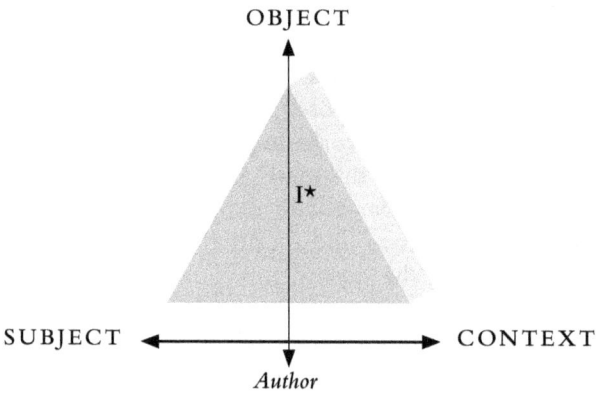

Fig. I.3. The authorial function (★ Literary Prize)

Stabilization does not, however, entail identity simplification or objectification and the traditional reading of the literary institution as an unproblematic ideological tool is, in this context, consequently challenged.

Indeed, considering the nature of identity creation entails acknowledging the fundamentally *dynamic* character of such a process, a dynamism emerging from its being inscribed within a temporal, evolving dimension. As literary competitions project the aesthetic choice in a constantly renewed cycle of aesthetic valuation and yearly selection, running parallel to constant transformations of the contextual and individual spheres, the identity-constitution process related to such a selection accordingly emerges as being inherently subject to never-ending displacement.

Identity, in such a perspective, becomes that 'which is not yet fulfilled',[61] nor ever will be, while the *utopian* dimension initially evoked in its *crystallising* potential is, in fact, to be understood in its *never-to-be-stabilised* essence. Within such a perspective, the literary institution, though arising from a need to cater to identity stabilisation, actually embodies the intrinsic impossibility of stalling identity dynamics. In other words, the literary institution is not seen as an identity-enforcing entity but as an identity-articulating framework which, far from validating an unproblematic model of personal and group identity, intervenes in the social discourse by modulating the social cognitive and discursive practices intervening in the *ever-changing* dynamics of identity formation.

Thus, the association of cultural nationalism or other expressions of identity construction and literary competitions, sustainable to an extent in the context of *static* reading of the utopian function of the selected works, is undermined once the literary competition is read in terms of its temporal, dynamic projection.

Methodologically speaking, the diachronic study of literary competitions, on which the current work is based, seeks to recapture and highlight the dynamic and ever-changing, problematic, nature of the process of identity articulation.

The problematisation of identity is embodied, as displayed by Italian literary competitions in the Fascist era, in the symbolic figure of the *Author*.

Indeed, from a historical perspective, as will be further discussed, the authorial figure has long been invested with a *liminarity-negotiating potential*. Symbolically set at the border of a group's cultural expression, it is at once projected toward the new and perceived as a guardian of the traditional, the transmitted, the inherited.

Within the context of Italian literary prizes, such a symbolic *locus* — the border — is embodied by the insertion of authorial figures' temporal and spatial displacements *within* the thematic and stylistic dimension of the winning works. Investigating the physical and historical frontiers of the Italian state, the *traveller-author* comes to question the separation and stable definition of one group from another, of one individual from another, projecting the aesthetic selection, enacted within the literary competitions, in a dimension of constant exchange between instances of group identity and instances of individual self-reflection and setting the literary institution, connected to the authorial figure it produces and validates on the social scene, at the edge of the fundamentally inter-related dimensions of individuality and community. The author is therefore seen as the prism through which not only does artistic form come to embody a community's foremost cognitive projections, but also through which such projections are simultaneously and inherently challenged.

Beyond the self-conscious thematic dimension of the Italian novels, acting as a negotiator of symbolic and, by extension, cognitive boundaries, the author figure comes to counter-balance the stabilising function and objectifying potential played by the metaphorical representation which is evoked in the first part of the study. Such a function is sketched in the *Author*/**OBJECT** binary link of the theoretical scheme. Indeed, the creation and projection of the authorial figure on the social sphere taking place on a yearly — or in any case temporal — basis, in literary competitions, modifies the nature of the *utopian* dimension which invests the literary institution by transferring the utopian focus away from the *crystallising* potential of art towards the projection of such a *potential* in a never-to-be-reached *future* dimension. In turn, the stabilising drive embodied by the selection of the aesthetic object is in turn renewed in a cyclical motion tending towards never-to-be-fulfilled stabilisation.

Chapter III: the process of categorisation — promoting social action

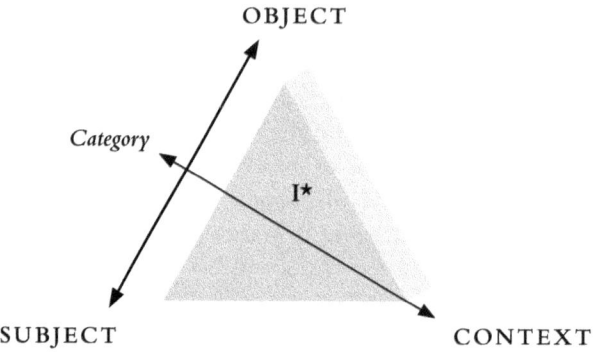

FIG. I.4. The process of categorisation (★ Literary Prize)

We have mentioned how, if identity emerges as a fundamentally *discursive* practice, inscribed within a process of constant symbolic renegotiation, the literary object which is in turn granted the social relevance at the basis of the identity-forming process is similarly inscribed within a cycle.

A turning point in such a cycle is marked when the temporary typifying and stabilising potential of the literary object is sanctioned by the inscription of the text/**OBJECT** within a process of categorisation whereby the elected text is defined as *literature* or *art*, a dimension illustrated by the *Category* element of the scheme.

Through such a definition, which can be either explicit or implicit in the act of aesthetic selection, the chosen text is endowed with a *typified* essence that, as with all categorisation, 'illuminates [the] relationship between the subjects and the objects of knowledge'[62] — as illustrated in the **SUBJECT/OBJECT** scheme relation — and intervenes directly in the **CONTEXT** dimension through its capacity of accomplishing social actions.[63]

Such a potential for *action* rests on the awareness that categorisation and the establishment of a hierarchical structure are tightly interwoven processes. The category of *art/literature* intervenes in the relation between **OBJECT** and **SUBJECT** by inserting the former within a hierarchically defined frame of values, whose function is that of providing the basis for the production of normative judgements.[64] Ultimately therefore, the text is set in a context in which it is endowed with an *ethical* function in that it is understood to 'perform *moral* work on the world described and, indexically, on the current interaction and participants who are producing and receiving' and, one might add, *valuing* 'the description'.[65]

Such a use of the act of categorisation appears to have been deliberately endorsed by the Francoist regime in the case of Spanish literary competitions. Indeed, the prizes examined in the third chapter can be seen as concrete embodiments of Francisco Franco's desire to shape the social structure and communal and individual identities through the means of 'el mito de la Cultura' [the myth of culture].[66] In such a perspective, the literary institution promoting the aesthetic categorisation process can be understood as being a concrete social materialisation of the governmental drive towards the undermining of cultural relativism.

However, the self-undermining potential of literary competitions — examined in the second chapter of the book — emerges again as the analysis of the novels having won literary competitions in Francoist Spain unveils a complex and multifaceted textual discourse. At the thematic level, realism and metafiction undermine, from opposite perspectives, the governmental drive towards the mythologizing of Spanish identity. The questioning of representation and perspective emphasised in the successful novels appears to highlight the arbitrary and subjective essence of the cultural sphere. The very social practices which intervene in the constitution of the latter appear to be ultimately and self-reflexively challenged.

Thus, the identity-forming social discourse tied to those self-same social practices emerges as a self-undermining and self-questioning dynamic drive and the ideological potential of literary competitions appears as being inherently undermined by the very functioning and by the nature of the competitions themselves.

Notes to the Introduction

1. Roger-Michel Allemand, *L'utopie* [Utopia] (Paris: Ellipses, 2005), cover.
2. Peter Stockwell, *Cognitive Poetics: An Introduction* (London: Routledge, 2002), p. 171.
3. Martin Page, 'Sous la surface' [Under the Surface], *Evene.fr Toute la Culture*, Livres (September 2005) <http://www.evene.fr/livres/actualite/interview-de-martin-page-180.php> [accessed 22 June 2017] (para. 8 of 8).
4. To focus only on the literary prizes considered in this work, Julien Gracq refused the *Goncourt* in 1951, while Miguel Delibes claimed to have rejected the offer made to him of winning the *Planeta* in 1994. Similarly, in 1950, Alberto Moravia rejected the *Viareggio Répaci* for *L'amore coniugale* [Conjugal Love] followed, in 1968, by Italo Calvino, winner for his *Ti con Zero* [Ti Zero], who communicated his decision with the following telegram: 'Ritenendo definitivamente conclusa l'epoca dei premi letterari rinuncio al Premio perché non mi sento di continuare ad avallare con il mio consenso istituzioni ormai svuotate di significato. Desiderando evitare ogni clamore giornalistico prego non annunciare mio nome tra i vincitori. Credete mia amicizia.' [Believing that the time of literary prizes is definitively concluded, I renounce the prize because I don't feel like endorsing, with my consent, institutions which are now empty of any significance. Wishing to avoid any journalistic clamour, I ask that my name be not announced amongst the winners. Please, do believe in my friendship.] Quotation by Italo Calvino in 'Le Polemiche' [Polemics], *Premio Letterario Viareggio Répaci* <http://premioletterarioviareggiorepaci.it/polemiche.htm> [accessed 13 April 2007] (para. 1 of 3).

5. See in particular: James F. English, *The Economy of Prestige: Prizes, Awards and the Circulation of Cultural Value* (Cambridge, Massachussetts: Harvard University Press, 2005); Richard Todd, *Consuming Fictions: The Booker Prize and Fiction in England Today* (London: Bloomsbury Publishing PLC, 1996).
6. Pierre Bourdieu, 'Le marché des biens symboliques' [The Market of Symbolic Goods], *L'Année sociologique* [The Sociological Year], 22 (1971), 49–126. Pierre Bourdieu, *Les Règles de l'art. Genèse et structure du champ littéraire* [The Rules of Art: Genesis and Structure of the Literary Field] (Paris: Le Seuil, 1992).
7. English (2005), cover.
8. Jacques Michon in 'Prix Littéraires' [Literary Prizes], *Le Dictionnaire du littéraire* [The Dictionary of the Literary], ed. by Paul Aron, Denis Saint-Jacques and Alain Viala (Paris: PUF, 2002), p. 488.
9. 'Premi Letterari: Un'inflazione ed una febbre che non accenna ad acquietarsi' [Literary Prizes: Inflation and a Fever which does not Seem to Abate], *Le reti di Dedalus*, La Newsletter del Sindacato Nazionale Scrittori, (n. 1, February 2005) <http://www.sindacatoscrittori.net/comunicazione/news/premiletterari.htm> [accessed 22 June 2017] (para. 1 of 2).
10. Guy Konopnicki, *Prix Littéraires: la grande magouille* [Literary Prizes: The Great Fraud] (Paris: Jean-Claude Gawsewitch Editeur, 2004).
11. Álvaro Palombo in Miguel Lorenci, 'Álvaro Pombo logra el Premio Planeta 2006 con una crónica familiar' [Alvaro Palombo Obtains the *Planeta* Prize with a Family Chronicle], *Gibralfaro*, Hemeroteca (n. 44, October 2006) <http://www.gibralfaro.net/hemeroteca/pag_1311.htm> [accessed 14 April 2006] (para. 10 of 18).
12. The Economist, 'Reflections of a Man Booker Prize Judge', *Economist.com* (21 October 2004) <http://www.economist.com/books/displayStory.cfm?story_id=3308497> [accessed 22 June 2017] (para. 3 of 9).
13. Ibid. (para. 3 of 9). A telling example of such a problematic rhetoric is provided in the explanation of choice criteria offered by Fiammetta Rocco, *The Economist* Literary Editor and 2004 *Man Booker Prize* judge (my emphasis): 'The third requirement, in addition to **courage** and **vision**, is about language. In order to capture a reader, an author must first **duel with them and force them to submit** to the writer's vision.'
14. English (2005), p. 187.
15. Tibor Fisher, 'Worthy but Forgettable', *The Guardian* (11 October 2005) <http://books.guardian.co.uk/bookerprize2005/story/0,,1589468,00.html> [accessed 22 June 2017] (para. 2 of 5) (my emphasis): 'In addition, one of the most important considerations as a Booker judge is: who do you want to hang out with? **Whose dinner parties do you want to be sitting at?** That's why the inclusion of Julian Barnes (dinner party-giver extraordinaire), Kazuo Ishiguro and Zadie Smith on the shortlist wasn't a surprise, and why the exclusion of Ian McEwan and Salman Rushdie was (but they had their long-listing so you can still scoff the sushi together at the book launches).'
16. Olivier Boura, *Un siècle de Goncourt* [A Century of *Goncourt*] (Paris: Arléa, 2003).
17. *Prix Goncourt, 1903–2003: essais critiques* [*Goncourt Prize*, 1903–2003: Critical Essays], ed. by Katherine Ashley (Oxford & Bern: Peter Lang AG, 2003).
18. *Goncourt: Cent ans de littérature* [*Goncourt* : One Hundred Years of Literature], ed. by Dominique-Antoine Grisoni (Paris: Noésis, 2003).
19. Maria Bellonci, *Il Premio Strega* [The *Strega* Prize] (Milano: Mondadori, 2003).
20. Marino Parenti, *Bagutta* (Milano: Casa Editrice Ceschina, 1928). See also, in the same line: *Milano degli scrittori. Bagutta 50 premi letterari 1927–1986* [Milan by Writers. *Bagutta* 50 Literary Prizes 1927–1986], ed. by Guido Vergani (Milano: Campari, 1986); Giovan Battista Angioletti and Orio Vergani, *Il primo Bagutta* [The First *Bagutta*] (Milano: Ceschina, 1955); Guido Vergani, *Bagutta e baguttiani* [*Bagutta* and Baguttians] (Milano: Lucini, 2005).
21. Antonia María Cabrera Santana, 'El Premio Eugenio Nadal y Carmen Laforet' [The *Eugenio Nadal* Prize and Carmen Laforet], *Vector Plus*, 18 (July-December 2001), <http://www.fulp.ulpgc.es/publicaciones/vectorplus/articulos/vp18_04_articulo01.pdf> [accessed 15 April 2007].
22. In particular, the following: Société des Ecrivains, *Guide des prix littéraires 2006* [The 2006 Guide

of Literary Prizes] (Paris: Société des Ecrivains, 2006); Bertrand Labes, *Guide Lire des prix et concours littéraires* [The *Lire* Guide of Literary Prizes and Competitions] (Paris: L'Express Editions, 2004); Bertrand Labes, *Guide Cartier des prix et concours littéraires* [The *Cartier* Guide of Literary Prizes and Competitions] (Paris: Le Cherche-midi Editeur, 1999); Bertrand Labes, *Guide Mont-Blanc des prix et concours littéraires* [The *Mont-Blanc* Guide of Literary Prizes and Competitions] (Paris: Le Cherche-midi Editeur, 1992).
23. *A Catalogue of Literary Awards*, ed. by Associazione Italiana Editori — Fondazione Maria e Goffredo Bellonci (Roma: Istituto Poligrafico e Zecca dello Stato, 1990).
24. Cinzia Tani, *Premiopoli* (Milano: Arnoldo Mondadori Editore, 1987).
25. Collectif, *Les prix littéraires. Programmes, valeurs, dates, jurys, historique* [Literary Prizes: Programmes, Values, Dates, Juries and History] (Paris: Jouve & Cie Editeurs, 1934).
26. Pierre Belfond, *La Délibération* [The Deliberation] (Paris: Lansman, 2002).
27. Ashley (2003).
28. Official Journal of the European Communities, C 035 (15/02/1990), 7–8.
29. Chris Shore, 'European Union and the Politics of Culture', *The Bruges Group* <http://www.brugesgroup.com/mediacentre/index.live?article=13> [accessed 15 April 2007] (para. 6 of 16). 'In 1984 the European Council meeting at Fontainebleau agreed to set up an ad hoc Committee to investigate ways of re-launching Community action in the 'cultural sector'. The Committee, chaired by Italian MEP Pietro Adonnino, produced two reports the following year outlining strategies promoting the 'European idea' — virtually all of which were subsequently implemented (Adonnino 1985). [...] The political aim behind these initiatives was ambitious: to reconfigure the symbolic ordering of time, space and education in order to stamp upon them the presence of EC institutions.'
30. In *Aristeion*, ed. by Patricia Cannellis (Brussels: The Commission of the European Communities, 1995), foreword.
31. Leonida Rèpaci quoted in 'Premio Viareggio' [*Viareggio* Prize], *Wikipedia*, <http://it.wikipedia.org/wiki/Premio_Viareggio> [accessed 22 June 2017] (introductory statement): 'Volevamo, noi che lo fondammo, creare un premio che avesse un respiro più ampio del Bagutta, nato qualche mese prima nell'osteria del Pepori a Milano, e circoscritto ad una vita di cenacolo' [We, who founded it, wished to create a prize with a wider reach compared to the *Bagutta*, born a few months earlier in Master Pepori's tavern in Milan and limited to a cenacle life].
32. In Massimo Gatta, 'Letteratura ai tavoli del Bagutta. Ritrovo di galantuomini' [Literature at the *Bagutta* Tables. A Meeting Place for Gentlemen], *MenSA* <http://www.mensamagazine.it/articolo.asp?id=740> [accessed 15 April 2007] (para. 2 of 11).
33. Ibid. 'Volevamo [...] farlo circolare assai più del Bagutta nella società letteraria italiana, e costituire intorno ad esso, con la prudenza richiesta dalla situazione, una possibilità di incontro e riconoscimento di tutte quelle forze, di quelle testimonianze, che meno avessero subito la pressione ideologica della dittatura [...]'. '[We wanted [...] to obtain a greater impact within Italian literary society and wanted to build around [the prize] — with the caution required by the situation — a possibility for meeting and for the acknowledgment of all those drives, those testimonies, which had suffered less from the ideological pressure of dictatorship].
34. 'Presentation' [Presentation], *Prix Renaudot* [Renaudot Prize] <http://www.renaudot.com/> [accessed 15 April 2007] (para. 1 of 3).
35. In line with such a view, studies such as Nathalie Heinich's *L'épreuve de la grandeur* have highlighted the relation between literary competitions and non-nationalistic forms of identity-forming by pointing, for instance, to the changes brought to authorial identity and to the writers' sense of the self by the social recognition which derives from literary competitions. Nathalie Heinich, *L'Epreuve de la grandeur: Prix littéraires et reconnaissance* [The Test of Greatness: Literary Prizes and Recognition] (Paris: La Découverte, 1999).
36. Boura (2003).
37. See, for instance: George Talbot, *Censorship in Fascist Italy, 1922–43* (London: Palgrave Macmillan, 2007); Guido Bonsaver, *Literature and Censorship in Fascist Italy* (Toronto: Toronto University Press, 2007); Guido Bonsaver and Robert Gordon (eds), *Culture, Censorship and the State in Twentieth Century Italy* (Oxford: Legenda, 2005).

38. Peter J. Burke and Jan E. Stets, *Identity Theory* (Oxford: Oxford University Press, 2009); André Gallois, *Occasions of Identity* (Oxford: Oxford University Press, 1998).
39. Elliot Aronson, Timothy Wilson & Robin Akert, *Social Psychology* (New York: Pearson Prentice Hall, 2007); Benedict Anderson, *Imagined Communities*, (London: Verso, 1991).
40. Francesco Cassata and Massimo Moraglio, eds, *Manicomio, società e politica* [Mental Institution, Society and Politics] (Pisa: BFS Edizioni, 2005); Francesco Cassata, *Molti, sani e forti. L'eugenetica in Italia* [Many, Healthy and Strong. Eugenics in Italy] (Torino: Bollati Boringhieri, 2006); Paolo Francesco Peloso, *La guerra dentro. La psichiatria italiana tra fascismo e resistenza (1922–1945)* [The War Within. Italian Psychiatry between Fascism and Resistance] (Verona: Ombre Corte, 2008).
41. Paolo Fornaciari, 'Lorenzo Viani e la grande guerra' [Lorenzo Viani and the Great War], *Comune di Viareggio* [City of Viareggio], <http://www.comune.viareggio.lu.it/index.php?option=com_content&view=article&id=911&Itemid=12> [accessed 22 June 2017] (paragraph 2).
42. Giorgio Bárberi Squarotti, *L'Orologio d'Italia — Carlo Levi ed altri racconti* [Italy's Clock — Carlo Levi and other Stories] (Limena: Libroitaliano World, 2001).
43. 'Mussolini contro Bacchelli: niente premio, non è fascista' [Mussolini vs. Bacchelli: He isn't a Fascist: No Prize], *Il Corriere della Sera*, <http://archiviostorico.corriere.it/1995/dicembre/19/Mussolini_contro_Bacchelli_Niente_premio_co_0_95121913688.shtml> (19.12.1995) [accessed 6 July 2015].
44. Foschini's antifascism was ultimately the cause of his deportation to Nazi concentration camps. He survived, but died an early death a few years after his liberation, owing to the effects of the physical and psychological tortures he had undergone and from which he never fully recovered.
45. Gemma Volli, *Le escluse* [The Excluded] (Empoli: Ibiskos Editrice Risolo, 2006).
46. Subsequently published as a text in its own right. See Michel Le Bris and Jean Rouaud, eds, *Pour une littérature-monde* (Paris: Gallimard, 2007).
47. Dora Capozza and Rupert Brown eds., *Social Identity Processes* (London: Sage Publications Limited, 2000).
48. Ibid. p. 6.
49. Considering the remarkable heterogeneity characterizing the interpretive methods and theoretical positions of cognitive literary criticism, it is perhaps necessary to specify here that, when referring to cognitive poetics, this study indicates in particular the theoretical and methodological approaches in literary criticism predominantly derived from research in the field of cognitive linguistics and cognitive psychology. As noted by Stockwell, cognitive poetics in this context are based on three principles: 'the notion that meaning is embodied, and that mind and body are continuous; the notion that [...] categories are provisional, situationally dependent and socio-culturally grounded in embodiment too; and the notion that language and its manifestations in reading and interpretation is a natural, evolved and universal trait in humans, continuous with other perceptual and tactile experience of the environment.' Peter Stockwell, 'Cognitive Poetics and Literary Theory', *www.academia.edu* <http://www.academia.edu/718974/Cognitive_poetics_and_literary_theory> [accessed 24 June 2015].
50. Andrew Janiak 'Kant's Views on Space and Time', *Stanford Encyclopedia of Philosophy* <http://plato.stanford.edu/entries/kant-spacetime/#IntPhiQueAboSpaTim> [accessed 22 June 2017] (2.2 — paragraph 2 of 3).
51. Stephen Engstrom, 'Understanding and Sensibility', *Inquiry*, 49 (2006), 2–25.
52. Nini Praetorious, *Principles of Cognition, Language and Action* (Dordrecht, The Netherlands: Kluwer Academic Publishers, 2000), p. 351.
53. Harold M. Proshansky, Abbe K. Fabian, and Robert Kaminoff, 'Place-identity: Physical world socialization of the self', *Journal of Environmental Psychology*, Vol. 3 (1), March 1983, 57–83.
54. *Cognitive Poetics in Practice*, ed. by Joanna Gavins and Gerard Steen (London: Routledge, 2003), p. 1.
55. Ibid. p. 1.
56. Stockwell (2002), p.170.
57. Ibid., p.170.

58. Marcel Mauss and Emile Durkheim, 'De quelques formes primitives de classification' [On Some Primitive Forms of Classification], *www.philagora.net* (Philosophie de Philagora, Epistémologie), <http://www.philagora.net/capes-agreg/mauss-durkheim4.htm> [accessed 17 April 2007] (part IV).
59. Charles Sanders Peirce, *Collected Writings* (8 vols), ed. by Charles Hartshorne, Paul Weiss, and Arthur W. Burks, vol. 2 (Cambridge, MA: Harvard University Press, 1931–1958), p. 228. The scheme is partially — but not wholly — based on C. S. Peirce's semiotic triangle. In particular, the OBJECT, the form taken by the sign, can be understood to represent Peirce's *representamen*. As will be further argued, Peirce's *interpretant* — the sense which is made of the sign — is here seen as the identity which is embodied in the SUBJECT. Peirce's *object* — that to which the sign refers — is here to be understood as the CONTEXT dimension.
60. Jack Zipes in Ernst Bloch, *The Utopian Function of Art and Literature* [1974/1975], trans. by Jack Zipes and Frank Mecklenburg (Cambridge, MA: MIT Press, 1988), p. xxxii.
61. Bloch (1988), p. 38.
62. Wikipedia, *Categorization* <http://en.wikipedia.org/wiki/Categorisation> [accessed on 23 June 2017] (para. 1 of 10).
63. Derek Edwards, 'Categories Are for Talking', *Theory and Psychology*, 1.4 (Sage, 1991), 515–42, (p. 517).
64. Jean-Jacques Wunenburger, *Questions d'étique* [Ethical Issues] (Paris: PUF, 1993), p. 26.
65. Edwards (1991), p. 518.
66. Leoncio González Hevia, *La Idea de Cultura durante la España franquista* [The Idea of Culture in Francoist Spain], El Catoblepas, 42 (August 2005) <http://www.nodulo.org/ec/2005/n042p01.htm> [accessed 21 July 2017] (para. 1 of 19).

CHAPTER 1

France 1900–1918: Utopian Society

Let us begin by considering, in this first chapter, the identity-forming and the identity-stabilising potential of literary competitions. As anticipated, the institutions to be examined in this section, focusing on the first years of the twentieth century, are the French *Prix Goncourt* and *Prix Femina*. Before turning to the specifics of the analytical discussion, let us briefly trace their historical origins.

The founding of the *Académie Goncourt*, which is the body responsible for the yearly implementation and award of the *Goncourt* literary prize, originated, as indicated by its official name of *Société littéraire des Goncourt*, in the naturalist writer Edmond Goncourt's (1822–1896) request — detailed in his will — to his friend and fellow author Alphonse Daudet, to constitute a yearly literary prize of 5000 francs to be awarded to a successful novelist. Additionally, each one of the ten members of the *Académie* forming the judging panel was originally entitled to a rent of 6000 francs a year, aimed at guaranteeing the members' financial independence.

The roots of Goncourt's wish have been traced to the novelist's hostility towards the aesthetic and literary choices enacted at the time of his life by the State-funded *Académie Française*. Additionally, Edmond and his brother Jules (1830–1870) allegedly sought to recapture in their life-time — and through their novelistic activity — the aesthetic and literary values of French eighteenth-century aristocratic *salons* [TN: cultural and social gathering spaces]. Through the elitist framework of the *Goncourt* Academy, the nineteenth-century novelist allegedly attempted the nostalgic preserving of a long-lost cultural, social and mental aristocratic landscape.[1]

The initial *Goncourt* Academy included Alphonse's son Léon Daudet (writer and journalist, 1867–1942), authors Joris-Karl Huysmans (1848–1907), Rosny senior (Joseph Henri Honoré Boex, 1856–1940) and Rosny junior (Séraphin Justin François Boex, 1859–1948), Octave Mirbeau (journalist, novelist, art critic, playwright, 1848–1917) Léon Hennique (novelist, 1851–1935), Paul Margueritte (novelist, 1860–1918), Gustave Geoffroy (novelist, 1855–1926), Elémir Bourges (novelist, 1852–1925) and Lucien Descaves (journalist, novelist, playwright, 1861–1949). On 21 December 1903, the first *Goncourt* prize was awarded to John Antoine Nau (Eugène Léon Eduard Joseph Torquet, 1860–1918) for his novel *Force Ennemie* [Enemy Force]. To this day, the members of the *Goncourt* Academy are entitled to a seat in the *Drouant* restaurant, where the voting procedure takes place.

The prestigious award has been granted, over the years, to some of the most famous authors of French literature — to name but a few, Marcel Proust in 1919 (*A l'ombre des jeunes filles en fleur* [Within a Budding Grove]), André Malraux in 1933 (*La condition humaine* [Man's Fate]), Henry Troyat in 1938 (*L'araigne* [The Spider]) or Simone de Beauvoir in 1954 (*Les mandarins* [The Mandarins]).

The *Prix Femina* was founded a year later, in 1904, by 22 contributing writers and editors of the magazine *La vie heureuse*. Led by countess Anna de Noailles (novelist, 1876–1933), Alphonse Daudet's own wife (Julia Allard, 1884–1940) and Judith Gautier (1845–1917), the founders hoped to counter the 'misogyny' which, they claimed, directed the *Goncourt* Academy choices.

According to *Le Nouvel Observateur*, the strife between the two institutions has never really ceased:

> En 1931, Antoine de Saint-Exupéry reçoit le Femina pour *Vol de nuit* alors qu'il pouvait avoir le Goncourt. En 1993, Marc Lambron, favori du Goncourt, est lauréat du Femina pour *L'œil du silence*. En 1959, c'est le Goncourt qui prend au Femina *Le dernier des justes* d'André Schwartz-Bart...[2]

> [In 1931, Antoine de Saint-Exupéry receives the *Femina* for *Vol de nuit* [Night Flight] when he could have got the *Goncourt*. In 1933, Marc Lambron, favourite for the *Goncourt*, is a laureate of the *Femina* for *L'oeil du silence* [The Eye of Silence]. In 1959, the *Goncourt* takes from the *Femina Le dernier des justes* [The Last of the Just] by André Schwartz-Bart...].

However, it is precisely by analysing the parallel choices of the two competitions in terms of the stylistic and thematic content of winning novels — focusing, for the purposes of the first chapter of this work, on the 1900–1920 period — that one notices how the supposed opposition between the two prizes is actually much less striking than what might be expected from competing institutions.

The Destabilisation of Identity

Indeed, in both competitions, in the 1900–1920 period, the contents of winning novels appear to reflect a wide-spread, anguished awareness of the destabilization of personal and social identities taking place in France, in those years. As will be demonstrated in the following section, it is thematically embodied in the binary opposition between *human* and *animal* lexical fields, which defines the literary discourse on *Frenchness* in the winning novels. In contrast with images of physical and mental destruction — culminating not only, as stated, in the repeated use of a lexical field relating to the *animal* world but also in the reiterated referring to the lexical field of *destruction* and *death* — French identity, in its ideal formulation, is posited as belonging to a *human* sphere fundamentally characterised by unsullied *wholeness*.

Such a literary thematic and lexical tension appears to be matched, in the context of contemporary non-literary discourses, by parallel references to structural dissolution. The case of Henri Louis Bergson's (1859–1941) theory of time, emerging in the cultural area in which the winning novels are written and judged, provides an illustration of the degree to which the destabilisation of form permeates in an extensive way the communal field of cognition.

If such discourses (both literary and non-literary) are moreover considered in the specific light of contemporary historical events — territorial transformations, movements of population, changes to the social and political landscape — one can highlight a diffuse sense of structural loss and an anguished acknowledgement of the dissolution of traditional identitary models.

Literary features

Focusing on the thematic content of the winning novels, one notices how indeed, in the years 1900–1920, French identity is challenged in many ways: physical wholeness, mental stability and spiritual identity are represented as being under the threat of dissolution.

In particular, the body is violated, its integrity attacked, and images of rape — both real and metaphorical — permeate the winning novels of Louis Pergaud (*Goncourt* 1910),[3] André Savignon (*Goncourt* 1912),[4] Claude Farrère (*Goncourt* 1905)[5] and Edouard Estaunié (*Femina* 1908).[6]

In Louis Pergaud's novel[7] and André Savignon's short stories,[8] actual rape is disturbingly and powerfully evoked; in Edouard Estaunié's *La vie secrète* [The Secret Life] verbal exchanges are fused and confused with physical aggression;[9] and in Farrère's following fragment, the sexual violation of the individual is used as the symbolic expression of the wider political, social and cultural destruction caused by colonialism:

> La contagion sanglante affolait les cerveaux. Fierce aussi enfonça une porte et chercha, féroce, une proie vivante. Il la trouva derrière deux planches dressées en barricade, dans un réduit sans toit que la lune éclairait impitoyablement: une fillette annamite cachée sous des nattes [...] Elle se jeta à ses pieds, lui embrassant les hanches et les genoux, elle le suppliait avec des sanglots et des caresses; il la sentait chaude et palpitante, collée à lui [...] Il trébucha, tomba sur la proie.[10]
>
> [A bloody contagion maddened the brains. Fierce, like the others, broke down a door and, ferocious, searched for a living prey. He found her behind two boards, erected as a barricade, in a roofless shelter mercilessly illuminated by the moon: a little annamite girl hidden under braids [...] She threw herself to his feet, embracing his hips and knees, she begged him with tears and caresses; he felt her, against him, hot and palpitating [...] He stumbled and fell on the prey.]

The reference to 'contagion' is indicative of a further referring to the individual's physical destruction through the use of the thematic and lexical fields of illness — both corporal and mental — and death. Thus, hunger alters Pergaud's Goupil, shaping him as a discarded rag, as a vagrant shadow whose ghostly appearance all but removes him from the realm of the living.[11] Mutilation — either self-imposed or externally caused — permeates both Pergaud's[12] and Savignon's tales.[13] If the physical deterioration of illness transmutes Savignon's characters into distorted and unrecognisable forms,[14] Farrère's protagonists, torn by self-destructive drives, are ultimately unable to recognise themselves in the ragged appearances reflected by mirrors:

> Il vit son visage, et s'inquiéta de le trouver pâle: quoi! c'était lui cette face plombée, ces yeux creux, ce regard terne? C'était lui ces lèvres exsangues, dont le baiser froid devait répugner comme le baiser d'un agonisant?[15]
>
> [He saw his face and worried to find himself so pale: What! Were this laden face, these sunken eyes, this dull gaze, really his? Were these bloodless lips his, whose cold kiss must be as repugnant as a dying man's kiss?]

Self-destruction,[16] physical and mental corruption[17] and violent death all symbolically articulate the degree to which the physical space of the body is penetrated, altered, deformed and ultimately destroyed[18] in a process which, albeit at times immediate[19] and surprising,[20] emerges in fact as a slow, all-pervading, ever-present, movement of decomposition:

> La mort est en chacun de nous, qui fait son oeuvre. Quand son travail cesse, nous disparaissons, mais nous mourons chaque jour un peu; la mort n'est pas une intruse, introduite par effraction, au déclin de notre vie, elle est notre compagne constante.[21]
>
> [Death is in each and every one of us, doing its work. When its work is done, we disappear, yet we also die a little each day; death is not an intruder, a trespasser, it is our constant companion.]

Such a corporeal deconstruction is moreover repeatedly projected onto a symbolic dimension in which the concept of form itself — human form — is openly dramatised and challenged, in particular through the pervading use of the lexical field of metamorphosis.

Such a lexical field is embodied in the proliferation of references to the animal world[22] emerging from the winning novels.[23] Thus, Edouard Estaunié's Monsieur Lethois sees nothing in humanity but 'une vaste fourmilière d'ordre inférieur et mal construite!' [a vast, badly-constructed anthill of an inferior order][24] and Pergaud's Goupil rests a paradoxically very human eye on the deformed and animalised hunters who capture him and who are described with 'les chicots de dents, jaunis par le tabac, trouant des mâchoires féroces, et des ventres qui bougeaient comme s'ils eussent voulu happer d'eux-mêmes une proie convoitée' [teeth stubs, yellowed by tobacco, piercing cruel jaws and bellies moving, as if they wished to snatch by themselves a coveted prey].[25] Similarly, de Miomandre's Jacques focuses on 'le passage félin d'une langue humide' [the feline passage of a humid tongue][26] while looking at Monsieur Paillon, and Savignon presents his characters as forever suspended between the human and the non-human dimensions: 'Quelque jour, chez cet objet qui vous paraît si aimable, la bête ardente reprendra le dessus, dans une frasque énorme' [One day, with a huge leap, the burning beast will overcome that which appears to be so lovely].[27] Again, if the metaphor of animalisation is used by Estaunié in order to unveil the social tensions opposing the developing workers' movement to the bourgeois preoccupations of the novel's protagonists in Jude Servin's address to Thérèse,[28] the young Marie-Claire appears to fill Audoux's text (*Femina* 1910) with imaginary monkeys[29] and bulls,[30] setting a fantastic animal realm in contrast to the stark reality depicted by the novel. The process is repeated by Edmond Jaloux in his filling the imagination of his young protagonists with sheep,[31] butterflies[32] and all kinds of other animals. Ultimately, Jaloux projects over the novel as a whole the sombre and apocalyptic vision of an inevitable and all-encompassing return to original bestiality:

> Alors la lumière diminuera comme une lampe qui manque d'huile, et ces êtres orgueilleux, qui ont cru progresser sans fin sous le ciel sans limites, remonteront à pas lents le chemin déjà parcouru. Venus de la bête, ils retourneront mornement vers leur origine.[33]
>
> [There will come a time when light will dwindle, like a lamp without oil, and these proud beings, who believed they would progress without limits under a boundless sky, will go back with slow steps on the trodden path. They come from the beast, and will gloomily return to their origins.]

Philosophical perspectives

The oscillation between the human and non-human dimensions, coupled with the sustained thematic referring to physical and mental dissolution we have evoked, project the literary production sanctioned by the *Prix Femina* and *Prix Goncourt* into a symbolic landscape where the very notion of *form* appears to be inherently destabilised. Significantly, one notices how contemporary non-literary discourses point to a similar process of structural destabilisation.

Taking the case of the Bergsonian theory of temporal flux, one notices how philosophical discourses chronologically close to the production of the literary texts we have considered[34] and, by extension, close to the emerging of the phenomenon of modern literary prizes in France, appear to match literary thematic concerns and, as further shown in following sections, a more generally diffused perception of the destabilisation of the structural notion of *space* occurring within the French cultural context.

In his *Essai sur les données immédiates de la conscience* [Time and Free Will: An Essay on the Immediate Data of Consciousness],[35] Henri Bergson famously lists the characteristics of the *spatial* dimension. Consisting of external elements, juxtaposed and deprived of any succession, space is defined by opposition to the *temporal* which is, on the other hand, conceived as an undivided and indivisible flux — pure 'durée' [duration].[36] The systematic process through which the spatial is projected onto the temporal produces the illusion of what Bergson defines as the 'temps homogène' [homogenous time],[37] that is, the belief that the temporal dimension can be distinguished in juxtaposed and successive moments. In fact, the synthetic process of consciousness produces the mistaken understanding of space as a succession of temporal subdivisions and the mistaken perception of time as a succession of spatial subdivisions.

In this context, one notices how Bergson sets up an opposition between the external dimension of space and the internal or individual dimension of time/consciousness. The external/spatial is thus defined by the absence of 'durée' or succession, while the definition of the internal/temporal dimension is based on the denial of the quantifiable and on the favouring of the concept of the qualitative.

What is significant for the current study, beyond the specifics of the Bergsonian theory, is that the conceptual deconstruction of the spatial dimension in Bergson's understanding of consciousness chronologically matches and thematically corresponds to the contextual drive towards formal destabilisation we have evoked in the context of French turn-of-the-century literary production.

Contextual dimension

Overall, the dominant mood appears to be that of an awareness, not to mention an anxiety, related to the absence, at the level of the communal cognitive sphere, of a stabilised, perceivable, structural dimension. One notices, incidentally, how critical positions which emphasise a pattern of spatial predominance in the field of cognitive perception, in the France of those years, might perhaps be reconsidered in the light of the problematisation of the formal — understood as *formed* — dimension which appears to invest the communal cognitive sphere and which emerges from both the literary and non-literary discourses we have considered.

Marxist critics, such as Uri Eisenzweig, have indeed argued that, between the end of the nineteenth century and the opening of the twentieth century, in France, the spatial dimension — in both cognitive processes and discursive practices — dominated the fluid, de-structured, ever-changing temporal dimension.[38] Such a process is read by Eisenzweig in parallel with the development of a politically significant colonialist drive:[39] the critic underlines what he considers as a crucial connection between the development of colonialist politics and processes of alleged dominance of the spatial dimension in the dynamics of cognition, representation and perception.

However, the critic's belief in a perception of the spatial dimension occurring 'sans problème' [without problems] can, in my opinion, be challenged. For instance, let us consider Eisenzweig's specific reference to colonialist politics in the light of the exponential growth of the prizes sponsored by the French *Société de Géographie* — 41 new prizes born between 1850 and 1950 — aimed at publications highlighting successes in geographical initiatives and explorations. On the one hand, it could be considered that such prizes are indeed the consequence of the ideological drive towards the cultural, geographical and political colonisation of foreign territories. On the other hand — and this is my contention — such a multiplication of prizes arguably points up a deep-seated anxiety with regard to the very stability of the evoked 'espace objectal' [objectal space]. It is the hope and desire to control an increasingly problematic spatial dimension that appears to be at the root of such a frenetic proliferation of geography-based competitions.

A similar argument can be made regarding the *Goncourt* and the *Femina*. A brief overview of these literary prizes points to the reiterated success of the so-called 'romans exotico-coloniaux' [exotico-colonialist novels].[40] Among the main examples, one notices *Les Civilisés* [The Civilized] by Claude Farrère (*Goncourt* 1905); *Dingley, l'illustre écrivain* [Dingley, The Famous Writer] by Jean and Jérôme Tharaud (*Goncourt* 1906); *En France* [In France] by the Leblond cousins (*Goncourt* 1909) and, to an extent, the early *Force Ennemie* [Enemy Force] by John-Antoine Nau (*Goncourt* 1903). Maurice Angenot underlines, in this context, the degree to which Euro-centric drives,[41] not to mention a Franco-centric worldview, offer the key for the reading of colonial-related narratives as attempts to crystallise a stereotyped landscape of nations and races.

Such attempts appear, however, to be highly problematic. Indeed, taking the example of Claude Farrère's *Les Civilisés*, set in the context of the French colonies, one notices how it introduces the early twentieth-century debate on the political crisis surrounding the colonial territories as well as expressing deep-seated anxieties related to the question of racial and national identities. If, on the one hand, it displays an apparently passionate criticism of the colonial world, it also inherently reinforces the stereotype it seeks to undermine by constructing the portrait of depravity and corruption of the French 'civilisers' against an ideal of purity and rectitude which is held to embody the true nature of what a civilising mission — understood within the colonialist model — should represent.[42] No single linear interpretation is offered by the novel, torn between contradictory representations and readings of the colonial experience. Farrère's association of colonialism, rape, contagion and death (as considered above) unveils the deep-seated ambiguity which characterises not only the discourse on colonialism but — perhaps more importantly for the purposes of this study — the discourse on the structural stability of bodies, geographical territories, nations and identities taking place in the France of those years.

Anticipating Eisenzweig's approach, in his *Qu'est-ce que la littérature*? [What is Literature?], Jean-Paul Sartre conflates stylistic choices, literary themes, ideological perceptions and historical events, in an overview of the end of the nineteenth and beginning of the twentieth centuries in France, which underlines the alleged *stability* of the cognised contextual sphere and which, in the light of the challenging position presented by this work, is worth quoting at some length (my emphasis):

> Pendant toute cette période, qui s'étend sur plusieurs générations, l'anecdote est racontée du point de vue de l'absolu, c'est à dire de l'ordre; c'est un changement local dans **un système en repos**; ni l'auteur ni le lecteur ne courent de risques, aucune surprise n'est à craindre: l'événement est passé, catalogué, compris. Dans une société **stabilisée**, qui n'a pas encore conscience des dangers qui la menacent, qui dispose d'une morale et d'un système d'explications pour intégrer ses changements locaux, qui s'est persuadée qu'elle est au-delà de l'historicité et qu'il n'arrivera plus jamais rien d'important, dans une France bourgeoise, cultivée jusqu'au dernier arpent, **découpée** en damier par des murs séculaires, **figée** dans ses méthodes industrielles, sommeillant sur la gloire de sa révolution...[43]

> [During the whole period, stretched over many generations, the anecdotal episode is narrated from within an absolute perspective, that is to say, order; it is a local change within a system at rest; neither the author nor the reader face any risks, no surprise must be feared: the event has passed, is classified, is understood. In a stabilised society, not yet aware of the dangers threatening it, endowed with a moral dimension and a system of explanations aimed at

integrating local changes, convinced that it is placed beyond history and that nothing important will ever happen, in a bourgeois France, cultivated up to its last yard [TN: *arpent* is a pre-metric French unit of measurement], cut as a draught-board by century-old walls, frozen in its industrial methods, sleeping on the glory of its revolution...]

Sartre thus establishes a multi-layered vision of the social cognitive field in which the geographical definition of the territory, the historical and political setting of national boundaries, the ideological framework of the bourgeoisie and the stylistic characteristics of literary expression are made to implode in a unique perception of *formal* stability. The form of the text, the geographical space of the historical landscape, the virtual pattern of social structures — all interconnect and appear as ostensibly stabilised in the critic's view.

Yet, as previously seen, the thematic content of the novels evoked displays an instability of the concept of form which challenges the stabilised cognitive pattern evoked by Sartre and Eisenzweig. The thematic pattern we have highlighted appears in fact to echo the numerous transformations occurring at different levels within the above-mentioned territory. These transformations, in turn, appear to deeply affect the cognitive dimension of the collective French national consciousness of the early twentieth century — the concept of *territory* being here understood as expressing not only France's external geographical and political frontiers but also its internal regional divisions and its social, human landscape.

In terms of the internal landscape, the relation between main cities and rural areas is irrevocably altered by an unprecedented urban development. With a process beginning at the end of the nineteenth century, Paris grows dramatically, seeing its population increase from 'just over half a million in 1801 [...] to over two million in 1877'.[44] The Parisian landscape itself undergoes massive architectural transformations in accordance with Georges Haussmann's planning.[45] Moreover, the distance between the urban setting and the traditional lifestyle of the countryside appears paradoxically to widen, just as technological developments allow for the exponential expansion of the railway network[46] and for its directly related perception of France in terms of reduced distances and easily accessible locations.[47]

Increasingly, the *France profonde* [TN: predominantly rural areas of the country, away from the main cities] is perceived as an internal frontier to be conquered, a space to be monitored and controlled. Among the preferred means stands out a process of enforced civilisation, based not only on the commendable effort to ensure the systematic diffusion of basic instruction and alphabetisation, but also on the somewhat less commendable systematic eradication of regional languages, local dialects and cultural traditions.[48] The 'instituteur' [teacher][49] becomes, in this context, a mythic figure, endowed with a missionary-like, quasi-religious aura, on whom the State can count 'to educate, cultivate, socialize, moralize, and modernise the Nation'.[50] Significantly, it is Louis Pergaud, 'instituteur' in the small hamlet of Maison-Alfort, who wins the 1910 *Prix Goncourt* with his *De Goupil à Margot*.

According to Maurice Angenot, the process of education finds its natural match in the systematic enforcement of compulsory military service, aimed not only at ensuring France's military potential but also at severing the links which still connect the average young farm labourer to the cultural reality of his local settlement. Thus, the State's educational campaign, together with the hardly resistible lure provided by an ever-widening job market offered by large urban settlements, lead to a massive phenomenon of internal migration. In a context of substantial displacements of population, old cultural prejudices and stereotypes against the rural world forcefully emerge in the urban social discourse[51] as, in turn, the city space is perceived by urban populations as being under threat of invasion.

To the widening of education and its related territorial, horizontal, movements of displacement, can also be added a vertical social mobility which is similarly articulated, within the social discourse, in a context of deep-seated anxiety. Thus, for instance, Paul Bourget's emphasis, in *L'Etape* [The Step],[52] on the tragic consequences of social promotion, is strongly echoed by Edmond de Goncourt's forceful criticism of the ongoing widening of basic education. The noticeable use of spatial metaphors is, in the writer's words, indicative of the degree to which territorial displacement and social mobility are indeed conflated in a unique fear of *structural* transformation (my emphasis):

> Toute mère du people veut donner, et à force de se saigner aux quatre veines, donne à son enfant l'instruction qu'elle n'a pas eue. De cette folie générale, de cette manie partout répandue dans le bas de la société **de jeter** ses enfants **pardessus soi**, de les porter **au-dessus de son niveau**, comme on **porte** les enfants au feu d'artifice, naît l'irrespect fatal de cet enfant pour les parents [...] Puis toutes les carrières **s'encombrent et se bouchent** par cette vulgarisation des aptitudes, des capacités. Un jour viendra où il n'y aura plus que des têtes, des plumes...[53]

> [Each and every mother of the populace wishes to give and — by bleeding herself dry — gives to her child the education she never received. A fatal lack of respect is born out of this general madness, this mania of the lower classes to elevate their children above themselves, as people carry children to see fireworks [...] As a result of such a vulgarisation of aptitudes and capacities, all careers are filled up and blocked. One day, only heads and pens will be left...]

To the anxiety linked to social mobility and its related expression of rhetorical resistance, one must add the concern with external frontiers to see how the triad which Maurice Angenot identifies with xenophobia, racism and patriotic rhetoric pervades the French social discourse at the opening of the twentieth century.

For instance, winners of the *Prix Goncourt* of the years 1900–1920 signal how the concern with regional, inner identity — in Emile Moselly's *Terres Lorraines* [Lands of *Lorraine*] (Goncourt 1907), and in André Savignon's *Filles de Pluie* [Daughters of the Rain] (Goncourt 1912) — merges with the anxious articulation of France's external borders in a process which nostalgically refers to a regional identity only to highlight the degree to which French identity, as a whole, is felt to be under threat.[54] Ethnocentrism and its obsessive focus on the notion of boundary, on the distinction between what is recognised and what is refused, on the attack on all that is foreign, seen as hostile, perceived as dangerously conspiring against the internal and external borders of France's unsullied identity, are central features of the discursive production of the years 1900–1920.[55]

At the national level, patriotism[56] articulates itself in the most varied discursive practices, ranging from children's literature to newspaper chronicles. After the critical Franco-German war of 1870, it dominates the greatest part of the social and artistic discourse. Thus, for instance, in the literary sphere, France increasingly embodies itself in the mythicised figure of a militant Joan of Arc.[57]

The symbolic significance of such an embodiment emerges in particular when considered in parallel with statements such as those contained in Maurice Barrès's (1862–1923) *Un homme libre* [A Free Man] (1889), which articulates the need for a specific and clearly delimited space of existence able to guarantee the exclusion of the *barbaric* — here understood in its original Greek sense of *foreign* (my emphasis):

> Simon et moi, nous comprîmes alors notre haine des étrangers, des barbares, et notre égotisme où nous **enfermons** avec nous-mêmes toute notre petite famille morale. Le premier soin de celui qui veut vivre, c'est de s'entourer de **hautes murailles**. Mais, dans son jardin **fermé**, il introduit avec lui ceux que guident des façons analogues de sentir et des intérêts communs.[58]

> [Simon and I understood then our hatred of foreigners, of barbarians, and the egotism in which we enclose ourselves and our little moral family. The first concern of someone wishing to live is to enclose himself within high walls. However, into his closed garden, he introduces those who feel just as he does and share common interests.]

True, in the specific case of Barrès' personal evolution, as the *barbarians* are increasingly perceived to press at the gates of the French spatial identity — the lexical field of enclosure being here particularly significant — patriotism and nationalism gain an increasingly threatening and virulent dimension which goes beyond the echoes evoked in this work.

With regard to the present study, however, one notices how the spatial discourse of enclosure and the discursive drive towards the symbolic embodiment of France in Joan of Arc's mythic form, both point to the desire of ensuring stability in the perception of the spatial field — the spatial dimension being here understood as both a *real*, territorial, political space and as a symbolic personified embodiment.

What emerges from such a discursive and symbolic practice is the desired immobilisation of French identity within clearly defined representative and territorial borders. In turn, such a stabilisation can be understood as ensuring the possible construction of a *stable Other* against whom to pinpoint and shape France's own identity. Indeed, as the Saussurean sign is defined through its difference from surrounding signs, the French semiotic dimension appears to be enforced through the construction of a distinct *foreign* semiotic sphere against which it can form a stable identity — an identity not threatened by formal dissolution.

As a consequence, the conception of France as an open symbolic and physical space appears to be hampered by a fear of penetration by external cultural identities, as manifested for instance with regard to the Americans by the ever particularly representative Goncourt brothers.

At the Universal Exposition of 1867, the Goncourt's diary accusingly registers 'le dernier coup au passé: l'américanisation de la France' [the last blow to the past: the

Americanisation of France], an observation rendered particularly evocative through the added use of the present participle 'rognant' [cutting short],[59] which projects the relation between the two countries on a spatial dimension where the symbolic body of France is mutilated. Goncourt's sombre prophecy culminates in the apocalyptic vision of Americans as 'les futurs conquérants du monde' [future conquerors of the world],[60] during a trip abroad to Rome, enacted in the same year.

Ultimately, the reader is presented with a catastrophic, apocalyptic vision of general destruction: 'Ce seront les barbares de la civilisation qui mangeront le monde latin, comme l'ont déjà mangée autrefois les barbares de la barbarie' [The barbarians of civilisation will devour the Latin world, just as the barbarians from Barbaric lands did a long time ago].[61] What is at stake is a framing process which will clearly delineate and encompass the foreign identity, preventing a threatening penetration of the different into the familiar, a deadly blurring of the limits between the self and the other.[62]

Utopia as Form: The Literary Institution

Thus the picture of the cognitive landscape, such as it is provided by literary prize winners, posits the problem of the widespread perception of a change of the essence of French identity, a change so deep it is expressed through metaphorical references to a process of metamorphosis, animalisation and dissolution. The social tensions reflected in the thematic dualism *human/non-human* testify, in this context, to a deep-seated destabilisation of the structural dimension in its multiple symbolic and non-symbolic embodiments, such as it is perceived and cognised by the social sphere as a whole.

The question posed is, however, not only that of the specific nature of the identity which is being discussed but also that of the fact that the social discourse on the nature of French identity appears to orient and shape specific cultural practices. In this context, it can be affirmed that the founding — and subsequent exponential development of literary competitions — is not a casual event. It appears, on the contrary, to be directly related to the cultural context we have evoked.

In particular, the institution of literary competitions can be understood as being a concrete instance of a *need-answering* social practice, emerging from a cultural dimension which at the social discursive level openly articulates, as shown, a wide-ranging need for both symbolic and non-symbolic *structuring*. In this light, the institution of literary prizes becomes symptomatic of the ways in which both discursive instances and social practices — influencing and reflecting each other — can be read as intending to restore and maintain *formal* stability.

Concretely, the literary institution appears to cater to the above-mentioned need for structural stability at multiple levels. First, in terms of its material organization and in its external dynamics — for instance, in its *occupation of physical space* — the literary competition appears to operate as the *institutional answer* to the needs of a social context in which both symbolic and physical spatial articulation and negotiation are central discursive and behavioural practices.

The specific case of the *Prix Goncourt*, read in the light of the biographical and autobiographical information relating to its founding members, provides moreover an example of a further dimension occupied by the literary institution. Beyond spatial organisation, it bridges the gap between *personal*, individual convictions and fears and *common* behavioural practices, through the negotiation of the relationship between group-related, wide-ranging, context-influenced, organisational drives and specific personal concerns. So, as highlighted by the *Goncourt* case, an apparently selective, elitist institution, whose aesthetic criteria arguably represent from the very beginning but a limited sector of the cultural landscape, can be read in terms of its capacity to embody a communal, nation-wide, aspiration to identity-structuring and stabilisation.

Thus, as the literary institutions under examination appear to reward those works which more emphatically or more openly articulate the anxieties permeating the whole of the social sphere, the very birth of the institution of modern literary prizes, which takes place precisely in the context of the late nineteenth-century social practices of the French cultural world, is *in itself* an expression and an embodiment of the need to counter-balance the destabilisation of cognised structural stability which we have evoked, a social practice which testifies to the self-conscious potential of the discourses we have previously considered.

However, a purely historical reading of the development of French literary prizes at the beginning of the twentieth century does not account for the long-term success of such competitions, not to mention the exponential development of similar prizes throughout Europe and beyond during the last hundred years. Transcending the historical and cultural limits of French prizes, literary competitions appear today to enjoy enduring popularity and success. The final part of this section will begin to consider why the phenomenon of modern literary prizes is able to transcend its historical origins. As will be further discussed below, it is my contention that such a potentially wide-ranging success emerges with particular strength if assessed in terms of the fundamentally 'utopian' nature (in the sense, as will be shown, of Ernst Bloch's definition of the term) of literary competitions.

The space of literature

It has been noticed how, at the end of the nineteenth century, in the French context, the space of literature is taken over by changing social groups who, in turn, stake their claim on the symbolic territory of the cultural sphere. In her analysis of the early twentieth-century French literary world, Priscilla Parkhurst focuses indeed on the characteristics that mark each different cultural organisation in this process of social construction and symbolic negotiation.

Significantly, considering the development of the French *cénacle* [TN: small group pursuing literary or philosophical interests], she underlines the intimacy and homogeneity of such group gatherings, defined in contrast to the mixed socialisation process enacted in the *salons*.[63] Characterised by militant dedication to specific aesthetic ideals,[64] the somehow informal *cénacle* often leads to the establishment of a more formal institutional framework — among which one can include the founding of newspapers, the annexing of publishing houses, and the institution of literary prizes — through which both human and economic resources can be more effectively mobilised.[65]

Yet such a perspective of potential market control is intrinsically destabilised, according to the author, by the systematic substitution of one group with another group throughout the nineteenth and early twentieth centuries: romantics, parnassians and naturalists. According to the critic, a constant process of social mobility[66] matches the strategic attempts to occupy the cultural territory: 'The first step towards self-definition was to claim intellectual and aesthetic territory [...] By such means groups took possession of literary space and made that space their own.'[67]

Significantly, such a reading reinforces the analysis of the cognitive destabilisation previously outlined, in its emphasis on both the ever-evolving nature of cultural gatherings and the expressed need for formal, organisational, structuring and spatial occupation.

In particular, in terms of the practical control of the social sphere, one notices how the claiming of symbolic space extends to the organisation of meeting places with a complex degree of interaction with the public sphere. As Paris increasingly offered '[...] those who lived there an unprecedented number of opportunities for relaxing, meeting people, and exchanging ideas',[68] in an ever-widening social space encompassing restaurants, theatres, newly lit avenues, squares and freshly planted parks, one notices how the perception of the transforming social space is matched by an increased need, expressed by cultural groups through their social behaviour, to establish firm symbolic and physical boundaries.[69] Thus, if, in their youth, the Goncourt could often be seen haunting the *Café Riche*, the *Café Helder*, or the *Brasserie des Martyrs*, dining in *Le Grand Balcon* on the *Boulevard des Italiens*, at the *Taverne Anglaise* or at the *Restaurant de la Terrasse*,[70] one notices how negatively they nevertheless later perceive '...ces arrière-fonds de café où se baptisent les gloires embryonnaires et les grands hommes sans nom, où chauffent ces succès de la bohème...' [these coffee-house back-rooms where embryonic glories and great men without a name are baptised, where bohemian successes are kept warm ...].[71]

In fact, the need to establish firm symbolic territories, characterised by spatial stability and a certain degree of closure, is paramount. Significantly, cultural life increasingly articulates itself in the context of closed circles and intellectual gatherings within private houses[72] or selected restaurants — as in the specific case of the *Académie Goncourt*, taking place in the *Drouant* restaurant. Although the restaurant is, in theory, an open and public space, it remains, in fact, a potentially private, limited, area within which the intellectual activity can be more securely framed. The negotiation of participation rights to the secluded sphere of the aesthetic decision-making process is articulated through the bias of entrance rights to the limited spatial dimension of the restaurant which, from a public, open space, is transformed into a closed arena marked by social structuring and hierarchical articulation.

Indeed, the creation of the *Prix Renaudot* in 1925 by a group of journalists who, excluded from the ritual *déjeuner chez Drouant* [lunch at *Drouant*'s] during which the

Goncourt is awarded, were impatiently waiting outside, is significant of the tactical uses that the limitation and delimitation of space have in a social context. Having moved to a neighbouring restaurant, the newly born *Renaudot* jury re-enacted the *Goncourt* strategic delimiting of an institutional space in order to validate its own identity as a social institution.

Such a process of boundary negotiation is significant of the need to set firm external limits[73] reinforcing the group's identity[74] and of the social practices triggered by the need for cognitive structuring, which we have highlighted in the context of early twentieth-century France. Thus, one notices how — in addition to the thematic concerns evoked by the winning novels — the physical, organisational reality of literary prize embodies in itself a concrete and operative process towards physical and symbolic territorial structuring and stabilisation.

Prix Goncourt

In the case of the *Prix Goncourt* and its contemporaries, one notices how such a need for symbolic and territorial spatial organisation — a kind of organisation which, as mentioned, aims to counter the perceived instability of the social dimension — is openly expressed by the creators of the prize themselves and self-consciously acknowledged in their autobiographical writings.

Inaugurating the long sequence of European literary prizes established in the twentieth century, the *Académie Goncourt*, stems — as mentioned above — from Edmond and Jules de Goncourt's idea of setting up a privately funded institution with the aim of supporting new authors in their attempt to establish themselves as novelists.

In this context, the creation of the *Académie Goncourt* has been considered as particularly expressive of the late nineteenth-century clash between poetry and prose in the context of the transformation of long-standing aesthetic hierarchies.[75] Allegedly, it marks the promotion of the novel — as opposed to non-fictional prose — to a higher aesthetic status on the artistic scene: 'le prix Goncourt n'est octroyé qu'à un roman ou un recueil de nouvelles — en général, un roman. Il couronne une prose exclusivement narrative, c'est à dire une prose dégagée du carcan de la rhétorique.'[76] [The *Goncourt* Prize is only awarded to a novel or to a collection of short stories — generally, to a novel. It is conferred on works in narrative prose only, that is to say prose freed from the weight of rhetoric.]

The idea took in all probability a substantial dimension following Edmond de Goncourt's 1873 participation to the Academy founded by Philippe de Chennevières, director of *Beaux-Arts*, at Bellesme dans l'Orne, and can certainly be understood to embody a particularly representative instance of the struggle for the control of the cultural territory we have previously mentioned.

The *Prix Goncourt* represents the struggle against cognitive destabilisation at a much deeper level, however, a dimension which is also shared by the other literary competitions considered in this study. Indeed, although officially founded on the 14 January 1903, the prize was in fact born on the death of Edmond de Goncourt in the late 1890s and its creation was strongly linked to the earlier death of Edmond's brother Jules. It was, specifically, after the tragic death of Jules de Goncourt that the desire to push ahead with the project took on a final urgency, as Edmond expressed in 1885:

> Idée de tous les moments, chez moi, de défendre dans l'avenir de l'oubli ce nom de Goncourt, par toutes les survies, survie par les oeuvres, survie par les fondations, survie par l'application de mon chiffre ou de ma marque sur toutes les choses d'art possédée par mon frère et par moi.[77]
>
> [It is a recurring idea of mine, that of defending from future oblivion this name of Goncourt, through all possible survivals, survival through the texts, survival through the foundations, survival through the application of my cipher or monogram on all the art objects possessed by my brother or by myself.]

What emerges from such a statement is, in fact, a drive towards the transcending of the mortal dimension by establishing a multiple system of cultural and social *structured* instances: aesthetic works, social institutions, visual signs. The shadow of death is significantly projected by the author not only on a personal level but on existing social institutions as well — as stated in a particularly straightforward manner in one of his much-discussed attacks on the official *Académie Française*, which is seen as 'se retirant de tout ce qui est vie et jeunesse' and 'cherchant le suicide' [[...] moving away from all that is life and youth [...] embracing suicide].'[78]

The dominant mood appears to be that of an anxiety which Heidegger recognises as 'that occurrence in human existence in which the nothing is revealed'.[79] Understanding the 'nothing' as an intrinsic instability of the *formed, formal, structured*, as the perceived absence, at the level of the social cognitive sphere, of a stabilised cognitive dimension, of the irresistible *flowing* dimension of a life irrevocably directed toward dissolution and self-annihilation, allows one to read the Goncourt sponsoring of the literary prize competition in the light of its echoing potential with regard to the social concerns and practices previously evoked. As expressed in terms of Goncourt's personal experience, the spectre of death and cognitive dissolution — *suicide* in the institutional framework, *oubli* in the personal dimension — shrouds the conception of the literary prize in an anxiety-laden subjective awareness of the necessity of ensuring life's survival through the medium of cultural expression.

Interestingly, in the specific case of the Goncourt brothers, the fear of death, dissolution and annihilation mentioned above, though particularly representative of their contextual dimension, also forms the basis for an understanding of the structuring potential of the studied institutional embodiments which transcends the historical context of the French case.

The history of modern literary prizes is, in this context, quite evocative. Not only is the fortune of the *Académie Goncourt* significant and quite immediate at home;[80] its emulators also quickly proliferate both in France and abroad. Thus as early as 1905 the *Prix du Cercle de la Vie Heureuse* (the future *Prix Femina*) is founded, shortly followed by the 1912 *Grand Prix de Littérature de l'Académie Française* [TN: French Academy prize for literature] and the 1914 *Grand Prix du Roman de l'Académie Française* [TN: French Academy prize for novelistic fiction], the creation of which comes — incidentally — as the ultimate recognition of the Goncourt's influence in the affirmation of the aesthetic and literary value of novelistic fiction. The *James Tait Black Memorial Prize* is simultaneously established in Scotland in 1919 and, after the First World War, the phenomenon grows exponentially with the second generation of prizes in both France — with the 1925 *Prix Renaudot* and the 1930 *Prix Intérallié* — and in Italy — with the 1927 *Premio Bagutta* and the 1929 *Premio Viareggio* — setting a trend of constant growth which, after more than a hundred years, shows as yet no sign of abating.

The key to understanding such a trans-cultural success is the assessment of the institution in terms of its capacity to fulfil a structuring function at the cognitive level which transcends the specifics of the historical context we have identified and yet caters for trans-national needs for structural stabilisation in whatever context those needs might emerge.

In fact, the literary prize institution, such as it was conceived by the Goncourt brothers and also such as it has developed beyond the Goncourt's specific cultural context, can be seen to express an *utopian* belief — utopian, as will be further explained, in Ernst Bloch's understanding of the term — through its capacity to promote a cultural form acting as a guarantee against the cognition of structural dissolution.

The 'utopian' drive according to Ernst Bloch

With regard to the latter element, the reference to a *utopian* projection in the context of death-related anxiety is here, as stated, specifically based on Theodor Adorno and Ernst Bloch's definition of the topic:

> [...] there is no **single** category by which utopia allows itself to be named [...] If one wants to see how this entire matter resolves itself, then [the question about the elimination of death] is actually the most important.[81]

In Adorno's and Bloch's view, utopia embodies indeed the need to construct and ideally preserve that which is threatened by dissolution and death, in a drive towards the transcending of a human, limited and temporally bound, dimension: 'There is something profoundly contradictory in every utopia, namely, that it cannot be conceived at all without the elimination of death; this is inherent in the very thought.'[82] From such a view emerges the understanding that the utopian consciousness 'means a consciousness for which the possibility that people no longer have to die does not have anything horrible about it, but is, on the contrary, that which one actually wants'.[83]

The possibility of embodying such a utopian perspective lies in Goncourt's desire to sponsor an expressive process which would be somehow preserved from life's flowing, that is to say its inherently self-annihilating, self-erasing and self-unforming dimension. Thus Goncourt's reference to the potentially enduring 'chiffre' [cipher], to the 'marque' [monogram] that he seeks to imprint on the reality which will follow his death, can be read in the light of Bloch's referring to a 'longing' toward construction or an ever-sustained process of 'reconstruction'.[84]

It is therefore ultimately not the actual content of the culturally defined category in which the utopian is described that is fundamentally *utopian* but the *categorising, framing, structuring* in itself which appears to be so, in that theoretically preserved by the *de-forming* power of temporal change, a dimension understood to escape 'un sensible changeant, divers, mêlé, ontologiquement dégradé' [a perceptible dimension which is ever-changing, diverse, mixed, ontologically degraded].[85]

The literary prize institution is, in this context, seen as an expression of such a utopian perspective through its capacity of simultaneously *embodying* and *producing* circumscribed, stabilised, cognisable structures. Such structures can be identified in the institution itself and, simultaneously, in the discourses which are generated through the bias of the institution, namely the winning works. A third aspect plays, moreover, a key role: the yearly re-formulation of the literary selection, the identification of a new winner, the projection of the literary institution towards a *future* dimension, where a new text, a new author, always need to be identified.

Such an emphasis on the 'future' similarly plays a key role in Ernst Bloch's reading of the utopian in terms of 'an **articulated newness** [which] appears as a breakthrough each time'[86] (my emphasis). Not only is the spatial, structured dimension here indicative, but the *future* emphasis is similarly functional for the theoretical assessment of literary competitions. Indeed, one notices how Goncourt's criticism of the *Académie Française* in the light of its disconnection from 'jeunesse' [youth] and the author's willingness to support emerging authors appear as particularly significant. The young, the new, ultimately reflect the utopian in that they are the symbolic embodiment of 'that which is not yet fulfilled'[87] but can *potentially* be fulfilled in the artistic context. In contrast to a temporal perspective understood to lead to dissolution and progression towards death, the literary institution, through its being inserted in a future-oriented structuring drive, embodies the idealised re-inscription of the temporal dimension in a manageable dimension. A form will emerge, will be socially sanctioned, will be mediated and controlled, will symbolise cultural and cognitive perfection.

Such a dimension takes concrete form through the belief that 'the journey of [a] time and [the] concerns of [a] time are manifested in images and ideas'.[88] Language becomes, in Bloch's as in Bergson's understanding, a tool which overcomes the otherwise meaningless personal flow of consciousness and the uncontrollable motion of time.

The structured essence, which the very notion of 'journey' — inscribed within the lexical field of *space* — lends to the concept of time, seems here particularly significant. Held to express an instance of the process of spatial domination, language is considered as a mechanism through which a symbolic representation substitutes the flowing reality of consciousness — in other words the dynamics of life — in order to sustain a common, socially agreed upon, ground of communication.

Goncourt relies precisely on the structuring function of language in order to construct his enduring *marque* [monogram]. Let us turn once more to Goncourt's words — '[...] par toutes les survies, survie par les oeuvres, survie par les fondations, survie par l'application de mon chiffre ou de ma marque [...]'[89] [through all possible survivals, survival through the texts, survival through the foundations, survival through the application of my cipher or monogram...]. One notices how the multi-level process of cognitive construction those words express — structuring of the social dimension through an institutional framework, marking of objects, framing of aesthetic works — also testifies to the social function of the literary prize as a social institution aimed at validating the structuring function of the linguistic tool.

What emerges is a two-level structuring drive which counters the cognitive destabilisation we have evoked on the double plane of the aesthetic object and of the social/institutional subject. Built on a *stabilising* understanding of the linguistic/cultural construct — the winning novel — the literary prize functions in turn as a structuring and stabilising framework on the social scene. In such a reading, the literary competition inscribes itself fully within the anxiety-laden cognitive dimension we have discussed and emerges as a *functional* answer to the highlighted and self-consciously perceived destabilisation of the cognitive landscape, while also being functional to any cultural situation in which the undermining of a stable cognised dimension is either traceable or self-consciously acknowledged.

In this light, the traditional understanding of the Goncourt approach to literary aesthetics in terms of a *naturalistic* relationship between literature and the real might be reassessed through the perspective of Itamar Even-Zohar's belief that the creation of a cultural *repertoire* — like that developed in the context of literary competitions — represents a drive towards the organisation, rather than the representation, of 'life'.[90] Life — echoing Goncourt's own observation on the importance of referring to 'la vie' in the context of aesthetic assessment — becomes, through the artistic structuring process as it is conceived in an utopian perspective, the *essence* of being, an essence which appears to be implicitly characterised by structural stability and all-encompassing wholeness.

In other words, arising from an avowed need to connect 'life' to cultural production, the *Goncourt* competition and its emulators intervene within the communal process of cognition by sanctioning the creation, at the symbolic level, of an artificially stabilised, symbolic dimension, embodied by each winning novel.

Objectified in the form of the literary work, authorial perception opposes the dynamics of the social arena by providing a structurally stable — written, unchanging, unaffected by dynamics — artistic framework. Such a framework, which will be considered in greater depth in the following section, is in turn sanctioned by the literary institution which determines its distinctiveness on the social cognitive landscape and, through this very act of sanctioning, the institution itself becomes promoter, controller and incarnation of cognitive stabilisation.

'Survie par les oeuvres'

In the following section, we will consider in greater detail exactly how the aesthetic object produced by the literary author — and celebrated by the literary competition — can fulfil such a role of cognitive stabilisation and, by extension, of identity generation.

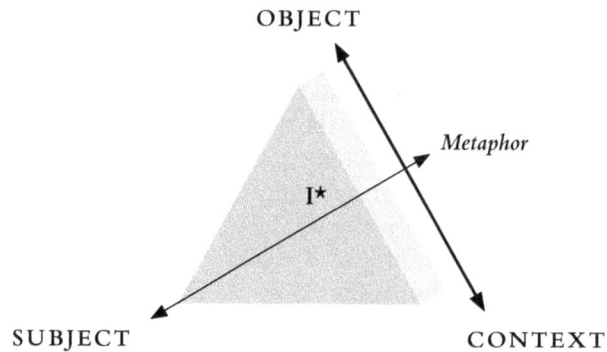

FIG. 1.1. The text as conceptual metaphor (* Literary Prize)

Focusing here on the link between aesthetic **OBJECT** and the structuring process, the literary text is seen as the embodiment of a conceptual metaphor. Such a metaphorical construction is read as a process of conceptual mapping through which properties from the external, contextual, dimension are projected from one perceptive domain, the world domain, to the written, internal, sphere of literary creation.

The literary text is, in turn, seen as a schema provider, allowing for the cognitive structuring of the self. A Lacanian reading of the metaphorical construct drives the integration of literary creation in the process of identity-shaping and assesses the metaphorical projection in terms of its utopian structuring function, in the context of the cognitive field. Such metaphorical mapping, running against the destabilisation of identity which can be evinced from the analysis of cultural and historical factors, is ultimately transferred through the institutionalisation of the aesthetic choice, on the social group as a whole. Thus the cultural institution is seen as being at once the product and the producer of stabilisation tendencies in a process which structures both self-identity and group identity.

The literary work as a conceptual metaphor

As stated, the understanding of the literary work as a cognitive stabilising framework must be articulated in the light of the relation tying the literary object to the contextual dimension from which it emerges. Indeed, affirming that a novel can fulfil a utopian function of structural construction entails positing a connection between contextual dimension, aesthetic object and the psychological articulation of the subject. In this light, the winning aesthetic object becomes the materialisation of the individual's attempt at opposing the *flowing* dimension of perception through an artificially constituted conceptual framework.

Significantly, such a view is already present in the Bergsonian understanding of the function of spatial predominance in the constitution of language which, contemporaneous with the development of French literary competitions, can be read in conjunction with Saussure's quasi-simultaneous conception of the linguistic in terms of a psychological trace. Both authors underline the importance of the framing, stabilising processes at work in the psychological constitution of language.

Repeatedly highlighted by Edmund Leach, through a structuralist approach to social anthropology strongly influenced by Saussure's work, such a process is based on the link existing between 'the meaning of expressive behaviour' and 'the relationship between observable patterns in the world out-there and unobservable patterns "in the mind"'.[91] In this context, the anthropologist notes how 'when we use symbols (either verbal or non-verbal) to distinguish one class of things or actions from another we are creating artificial boundaries in a field which is naturally continuous'.[92] As a result, representation consists in tracing a symbolic 'map' of the perceived which 'serves as a metaphoric description of the terrain'.[93]

The act of perception, like the act of artistic creation, is therefore understood to be based on the simultaneous apprehension of signification, intended as the awareness of the potential structured dimension of reality, and on a drive towards stabilisation and closure, embodied by the creative act of metaphorical structuring brought forward by the individual. 'Perception as artistic creation is thus based on the paradox of simultaneously perceiving a form and "bringing" a form to the world'.[94] Thus, according to Merleau-Ponty,

> the miracle of consciousness consists in bringing to light, through attention, phenomena which re-establish the unity of the object in a new dimension at the very moment when they destroy it. Thus attention is neither an association of images, nor the return to itself of thought already in control of its objects, but the active constitution of a new object which makes explicit and articulate what was until then presented as no more than an indeterminate horizon.[95]

The understanding of the perceived — and the represented — in terms of a structural form can be dated back to ancient Greek philosophy. True, from the Platonic tradition arises a disconnection between form as it can be externally perceived and *Form* understood as the idealised conceptualisation of ultimate reality, 'that which is beyond hypothesis, the first principle of all that exists'.[96] *Noesis*, understanding, grasps forms in a dialectical perspective which, if it is seen as distinct and non-comparable with the *pistis* level of sense perception, is all the more remote from the *eikasia* level of image-making.[97] The ultimate platonic *Form* does not therefore belong to the everyday dimension of cognitive understanding and perception.

In complete opposition to such a view, the Aristotelian understanding of form does not enforce a disconnection between the level of the image and the level of an idealised understanding of *Form*. It shifts the discussion away from such a dual opposition by highlighting a feature which is relevant to both the level of the visible and the levels of the intelligible: the notion of structure.[98] Crucially, this entails that 'the iconicity of the enactive or impersonatory mode need not involve a perceptual match between representational media and its object'[99] as it is the *structure* which links the object and its representation. This model, according to Stephen Halliwell, treats mimesis 'as not only a matter of the representational properties of an object, but also a form and a vehicle of experience'.[100] Joining the levels of sense perception, conceptual understanding and representation is thus the understanding of form as *structure*.

Such a position crucially entails a re-definition of the notion of mimesis — as anticipated above by the reassessment of Goncourt's association between 'vie' [life] and literature. The work of art — or, in the case under examination, the literary work — is not held to represent any given reality but is seen as uncovering the articulations of reality.

Turning back to literary competitions, the novel that is selected embodies therefore a stabilisation of the cognitive sphere in that it offers a fixed, framed, trace capturing the essence of reality, through which the world can be apprehended in a stable cognitive framework. Such a view has been particularly investigated by the cognitive approach to poetics which defines human expression in terms of a metaphorical mapping able to conceive everyday experience through conceptual categories.[101]

Incidentally, in the specific case of the *Goncourt*, reading the literary prize in such a perspective, rather than focusing on the traditional *naturalistic* dimension, allows for the understanding of the continuous success of the literary institution and its capacity to remain tuned to the wider social group's evolution and changing aesthetic appreciation.

Indeed, the literary institution appears to be founded on an understanding of art that — far from being mimetic — is, on the contrary, related to the external dimension in a fundamentally *metaphorical* relationship, understood as a transferral of structural form from a domain of cognitive experience to a domain of artistic articulation. In the specific case of French cultural production, the referring to the binary opposition between *human* and *animal* dimensions echoes the spatial/formal alterations perceived in the social, geopolitical, territorial landscapes. Stabilised in the metaphorical *form* of animalisation, the anxieties expressed by the social sphere find a stabilised mode of expression.

Art, literary art, fulfils in this view an idealised function of embodiment which ensures the stabilisation of the ever-shifting cognitive process through the tracing of a momentarily stabilised metaphoric map of the perceived world. In the context of early twentieth-century literary competitions, the selected novels are the embodiment of such a map. Art is ultimately seen here as a stabilising tool and the control of such cultural articulation is seen as the means through which the literary institution fulfils a need to guarantee the control of a stabilised social sphere. Seen within this framework, the process of aesthetical judgement that takes place in the context of a literary competition can be viewed as an attempt at validating, at the social level, the semiotic relation between artistic form and external contextual dynamics, such as they are perceived at the cognitive level.

The paradox of representation

The *metaphorical approach* which the current study has evoked is, however, apparently characterised by an inner contradiction. On the one hand, we have underlined how the metaphorical relation occurring between the novel and the world, in that relying on a non-mimetic relation, cannot be assessed in terms of representativeness. As a consequence, in the context of the *Goncourt* prize, the traditional emphasis on naturalism has been redefined. On the other hand, we have highlighted the degree to which a *representative* potential is indeed at the basis of the constitution of the work of art in that expression of a dynamic contextual articulation which is apprehended at the level of space-temporal perception. In the light of such an approach, the work appears at once, from such a critical perspective, as both representative and non-representative, and, to a degree, as both mimetic — at least from a structural perspective — and, simultaneously, non-mimetic.

Such a contradiction, in fact inherent in the conception of a metaphorical relation, is resolved when considering the novels selected in the context of literary prizes in the light of Nelson Goodman's understanding of the notion of *exemplificatory metaphor*. Indeed, the critic refuses the traditional understanding of mimesis as *resemblance*, pointing to how 'denotation is the core of representation and is independent of resemblance'.[102] In this light, the traditional rhetoric of naturalism is unveiled as the artificial construction of 'the myth of the innocent eye'[103] aimed at hiding the fact that 'reception and interpretation are not separable operations'.[104] Representation is thus inserted in a process where the work of art is marked by the artificiality of its construction, by its fundamentally *symbolic* essence. Whether or not 'transparent',[105] that is to say marked by a greater or lesser degree of realism, the artistic symbol is, in fact, to be seen as unrelated to the context which it is held to represent.

Yet, analysing the relationship between the object and the symbol which represents it, the critic also notes how 'an object that is [...] metaphorically denoted by a predicate [...] may be said to exemplify that predicate or property'.[106] Specifically, 'an exemplified property is one that is both possessed and referred to by a symbol'.[107]

Such a position presents, therefore, the artistic symbol — the novel — as linked to the contextual system from which it emerges by a metaphorical relation, while it also recognises in the relation between the object and the predicate which denotes it, an exemplificatory dimension. In this light, in its relation to the context, the novel

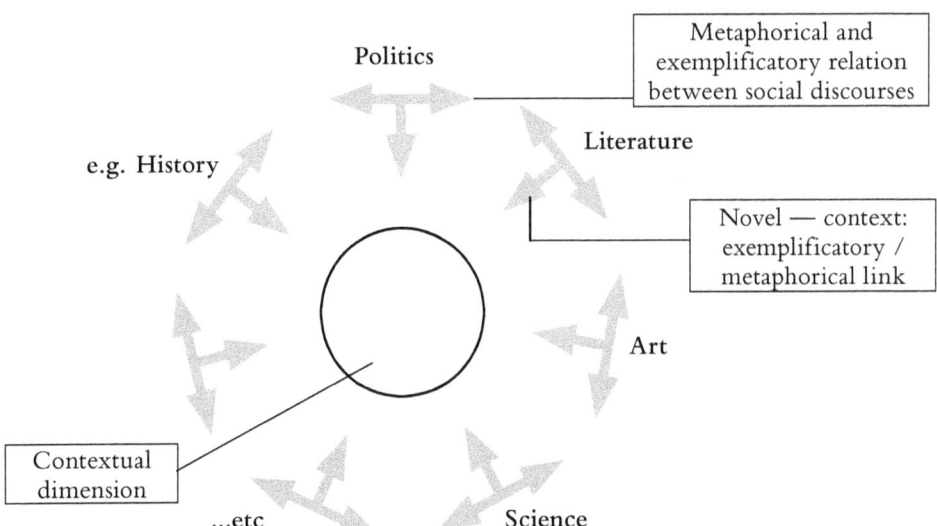

FIG. 1.2. Metaphorical and exemplificatory relation between social discourses

fulfils indeed an expressive, direct, dimension through its exemplificatory potential in that exemplification is based, according to Goodman, on the 'possession'[108] of shared characteristics. But it remains simultaneously disconnected from its context through its metaphoric — non-resembling — essence.

The exemplificatory dimension is related to the sphere of structural articulation in that it is shared by both the symbol and the context it refers to. The metaphorical dimension is, on the other hand, linked to the non-mimetic relation between symbol and object. George Lakoff and Mark Johnson point, in this context, to how the cognitive content of the metaphor is constituted by the transference of a mapping of one distinct domain of experience onto another.[109]

Read in this light, the novel is seen as an exemplificatory metaphor of the contextual dimension, at once tied to it and detached from it. Such a detachment is essential to its stability as a symbol in that it allows for the isolation of the metaphoric sign from the shifting dynamics we have previously discussed. The separateness of the symbol allows for its temporary closure and stabilisation and lets the metaphor fulfil its idealised, utopian function.

A further dimension of stability is granted by the literary competition to the selected novel through the projecting of the chosen aesthetic structure on a plane of *artistic* value. In this context, the literary work becomes endowed with a relation supplementary to that which characterises its metaphorical/exemplificatory link with the contextual dimension, namely that which links the chosen novel with the socially acknowledged label/signified/category of *Art* or *Literature*.

As it is chosen to embody the expression of an aesthetic judgement, the novel is granted a symbolic dimension. It becomes the *signifier* of the *ART signified* in a process which transforms the signifier into a cognitively stable framework.

FIG. 1.3. Labelling process

From that moment, through its enhanced social visibility, the chosen novel embodies that *other* stabilised, circumscribed, structural dimension, to which Ernst Bloch refers when defining his utopia.[110]

Utopia, in Ernst Bloch's reading of the combination of the Greek *ou* [non] and *topos* [location],[111] expresses indeed an *other* space, which is a psychological rather than geographical structure. Distinguishing his understanding of the utopian from the traditional emphasis on imagined locations, Bloch underlines how 'l'utopie n'est pas, de prime abord [...] un topos géographique ou spatial, mais un **topos psychologique**; et seulement en second lieu, un topos idéologique, politique, social, éthique, et religieux'[112] [Utopia is not, in the first instance, a geographical or spatial topic, it is a psychological topic; only in a secondary perspective does it become an ideological, political, social, ethical and religious topic]. Crucially, such an *other*, framed space is indeed a dimension characterised by identity-shaping dynamics, as will be argued in the following section.

The novel as mirror: constructing identities

Having established the connection tying the development of literary prizes to the destabilisation of the cognitive sphere, the question waiting to be asked is that of the possible connection linking the perception of a stabilised cognitive construct to the resolution of the identity issue. In other words, how can the social endorsement of a given metaphoric construct enter the process of identity-formation and stabilisation?

We have so far considered the degree to which an *identity* relation could be traced between the metaphorical construct (*object*) and the external, *contextual*, dimension. It remains to be seen, however, how such an *identity* relation can be projected onto the *subject* in a process of personal/cultural/social identity formation, thus closing the first trilateral relation we have traced around the literary institution.

We will start by considering the ways in which an *identity creative* potential emerges in the context of art production. Indeed, as stated, positing that the cultural work produces or interacts with the conception of a specific cultural identity — in the *Goncourt* and *Femina* cases, *French* identity — signifies also that the cultural work intervenes in the construction of identity in the wholeness of its complex articulation — identity being therefore understood not only in terms of cultural specificity but also in terms of general psychological structuring.

In this context, one notices a long tradition, going back to the Platonic condemnation of untruthful representation, which emphasises the degree to which the individual can be *formed* through the immediate impressive potential contained by the work of art, which is endowed with the capacity of presenting exemplary models — at the thematic level — for the shaping of the individual's personality.[113] Art becomes, in this reading, the practical link between the knowledge of the world and the conceptualisation of the self. It 'is not a luxury, and bad art is not a thing we can afford to tolerate. To know ourselves is the foundation of all life that develops beyond the mere psychical level of evidence'.[114]

The expressiveness[115] characterising Blochean aesthetics emphasises, however, specifically 'un principe **mimétique** cherchant le dédoublement du moi-créateur dans les objectivations figuratives, ornementales, architecturales, etc. de la matière (transformée, sculptée), etc'[116] [a mimetic principle, seeking the duplication of the I-creator in the figurative, ornamental, architectural, figurative objectivations of matter (transformed matter, sculpted matter), etc.]. The relation between the self and the object is thus redefined and refined in terms of a parallelism between creator and created which can be made explicit through the referral to an identitary structural dimension.

Such a parallelism can be defined through Lakoff and Johnson's[117] thesis on the degree to which all abstract conceptualisation — thoughts, linguistic projections and, by extension, artistic creations — is related to the psychological dimension of the individual — a process which is, for the authors, concretised in the concept of *embodiment*. Metaphor is not simply seen as a linguistic construction but as a conceptual embodiment which sees the projection of individual cognition in the linguistic sphere.

Thus the Blochean 'dédoublement' [doubling] can be read in the light of the metaphorical relation between individual cognition and linguistic/artistic medium: a relation based on the projection of structured form. A link between identity and artistic form is indeed acknowledged by Ernst Bloch himself in a particularly expressive, not to mention poetic, evocation which it is worth quoting at length (my emphasis):

> My dancing, my morning stars sing and all transparent formations of this kind reach the same **egoistic architectural horizon** and also the same **subjective** ornament of their entelechy: to be a trace, a sign of Makanthropos, to be a seal of its secret figure, of its hidden emotional Jerusalem. Here nothing is left that can be borrowed from the outside. The soul does not have to borrow alien prescriptions anymore. But the soul's own need is strong enough to attract the cortex and marks to assume its own position, **the pictures only become our own emergence at a different place.**[118]

In other words, by stating that 'no other relation to an object can occur than one that reflects the secret contour of the human face all over the world and connects the most abstract organic with the longing for our hearts, for the richness of the self-encounter',[119] the philosopher highlights the fundamentally *self*-shaping function fulfilled by the artistic medium.

Excluded from the Platonic city because of his capacity, through the representation of given emotions, of *transforming* the human soul,[120] the artist is thus alternatively accused or celebrated for the relation of *identity* he constitutes between the object and the subject: 'car il faut se rendre semblable à l'object vu pour le voir'[121] [one needs to make himself similar to the object which is seen in order to actually see that object]. True, in this view, the metaphorical projection which forms the aesthetic work is seen in the light of its corresponding not, as previously stated, to the structural dimension of reality, but to the inner individual cognitive framework, as corresponding therefore to a *reflection of the self*. However, should *both* views be simultaneously taken into consideration, the literary/artistic object is seen as a prism which mediates between the subjective and the external through the negotiation of a *structural identity*.

Significantly, the *reflection*-relation between object and self can be examined in the light of Lacan's theory of identity construction. Indeed, Lacan's understanding of identity construction through the metaphorical framework of the *mirror* phase is evocative of the process of identity-structuring enacted, through the selected aesthetic object, by literary competitions. Understanding the chosen novel as the cognised structure which the Lacanian mirror embodies, is to read the relationship between novel and subject — both subject *author* and subject *reader* — as one in which the structural stability obtained in the closed and finished form of the novel allows for the structuring and the closure of subjective identity.

In his *Le stade du miroir comme formateur de la fonction du Je telle qu'elle nous est révélée dans l'expérience psychanalytique* [The Mirror Stage as Formative of the Function of the I as Revealed in Psychoanalytic Experience], Lacan highlights how the fragmented infant identifies with — and wishes to be like — an image of wholeness. The *stade du miroir* [the mirror stage] est un drame dont la poussée interne se précipite de l'insuffisance à l'anticipation — et qui pour le sujet, pris au leurre de l'identification spatiale, machine les fantasmes qui se succèdent d'une image morcelée du corps à une forme que nous appellerons orthopédique dans sa totalité...[122]

[is a drama where the internal drive oscillates between insufficiency and anticipation — and which produces for the subject, taken by the illusion of spatial identification, a series of fantasies where a broken image of the body is followed by a form which, in its totality, can be defined as orthopedic].

Such a process of identification between structural form and cognition leads to the manufacture of the subject identity and self-perception as a stabilised whole. According to Lacan, this is in fact the start of a lifelong process of identifying the self in terms of the *other* and of constituting the *imagined* dimension of the self, such as it is embodied in the *ego*. Relying on a division between the self and the other, the imaginary is therefore fundamentally constructed through the apprehension of the other and is reciprocally related to the existence of the other.

Understanding the Lacanian *other* in terms of Bloch's utopian, artistic *other*,[123] and in the light of the three-fold relation between *context*, *subject* and artistic *object* we have illustrated, leads us to the conclusion that the identity-structuring relation between individual and artistic object is ultimately reciprocal and interactive.

Thus knowledge of the world, originating from perception and/or representation and providing in turn further representative instances, leads to knowledge and to the cognition of the self through a process of self-fashioning directly related to that very conceptual framework through which the world has, in turn, been constructed and represented. The literary institution, which validates the artistic — thus cognitively stabilised — object-status of the winning novel is, in this context, ultimately inserted at the heart of such a cognitive process and is endowed with social empowerment in that it *determines* at the social level, the emerging instances of identity creation.

What such a reading of the aesthetic function entails, though, as mediated through the literary institution, is at once a shift from personal identity to communal identity (positing by extension the problem of the boundary between non-cultural and cultural identity), and a view of the trilateral relation between object, subject and context as a *static and fixed* network which fundamentally ties identity and artistic production within an enclosed frame of self-definition and self-validation.

Crucially, the latter observation actually accounts for the critical assessments which have related the institution of literary prizes to cultural nationalism and reveals the extent to which the issue of the system *stasis* and the view of literary prizes as products and producers within a closed *cultural* dimension belong to the same theoretical framework and theoretically sustain one another.

However, as will be demonstrated in the following chapter, the reading of literary prizes in terms of a static system is understood to account for only a part of the social, cultural and symbolic functioning of the institution under examination.

Notes to Chapter 1

1. André Billy, *Les Frères Goncourt* [The Goncourt Brothers] (Paris: Flammarion, 1954).
2. 'Jean Paul Dubois: Prix Femina', *Le Nouvel Observateur* (Littérature) < http://tempsreel. nouvelobs.com/culture/20041103.OBS0648/jean-paul-dubois-prix-femina.html> [accessed 22 June 2017] (para. 4 of 4).
3. Louis Pergaud, *De Goupil à Margot: histoires de bêtes* [From *Goupil* to *Margot*: Animal Stories] [1910], 13th edn (Paris: Mercure de France, 1914).
4. André Savignon, *Filles de la pluie: scènes de la vie ouessantine* [Daughters of the Rain: Scenes of Life in *Ouessant*] (Paris: Bernard Grasset Editeur, 1912).
5. Claude Farrère, *Les Civilisés* [The Civilised] [1905] (Paris: Ernest Flammarion, 1921).
6. Edouard Estaunié, *La Vie secrète* [The Secret Life] [1908], 33rd edn (Paris: Librairie Académique Perrin, 1935).
7. Pergaud (1914), p. 82.
8. Savignon (1912), p. 233.
9. Estaunié (1935), p. 315.
10. Farrère (1921), pp. 291–92.
11. Pergaud (1914), p. 65.
12. Ibid., p. 98.
13. Savignon (1912), p. 239.
14. Ibid., p. 239.
15. Farrère (1921), p. 334.
16. Pergaud (1914), p. 161.
17. Ibid., p. 253.
18. Farrère (1921), p. 289.
19. Marguerite Audoux, *Marie-Claire*, [1910] (Paris: Arthème Fayard & Cie, [193(?)]), p. 47.
20. Edmond Jaloux, *Le Reste est silence* [The Rest is Silence] (Paris: Editions Lapina, 1924), p. 33.
21. Ibid., p. 149.
22. Audoux, [193(?)], p. 8.
23. Francis de Miomandre, *Ecrit sur de l'eau* [Written on Water], [1908], new edn (Paris: Emile-Paul Frères, 1919), p. 39.
24. Estaunié (1935), p. 28.
25. Pergaud (1914), p. 34.
26. Miomandre (1919), p. 56.
27. Savignon (1912), p. 182.
28. Estaunié (1935), p. 194.
29. Audoux, [193(?)], p. 19.
30. Ibid., p. 21.
31. Jaloux (1924), p. 33.
32. Ibid., p. 81.
33. Ibid., p. 148.
34. Frédéric Worms, 'Henri Bergson', PUF <http://www.puf.com/Espace_Bergson/Henri_ Bergson> [accessed 22 June 2017] (para. 23 of 45). '[1911–1912] C'est aussi le moment où la philosophie de Bergson rencontre ses premiers relais de grande vulgarisation' [It is also the time when Bergson's philosophy finds its first channels leading to great popularisation].
35. Henri Bergson, *Essai sur les données immédiates de la conscience* [Time and Free Will: An Essay on the Immediate Data of Consciousness] [1888], 144th edn (Paris: Presses Universitaires de France, 1970).
36. Ibid., p. 32.
37. Ibid., p. 40.
38. Uri Eisenzweig in Claude Duchet, *Sociocritique* [Socio-criticism] (Paris: Nathan, 1979), p. 186.
39. Ibid., p. 186.
40. Norbert Dodille in Ashley (2004), p. 60.
41. Angenot (1989), p. 213.

42. Farrère (1921).
43. Jean-Paul Sartre, *Qu'est-ce que la Littérature?* [What is Literature?] (Paris: Gallimard, 1948), p. 179.
44. *French Cultural Studies: An Introduction*, ed. by Jill Forbes and Michael Kelly (Oxford: Oxford University Press, 1995), p. 15.
45. Billy (1954), p. 237. As reflected in the deep-seated dismay of the ever-observing Goncourt: 'Le progrès, qu'est-ce que lui doit au fond Paris? Des boulevards, des grandes artères... oui, il n'a plus laissé de coins dans les rues ignorées, où l'on pouvait jadis vivre caché et heureux...' [What does Paris owe to progress, in the end? Boulevards, large avenues... yes, it did not leave one single place in ignored streets, where one could at one time live hidden and be happy...].
46. Significantly, it is the railway line which indeed dominates the ending of Marguerite Audoux's *Marie Claire*, leading the protagonist towards the new and threatening space of the city.
47. Forbes and Kelly (1995), p. 21. In relation to the development of the railways and the transformed perception of space, the authors point to the related development of local and national tourism which occurs at the beginning of the twentieth century.
48. Maurice Angenot, *1889: Un état du discours social* [1889: A State of the Social Discourse] (Longueuil: Le Préambule, 1989), pp. 160–62.
49. Ibid., pp. 168–69.
50. Forbes and Kelly (1995), p. 39.
51. Angenot (1989), p. 209. It is precisely such a 'bestialité villageoise' [village bestiality] which is enacted in Louis Pergaud's *De Goupil à Margot* as farmers and inhabitants of the countryside are represented as characterised by a violence, not to say viciousness, which at times equates, at times surpasses, that of the animal protagonists of the winning novel.
52. Paul Bourget, *L'Etape* [The Step] (Paris: Plon-Nourrit, [1902 (?)]).
53. Billy (1954), p. 238.
54. Norbert Dodille significantly points to a connection between the diffusion of colonial literature and the contemporary development and success of regional literature in early nineteenth-century France (my emphasis): 'Par exemple, le développement de la littérature régionaliste doit bénéficier de conditions qui sont tout à fait comparables à celles que l'on va tenter de développer pour la littérature coloniale: création de Sociétés, de chaires universitaires, d'associations, de **prix littéraires**.' [For instance, the development of regionalist literature must benefit from the same conditions as those which will be developed for colonial literature: creation of societies, university positions, associations, literary prizes.] Norbert Dodille, 'Les théories du roman colonial' [The Theories of Colonialist Novels], *Introduction aux discours coloniaux* [Introduction to colonial discourses], <http://unt.univ-reunion.fr/fileadmin/Fichiers/UNT/UOH/idc/co/Cours102.html> [accessed 3 February 2017].
55. Angenot (1989), p. 213.
56. Angenot (1989), p. 217.
57. Ibid., p. 222.
58. Maurice Barrès, *Un homme libre* [A Free Man], [1889] (Paris: Perrin, 19[?]), electronic edition in 'Barrès, Maurice', *Gallica*, <http://gallica.bnf.fr/ark:/12148/bpt6k87498z.item> [accessed 6 April 2008] (Livre II — L'Eglise militante, p. 102).
59. See Billy (1954), p. 238.
60. Billy (1954), p. 239.
61. Billy (1954), p. 239.
62. Anthony P. Cohen, *The Symbolic Construction of Community* (London: Tavistock, 1985), p. 109. (my emphasis): '[...] their members find their identities as individuals through their occupancy of the community's social space: if outsiders trespass in that space, then its occupants' own sense of self is felt to be **debased and defaced**. This sense is always so tenuous when the physical and structural boundaries which previously divided the community from the rest of the world are increasingly blurred. It can therefore easily be depicted as under threat: it is a ready means of mobilising collectivity.'
63. Priscilla Parkhurst Clark, *Literary France: The Making of a Culture* (Berkeley: University of California Press, 1987), p. 68.

64. Ibid., p. 69.
65. Ibid., p. 69.
66. Ibid., p. 69. Incidentally, the author points to how the process of social mobility is not only an horizontal but also a vertical one: 'The eminently bourgeois Balzac stood out among the aristocratic romantics. The end of the century reversed the situation and made the aristocratic Goncourt the misfits.'
67. Ibid., p. 82.
68. Forbes and Kelly (1985), p. 15: 'It is estimated that by the turn of the century there were a staggering 24,000 cafés in the greater Paris area alone.'
69. Walter Benjamin, *The Arcades Project*, [1982], ed. by Roy Tiedemann, trans. by Howard Eiland and Kevin McLaughlin (Cambridge, MA: Harvard University Press, 1999). When assessed in the light of Walter Benjamin's study of late nineteenth-century Parisian architecture in *The Arcades Project*, and in the light of his 1939 *Paris, capitale du XIXème siècle* [Paris, a Nineteenth Century Capital], one notices how the transformations brought by Haussmann's planning, the strategic favouring of open spaces and fluid networks of paths, can be assessed in relation to the previously mentioned anxiety about shapelessness, penetration and change.
70. Billy (1954), p. 111.
71. Ibid., p. 99.
72. Forbes and Kelly (1985), p. 15.
73. Amos Rapoport in *Companion Encyclopedia of Anthoplogy,* ed. by Tim Ingold (London. Routledge, 2002), pp. 477–78: 'Making markers stronger increases clarity and the strength of cues, and hence reinforces the organisation of meaning. [...] Institutions, such as those of recreation, commerce, government, and so on, and the ways in which they operate, are intimately linked with systems of settings, are fairly easily analysed and have profound consequences for spatial organisation and built form [...] Roles are often associated with particular activities and settings; again they can readily be related to the built environment. Social groups of various sorts can be easily connected to spatial organisation, which is, in effect, the uneven distribution of such groups in space [...] [S]ocial structure and spatial structure are closely related.'
74. Ibid., p. 486.
75. Stéphanie Smadja, in Ashley (2004), p. 46.
76. Ibid., p. 49.
77. See Billy (1954), p. 408.
78. Ibid., p. 407.
79. Martin Heidegger in David Farrell Krell, *Basic Writings: Martin Heidegger* (London: Routledge, 1993), p. 101.
80. Stéphanie Smadja, in Ashley (2004), p. 45.
81. A discussion between Ernst Bloch and Theodor W. Adorno on the 'Contradictions of Utopian Longing', in Bloch (1988), p. 8.
82. Ibid., p. 10.
83. Ibid., p. 8.
84. Ibid., p. 6.
85. Carole Talon-Hugon, *L'Esthétique* (Paris: Presses Universitaires de France, 2004), pp. 13–14.
86. Bloch (1988), p. 8.
87. Ibid., p. 39.
88. Ibid., p. 38.
89. Billy (1954), p. 408.
90. Itamar Even-Zohar, 'The Making of Culture Repertoire and the Role of Transfer', *Target*, 9–2 (1997), pp. 373–81.
91. Edmund Leach, *Culture and Communication: The Logic by which Symbols are Connected* (Cambridge, Cambridge University Press, 1976), p. 17.
92. Ibid., p. 33.
93. Ibid., p. 51.
94. Adrienne Dengerink Chaplin, in *The Routledge Companion to Aesthetics*, ed. by Berys Gaut and Dominic McIver Lopes (London: Routledge, 2005), p. 167. 'Hence, in order to perceive, we both **discover** meaning and **bring** meaning to the world.'

95. Maurice Merleau-Ponty, *Phenomenology of Perception*, [1945], trans. by Colin Smith (London: Routledge, 2005), p. 35.
96. Plato, *The Republic*, trans. by Georges M. A. Grube and rev. by C. D. C. Reeve (Indianapolis: Hackett Publishing Company, 1992), p. 165.
97. Ibid., p. 164.
98. Aristotle, *Poetics*, trans. with notes by Richard Janko (Indianapolis: Hackett Publishing Company, 1987), p. xv. According to Aristotle, recognising that something is a representation is an intellectual process — we identify what is represented because it has some features of the actual object [...] Thus we recognise a sketch of a cow because it has four legs, horns, and so on. To the complaint that such a sketch involves a loss of detail, Aristotle would reply that this loss is accompanied by an increased clarity of the basic form. This explains his high valuation of plot, the structure of the action which poetry represents...
99. Stephen Halliwell, *The Aesthetics of Mimesis: Ancient Texts and Modern Problems* (Princeton: Princeton University Press, 2002), p. 169.
100. Ibid., p. 161.
101. Stockwell (2002), p. 109.
102. Nelson Goodman, *Languages of Art* (Indianapolis: Hackett Publishing Company, 1976), p. 5.
103. Ibid., p. 8.
104. Ibid., p. 8.
105. Ibid., p. 36.
106. Ibid., p. 52.
107. Jennifer Robinson, in Gaut and McIver Lopes (2005), p. 189.
108. Goodman (1976), p.53.
109. Garry L. Hagberg, in Gaut and McIver Lopes (2005), p. 376. See also George Lakoff and Mark Johnson, *Metaphors We Live By* (Chicago: Chicago University Press, 1980).
110. Bloch (1988), p. 12. 'That means that the true thing determines itself via the false thing, or via that which makes itself falsely known. And insofar as we are not allowed to cast the picture of utopia, insofar as we do not know what the correct thing would be, we know exactly, to be sure, what the false thing is.'
111. Michèle Riot-Sarcey and Paul Aron, in Paul Aron et al. (2002), p. 633.
112. Arno Münster, *Figures de l'Utopie dans la pensée d'Ernst Bloch* [Figures of Utopia in Ernst Bloch's Thought] (Paris: Aubier, 1985), p. 45.
113. Plato, *Complete Works*, ed. by John M. Cooper and D. S. Hutchinson (Indianapolis: Hackett Publishing Company, 1997), pp. 325–26.
114. Robin G. Collingwood, *Principles of Art* (Oxford: Oxford University Press 1938), p. 284.
115. Münster (1985), p. 153.
116. Ibid., p.155.
117. Lakoff and Johnson (1980).
118. Bloch (1988), p. 102.
119. Ibid., p. 102.
120. Talon-Hugon (2004), p. 24.
121. Ibid., p. 17.
122. Jacques Lacan, 'Le Stade du miroir' [The Mirror Stage] [1936/1949], in *Écrits* [Writings] (Paris: Editions du Seuil, 1999), p. 96.
123. In this context it is interesting to note how both Lacan and Bloch refer to the structuring process in terms of 'anticipation' (p. 96) and express a belief in a forward projection of cognition which can be associated with the conception of an *idealised* structure. Thus Jacques Lacan refers to a 'Je-Ideal' [I-Ideal] (p. 93) which is born out of a movement of 'anticipation' while Bloch points to the 'future-oriented' nature of the utopian construct.

CHAPTER 2

Italy 1920–1945: Utopian Travels

The second chapter, focusing on Italian literary competitions in the Fascist era, will highlight the degree to which the analysis unveiling the *static* dimension of identity-formation processes in literary competitions does not explain, in its entirety, the functioning and aesthetic choices of such organisations. Such a redefinition and reframing of the theoretical model sketched so far takes place in two main steps.

The chapter will begin with a consideration of the *Weltanschauung* [worldview] theory which, through its tying of identity and cultural production within a closed and self-referring circle, echoes — from a different yet arguably related perspective — the *static* system sketched in the initial chapter.

It will be demonstrated how an analysis of the *Weltanschauung* view, apparently celebrated and enforced by Italian literary competitions in the Fascist era, actually unveils a permeating and diffused referring — in the winning novels — to a problematisation of the very ideological representations which are allegedly celebrated. Such a problematisation is understood to express the degree to which the *Weltanschauung* position must be understood as belonging to the field of the rhetorical self-validation, on the social scene, of the literary institutions, in a context which is correlated to specific political instances, and not to the functioning of the institution as such. In fact, the analysis of the functioning of literary competitions is understood to transcend such self-generated rhetoric to embrace wider and more contradictory dynamics.

Concretely, such contradictory dynamics emerge through the taking into consideration of the *diachronic* nature of literary competitions, and of the degree to which such a diachronic perspective can recapture and highlight the dynamic and ever-changing, problematic, nature of the process of identity articulation.

At the level of the theoretical framework, this translates into aiming the analysis at a reformulation of the theory of metaphorical mapping by introducing the one factor which, in the section illustrating the *stabilising* potential of the metaphorical construct, has been deliberately left unmentioned: the *time factor*.

Indeed, if, as stated by Edmund Leach, the 'metaphoric description of the terrain' that ties the object to the contextual dimension is 'also a metaphoric representation of time',[1] understanding the object in terms of its unity can only be based 'on the foreshadowing of an imminent order',[2] which matches the *future-oriented* quality of the Blochean conception of the utopian dimension.

The structuring process becomes here an ordering *motion*[3] which, significantly enough, is specifically attributed, by Maurice Merleau–Ponty, to the act of artistic creation. Thus, according to the philosopher, the cognitive act, understood as 'not the bringing to explicit expression of a pre-existing being, but the laying down of being', finds its reflection in artistic creation understood as 'the act of bringing truth into being', 'truth' being here understood as the essence we have previously evoked and 'being' emphasising here the ever-proceeding nature of such dynamics.

Identity, in such a perspective, becomes that 'which is not yet fulfilled',[4] nor ever will be, while the utopian dimension initially evoked in its *forming* potential is to be understood in its *never-to-be-fulfilled* essence. Within such a perspective, the literary institution, though arising from a need to cater to identity stabilisation, in fact embodies the intrinsic impossibility of stalling identity dynamics.

In this view, the literary institution is not seen as an identity-enforcing entity but as an identity-articulating framework which, far from validating an unproblematic model of personal and group identity, intervenes in the social discourse by modulating the social cognitive and discursive practices which intervene on the *ever-changing* process of identity-constitution. As a result, the association of ideological cultural nationalism and literary competitions, sustainable to an extent in the context of a *static* reading of the utopian function of the selected works, is undermined once the literary competition is read in terms of its temporal, dynamic projection.

As literary competitions reiterate their choices in a constantly renewed cycle of aesthetic valuation and yearly selection, running parallel to constant contextual and subjective transformations, the identity-constitution process related to such a selection accordingly emerges as inherently submitted to never-ending displacement.

A two-step renegotiation of the theoretical framework has been announced. The second reformulation of the theoretical framework presented in the preceding chapter — taking into consideration the dynamism which is understood to characterise the process of identity construction — will be based on the introduction of a new element in the theoretical scheme, namely the figure and function of the *authorial* subject.

In particular, the author figure is understood to undermine and challenge the specific and apparently *locked* exchange occurring between artistic object and cognising subject, through his projecting of such a relation on a temporal — thus ever-flowing and ever-evolving — dimension and through his undermining of the structural boundaries which, as shown in the initial chapter, form the basis for the constitution of the aesthetic 'mirror' at the roots of the process of identity-creation.

In the example provided by Italian literary prizes, investigating the physical and historical frontiers of the Italian state, the *author-traveller* challenges the separation and stable definition of one group from another, of one individual from another, projecting the aesthetic selection, enacted within the literary competitions, in a dimension of constant exchange between instances of group identity and instances of individual self-reflection and setting the literary institution, embodied in the authorial figure it produces and validates on the social scene, at the edge of the fundamentally inter-related dimensions of individuality and community.

The author is therefore seen as the prism through which not only does artistic form come to embody a community's foremost cognitive projections but also through which such projections are simultaneously and inherently challenged. Acting as a negotiator of symbolic and, by extension, cognitive boundaries, the author-figure counter-balances the stabilising function and objectifying potential played by the metaphorical representation, which is embodied in the artistic object and which has been considered in the initial part of the study.

The problematisation of communal and individual identities can be read in parallel with the problematisation of the artistic object itself. In the theoretical scheme, such a relation is illustrated through the visual link between authorial subject and aesthetic object.

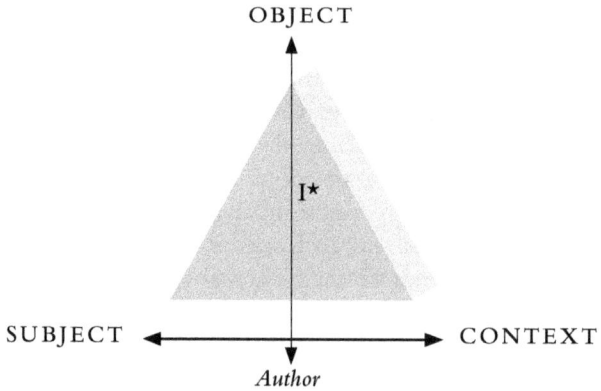

FIG. 2.1. The authorial function (★ Literary Prize)

With regard to the formation of the subject's identity, as illustrated by the case of Italian literary competitions, the *Author* figure, by intervening between the **SUBJECT** and the **CONTEXT**, negotiates at the physical/territorial level the definition of structural boundaries, challenging the rhetorical presentation of a fixed and communally perceived 'Italian' space through the territorial exploration and problematisation of the physical space which the author depicts himself as performing.

With regard to the constitution of the aesthetic **OBJECT**, the hybrid nature of winning Italian literary compositions, fundamentally shaped and influenced by the journalistic and pictorial genres, reveals that the aesthetic object — as opposed to the way in which it has been introduced in the initial presentation of the scheme — is in fact a much more dynamic and unstable element. In particular, the mixed generic nature of the literary/journalistic/pictorial construct is related to the ambivalence pervading the social identity of the *Author* figure and, by extension, the identities of the **SUBJECT** which, through such an aesthetic **OBJECT**, should theoretically find the stabilisation of his/her cognitive sphere and of his/her identitary dimension.

As a result, not only is the fixed identitary relation between **SUBJECT** and cultural **OBJECT** inherently challenged, but the very concept of communal identity is unveiled as being a fundamentally unstable, shifting — in the Derridean sense, an essentially deferred — projection. The utopian focus moves away from the *forming* potential of art towards the projection of such a forming potential in a *never-to-be-reached* future dimension.

Questioning the Weltanschauung: Utopia as Hope

As briefly anticipated, reading the cultural object in terms of the specific cultural identity of its creators and reading the identity of cultural producers in the sole light of the 'mirroring' — identity-shaping potential — of the aesthetic objects to which they give form, entails sustaining a view of literary competitions as based on a fundamentally *static* and *closed* framework.

As will be seen, not only does the mechanism outlined not account for the specifics of an individual identity's ever-proceeding displacement, but it also appears as inadequate to explain the processes of *communal* identity negotiation, which follow the same inherently self-undermining and dialectic dynamics.

Accounting for the constitution of communal identity is central to the analysis of literary prizes in that, in the social rhetoric enforced by the competitions themselves or, alternatively, used to analyse such competitions, it is through the specific aesthetic claim as to the *universality* of judgement,[5] which the literary prize displays, that the identity is projected through the institution on the social group as a whole. Such a process can be read as being, in turn, aimed at stabilising and reinforcing a communal perception of identity and reinforcing the belief in a 'universally communicable'[6] state of mind from which aesthetic production and aesthetic assessment emerge and to whose formation they, in turn, contribute.

Challenging such a reading entails seeing the literary institution itself as a social phenomenon which transcends specific political and ideological boundaries to embrace a dialectical — rather than an un-problematically affirmative — social practice. From such a perspective stems the understanding of social phenomena such as literary competitions as articulating frameworks which, far from enforcing a uniform view of identity content, allow for the discursive problematisation of the attempt at identity-stabilisation.

'Weltanschauung' as cognitive enclosure

The perception of a static and self-referring cognitive framework is in line with the theory in which language is seen as fixing the process of consciousness within a symbolic frame of spatial projection and directly influencing the process of perception itself. Through the *solidification* of the external dimension in the symbolic linguistic trace, the mind is led to perceive and conceive within the very limits imposed by the linguistic — and one might add structural — frame.[7]

In this view, the positioning of the literary prize in terms of an ideologically influenced rhetoric can indeed be justified in the sense that the literary institution, by validating a cultural framework designed to stabilise the perception of identity, enters a process in which additional and subsequent perceptions of cultural identity are allegedly developed from *within* the cultural frame that has been validated.

Such a perspective corresponds therefore to the view that cultural expressions and cultural identity arise from one another and that the specificity of cultural identity allows for the specificity of cultural expression.

Positing the artistic work as valuable in that expression of a definite cultural identity[8] is a critical approach which finds its historical foundations in Ancient Greece, more specifically in the Epicurean belief in the existence of a connection between names and the feelings and impressions from which they are generated. What Epicurus (342–270 BC) outlines, in his *Letter to Herodotus*, is a theory that can be understood in opposition to the Saussurean view of the arbitrary nature of signs. While recognising that meanings can, to an extent, be made more specific by common consent and convention and additional words can be created by reasoning with the prevailing mode of expression,[9] Epicurus points nevertheless to how, in its hypothetical origins, language emerges from a *non-arbitrary* system of name attribution.

Thus the bases are laid for the opposition between the *naturalistic* theory, partly sustained in Plato's *Cratylus*,[10] defending the existence of an intrinsic connection between a sound and the notion it signifies and the Aristotelian *conventionalism* underlining, on the contrary, the arbitrariness of language[11] — a view which will subsequently find its main expression in Saussurean linguistics.

Throughout the centuries, the controversy regularly manifests itself. For instance, in the seventeenth century, in opposition to the Lockean emphasis on the semiotic nature of words and on the conventionality of the relationship existing between word and object, Leibnitz defines language as the mirror of the human mind, relying on the metaphor of the prism in order to illustrate the degree to which each single language illustrates a determined, distinct, specific view of external reality.

It is, however, in Humboldt's Romantic theories on the specificity of cultural identity which such an approach finds perhaps its most articulate form. Influenced by eighteenth-century views of the relation between thinking and language, Humboldt sees the essence of thinking as ultimately consisting in a process which divides and sub-divides the unbroken flux of sensations and feelings, forming a *totality* out of an indistinct and shifting dimension and attaching a *name* to such reflexively defined entities. Pointing to the *representational* dimension of such an approach, Martin Manchester underlines how, in this perspective,

> words (or at least 'naming' words like nouns) designate directly <u>ideas</u>, and that ideas (at least some of them) designate <u>objects</u> [...] The guiding intuition of representational semantics is that language represents thoughts.[12]

Such a position plays a fundamental role in sustaining the Humboldtian belief in the existence of a relationship between the culturally specific thoughts of a defined community and the linguistic and, by extension, artistic production to which they can give birth. The extent to which Humboldt retains a belief in the *original* arbitrariness of the relation between signifier and signified, and thus follows the

Lockean position, remains unclear.[13] However, when focusing on the successive steps of language formation, not on the *hypothetical* origins of language, therefore, but on the day-to-day linguistic *practice*, he heavily relies on the Leibnizian vision of language as emerging from a *motivated* pattern of associations, tracing a connection between linguistic utterance and cultural identity.

A nation's linguistic expression, be it literary or non-literary, oral or written, becomes representative of the nation's identity, thoughts — in other words its *worldview*. Ultimately, what language represents are not the objects themselves but the conceptual framework through which the external world is perceived.[14] As a consequence, the act of thinking is seen as being dependent on language, 'the total lexicon at any given time represent[ing] the total available constituent elements for any potential thought of the speaker of that language'.[15]

On the one hand, this leads us to a conception of the realm of ideas as marked by an historical framework where thoughts can no longer be held to be independent of words. On the other hand, one might reverse the equation and point out the degree to which words — in the sense of the form and content of literary production — cannot be held to be independent of the conceptual sphere of a given society.

While relying on what will become Saussure's definition of the sign through a process of differentiation, Humboldt's approach undermines the closure of the Saussurean system by connecting each differentiated term to an external dimension in which signified and signifier are linked through a non-arbitrary system, pointing not only to how words such as 'hippos, equus, and Pferd' [horse] are different in relation to one other but to how they 'do not say throughout and completely the same thing'[16] in different cultural and cognitive settings.

The closed nature of the system is, however, recuperated in the understanding of a virtual circle enclosing external cognitive dimension and linguistic-cultural dimension in a unique dynamic of reciprocal fashioning.

Humboldt's thought thus inscribes itself within a wider German tradition, stretching back to Herder, permeating both literature and philosophy, underpinning for instance Heidegger's aesthetic theory[17] which has been considered as fundamental in the development of twentieth-century nationalistic doctrines.

It can hardly be denied that a strong part of twentieth-century nationalist views on culture relied on the nineteenth-century German Romantic emphasis on the link between culture and national identity. Yet reading the appearance of literary prizes at specific historical moments as the articulation of national identity ideologies, when taken together with an awareness of the identity-framing potential which the institution activates within the social scene, means endorsing an unproblematised view of such a connection.

It does not appear to account for the complexity and dynamism of the process through which 'people construct community symbolically, making it a resource and repository of meaning, and a referent of their own identity',[18] and of the limits which such a process meets in the self-same community that enacts it.

Thus if the institution of literary prizes rests, at least in part, on an understanding that language, and all the more so figurative language, 'can be inaccessible to all but those who share information about one another's knowledge, beliefs, intentions and attitudes',[19] it also enters into a process whereby the chosen text reveals 'where the paths of [an individual's] various experiences intersect'[20] and 'where [an individual's] and other people's [experiences] intersect and engage each other like gears.'[21] Crucially, as will be shown, such intersections are shifting boundaries rather than stable circuits internal to the community.

At the opening of the previous chapter, we saw how literary institutions appear to stem from a community's ontological drive in specific temporal moments, during which external political and social factors undermine the stability of the community's cognitive sphere. An analysis of the development of Italian cultural production in the light of the country's early nationalist drives might, in the first instance, appear to confirm such a position. In particular, it will highlight the degree to which literary competitions can, to an extent, be assessed in the light of how not only the pleasure but also the recognition and/or definition of the *beautiful* rests on a view of art as an articulated expression of the community's own specific ontological drives, such as they are expressed and acknowledged within a specific linguistic discourse/worldview. In other words, literary competitions appear to support the view that 'a pleasure can be universally communicable only if it is based not on mere sensation but rather on a state of mind that is universally communicable'.[22]

However, the simultaneous challenging of territorial, historical, cultural and social boundaries, effected through the authorial figure and taking place in parallel with the articulation of such a rhetoric, inherently undermines such a static relation between cognition, art and identity and ultimately denies the existence of a linear and unproblematic binary relation between *cultural* object and *natural* subject.

Such challenging allows for a modified understanding of the functioning of literary competitions and highlights the degree to which the studied cultural institutions operate in the process of cultural negotiation not by closing the cognitive sphere but by articulating a dynamic between drives towards stabilised closure and drives towards openness and transformation.

Italian aesthetic nationalism in literary competitions

Italian twentieth-century nationalism emerged from the ashes of the *Risorgimento*[23] [TN: revolutionary movement linked to the Italian unification process] national unity ideals. In opposition to the New Left *real-politick*, aimed at securing government stability through pragmatic policies and general ideological compromises with the influential Catholic and Socialist social sub-groups,[24] nationalists referred back to the Mazzinian idealised[25] — and somewhat un-compromising — vision of a united people in order to overcome 'both territorial and class cleavage'.[26]

Emerging in the context of the lively late-1890s Florentine intellectual scene, early modern Italian nationalism was thus strongly influenced by Romantic ideals and was first articulated in *riviste* [TN: cultural magazines] which often merged aesthetic preoccupations with political discussions. In fact, aesthetic publications became increasingly *political* in both their conception and implementation, as fears of moral, political and social *decadence* led the Italian intellectuals of the early years of the twentieth century to attempt to undermine the political forces in power.[27] For instance, in the 1903 prefatory statement to his new journal *Il Regno*, Florentine writer Enrico Corradini (1865–1931) declared that the editors were united in their common purpose to rail against the degeneracy into which they believed the country had recently sunk'.[28] The 1908 foundation of *La Voce* by Perugia-born Giuseppe Prezzolini (1882–1982) marks, in this context, a significant defining moment in the evolution of the Italian early twentieth-century intellectual scene, in that it not only illustrates the exponential growth of the politicised *riviste* phenomenon but also testifies to the growing diversification within nationalistic trends[29] such as it is expressed by the 1910s proliferation of nationalist newspapers: *Il Tricolore* from Turin (1909), *La Grande Italia* in Milan (1909), *La Nave* in Naples (1909) or *Mare Nostro* in Venice (1909).

Beyond political distinctions, however, the emphasis given by Italian nationalism to the construction of an idealised picture of a *united* Italy, conceived as an autonomous and structured entity, was to prove fundamental in the subsequent articulation of Fascist national ideology:

> When reflecting in 1923 on the fortunes of nationalism in Italy, Corradini wrote that his movement had breathed new life into 'the true myth of the nation'. He suggested that the idea, which he and his followers had propagated, of a nation or imagined community which asserted its identity through violent struggle against other nations, was one that had inspired vast swathes of Italian society.[30]

The link with the nationalist development in France in the early years of the twentieth century (discussed in Chapter 1) would seem obvious. The specific reference to the influence of the autochthonous Italian *Risorgimento* ideals is, though, significant here in that it highlights the parallel yet fundamentally unrelated development of Italian and French political nationalist contexts.

Specifically, scholars such as Francesco Perfetti, in line with Benedict Anderson's focus on the gradual nature of the process of formation of a nationalistic perspective, minimise the potential influence of French nationalism on the shaping of Italian nationalistic movements,[31] opposing, for instance, Charles Burdett's theory[32] of a Barresian or Sorellian influence over Corradini's discourses in *Il Regno*. Pointing to the *Risorgimento* roots of the nationalistic ideology, Perfetti highlights how, in fact, the Italian and French nationalisms are to be read in the context of a parallel development rather than in terms of a hierarchical influence.[33] Thus, even where the French influence of Maurras could be identified in the emergence of certain Italian anti-parliamentarian and anti-democratic positions, the origin of Italian twentieth-century nationalism can be traced to the country's own ideological background.

Such a perspective bears a direct relation to the issue of literary competitions in that, though inspired by their French neighbour's quasi-contemporary founding of literary prizes, Italian intellectuals giving birth to the *Bagutta* and, subsequently, to the *Viareggio* prizes were reacting to *specific* geopolitical and cultural contextual instances and — in the *Bagutta* case — explicitly distinguished the newly-born Italian prize from the contemporary *Goncourt*.

The *Premio Bagutta* was founded in Milan in Alberto Pepori's *trattoria* in the eponymous *Via Bagutta*. Writer and playwright Riccardo Bacchelli (1891–1985) and film critic and screenwriter Adolfo Franci (1895–1954), together with a group of friends, writers and journalists from the circle of Umberto Fracchia's (1889–1930) *rivista La Fiera Letteraria* and of the *Corriere della Sera*, as well as painters and intellectuals of the Milanese cultural scene — including, among others, Orio Vergani (journalist, photographer 1899–1960), Paolo Monelli (journalist 1891–1984) and Mario Vellani Marchi (painter 1895–1979) — met on 11 November 1926 for what had become a customary dinner at the *trattoria Bagutta*.

It was during that rainy evening in autumnal Milan that the first contemporary Italian literary prize was born, as fondly recalled by Orio Vergani:

> L'inverno è precoce, a Milano. La sera del giorno di San Martino, 11 novembre 1926, pioveva, e già l'attaccapanni di Bagutta era carico di pastrani. Si preannunciava una serata di pioggia interminabile. Il sor Pepori aveva messo sul fuoco le prime caldarroste. Fuori, via Bagutta, sull'acciottolato, grondava d'acqua come una chiavica, e i vetri della porta erano appannati dal fiato. Ci si guardava in faccia, nel gruppo che s'era attardato a tavola. L'ora era troppo inoltrata per andare a un teatro o a un cinematografo: non si sapeva come passare il tempo che ci separava dall'ora 'ragionevole' per trasferirci al Savini [...]. Uno di noi disse 'perché non fondiamo un premio letterario?' 'Come lo si chiamerebbe?', domandò uno degli amici che aveva cominciato a sbucciare una castagna. 'Si potrebbe chiamarlo Premio Bagutta. In Italia non c'è nessun premio letterario e questo avrebbe il merito, soprattutto, che lo daremmo noi, con i nostri soldi, senza aspettare l'eredità dei Goncourt, senza costituire un'Accademia, senza servire l'interesse di nessuno'.[34]

> [Winter comes early to Milan. On the evening of St. Martin's Day, on the 11th of November 1926, it rained and the cloak rack at Bagutta's was already covered in coats. An evening of endless rain was expected. Master Pepori had put the first chestnuts to roast on the fire. Outside, in the street, rain poured down and the glass panel on the door was fogged up. We looked at each other, we who were still sitting at the table. It was too late to go to the theatre or to the cinema: how could we pass the time while waiting for a 'reasonable' hour to move to Savini's? [...]. One of us said 'why don't we create a literary prize?' 'What would we call it?' asked one of the friends, peeling a roasted chestnut. 'We could call it *Premio Bagutta*. There are no literary prizes in Italy and this prize would have the merit, in particular, that it would be our gift, made with our money, without waiting for the *Goncourt*'s legacy, without creating any academy, without serving anybody's interest'.]

Paradoxically, when one considers the highlighted 'Italian' dimension attributed to the newly-born literary prize, the *Bagutta* was perceived by contemporary observers as having an excessively 'local' origin and impact and the *Viareggio* prize, founded in 1929 by Leonida Répaci (writer and painter 1898–1985), Carlo Salsa (journalist and screenwriter 1893–1962) and Alberto Colantuoni (writer and actor 1880–1959), was born with the avowed intention of countering the *Bagutta*'s allegedly restricted cultural milieu. In Leonida Répaci's own words:

> Volevamo, noi che lo fondammo, creare un premio che avesse un respiro più

> ampio del Bagutta, nato qualche mese prima nell'osteria del Pepori a Milano, e circoscritto ad una vita di cenacolo. Volevamo [...] farlo circolare assai più del Bagutta nella società letteraria italiana...[35]
>
> [We, who founded it, wished to create a prize with a wider reach compared to the *Bagutta*, born a few months earlier in Master Pepori's tavern in Milan and limited to a cenacle life. We wanted to obtain a greater impact within Italian literary society...]

From a certain perspective, one notices a degree of correspondence between the emergence of literary prizes on the Italian cultural scene and the hostility which the self-same cultural scene expressed, in part, toward the phenomenon of cultural cosmopolitanism.

The early decades of the twentieth century indeed saw the *foreign* become, both in Italy and perhaps even more spectacularly in France,[36] a synonym for the degenerate and the corrupted. As in France, Italian internal identity was shaped in opposition to the external *other* in a process where any internal variation of the model was perceived as threatening the homogeneity and reliability of the nationalistic symbolic ideal being constructed.

If, in Paris, foreign artists met with an increasingly hostile reaction from native intellectuals, in Italy, the literary milieu was split between the partisans of the cultural provincialism of the *strapaese* and the supporters of the broadly cosmopolitan *stracittà* position[37] [TN: early twentieth-century literary and cultural movements].

If a publication like the 1926 *Solaria,* under the editorship of Alberto Carocci (1904–1972), attempted to maintain itself above the most narrow-minded trends of cultural provincialism,[38] Corradini's previously evoked emphasis on the definition of a group's own identity through violent opposition to other social realities is significant of the 'oppositional character'[39] of the procedure through which the Italian symbolic community was predominantly articulated.

A short fragment from Vincenzo Cardarelli's 1929 Bagutta winner, *Il Sole a Picco*, displays a rich layering of stylistic strategies aimed at establishing precisely such a symbolic opposition. Relying on the diffused knowledge of popular, national stereotypes, which present the Italian nation as a land of *poeti, santi, navigatori* [poets, saints and sailors], he evokes the fantastic descriptions of Marco Polo's *Il Milione* [The Travels of Marco Polo] in order to create a sense of estrangement and disconnection between the Italian reality and the actually not so exotic or distant Netherlands:

> In gioventù, aveva girato anche un po' il mondo, a scopo di lavoro, spingendosi fino in Olanda: del quale paese ricordava costumi ed eccessi mirabili, parlando degli olandesi, che quando sono ubriachi si divertono a far incendiare il loro fiato alla fiamma delle lucerne, a quella maniera che Marco Polo parla dei Tartari o dei Persiani.[40]
>
> [In his youth, he had travelled a little, looking for work, going as far as the Netherlands. Of that country, he remembered the extraordinary habits and excesses. He spoke of the Dutch who, when they are drunk, enjoy setting fire to their breath with the flames of the lanterns, just as the Tartars or Persians do, according to Marco Polo.]

The reality of the Netherlands becomes, through the poet's representation, doubly transformed and, in fact, twice removed from the Italian reality: first, through the character's exaggerated memories and his deformed presentation of northern life, and second, through the parallel and superimposed literary association with the fantastic and exotic world of Marco Polo, legendary explorer. Italian identity is, by contrast, doubly affirmed, through the parallel reading of the normal *italianity* of the narrating characters — the illustrious Marco Polo anticipating and at the same time validating the later description of Cardarelli's character — and through the implicit distinction established from the super-human/non-human behaviour of the Dutch, meaningfully associated with barbaric and exotic populations: 'Tartari', 'Persiani'.

The nationalist rhetoric appears under many forms in the novels having won the Italian literary prizes of the period. Critics have underlined, for instance, in the context of the above-mentioned nationalist trend, the development of a new aesthetic classicism[41] fuelled, at the European level, among other factors, by a depreciation of Germanic culture in the wake of the First World War. Permeating the debate on Italian aesthetics, a renewed classicism[42] became indeed the cultural model on which the symbolic community, or in Rita Baldassarri's terms, the 'paese ideale' [the ideal country] was constructed.[43] Classicism can certainly be understood in terms of a proliferation of direct allusions to ancient classical cultures, as openly expressed by Carlo Emilio Gadda's statement taken from the 1934 *Bagutta* winner *Il Castello di Udine* [The Castle of Udine]:

> Voglio un'avventura mediterranea! Troppo abbiamo negletto la culla della civiltà! Voglio Eschilo, voglio Nausicaa, voglio le Sirti, voglio Scilla, voglio Cariddi, voglio venti Sicani, voglio l'Imetto, voglio l'Eretteo![44]
>
> [I long for a Mediterranean adventure! We have neglected way too much the cradle of civilization! I long to see Aeschylus, Nausicaa, the Sirtae, Scylla, I long for Charybdis, I long for Sicilian winds, for the Imetto mountain, I long for the Erechtheyon!].

Ironically, Gadda's Mediterranean cruise, far from mimicking any Ulyssean wandering, is in fact an instance of the tour-operator organised, ordered, travel which was swiftly made possible in the newly conquered Italian colonies in Libya. The improvised neo-conqueror carefully spells out the trajectory of his trip 'Tirreno in Crociera' [Cruise in the Tyrrenian], 'Dal Golfo all'Etna' [From the Gulf to the Etna], 'Tripolitania in Torpedone' [Tripolitania by bus] and 'Sabbia di Tripoli' [Sands of Tripoli], sketching a surprising Grand Tour in which tourism and colonialism blend and mix. Such a fusion of views is moreover expressed at a stylistic level in the merging of nationalistic rhetoric and poetic description which sketches the Libyan shore: 'Una cruda bianchezza di parallelepipedi ammodo, di là dal mare, definì Tripoli italiana.' [A raw whiteness of ordered structures, across the sea, defined the Italian Tripoli].[45]

The reference to Italy's classical past similarly emerges from the referring to a wide, all-encompassing, Mediterranean territorial and symbolic dimension, which encloses, in the cultural echoes it evokes, both the Greek and Latin ancient worlds. Classicism, in this context, is also to be understood as an aestheticised longing for idealised cultural precursors of a similarly idealised contemporary Italian identity, precursors which are to transcend Italy's actual territorial frontiers and encompass not only external and internal physical territories but also past cultural realities and imagined artistic projections. References ranging from ancient Etruscan civilisations to Dante and to late nineteenth-century *Risorgimento* authors thus characterise the literary production of the second and third decade of the twentieth century.[46] Through such references, an idealised *Italian* heritage, a specific tradition, is rebuilt, in contrast to the factual territorial and political divisions marking the historical progress towards a united Italian state. The tracing, the re-creating of a (to an extent) fictionalised 'historical' past 'reinforc[es] the cultural boundaries of the community'.[47] That which finally emerges is a narrative endowed with strong didactic potential, in which the processes of remembering, re-creation, recognition and acquisition[48] of culture appear as impossible to separate.

In Cardarelli's *Il Sole a Picco* [The Blazing Sun] specific regional history is thus extended to express national identity as a whole. As highlighted by the term 'paese', the evocation of the Etruscan past of the poet's own region — Maremma — becomes a celebration of the idealised character of the Italian nation's ancestor-civilisation. Significantly, the specific identity of the Etruscan people is established in opposition to the *foreign* which, in the following example and in contrast to Gadda's references, is represented by the Greek world. And so, Etruscan artists are described as:

> ...mestieranti insigni e corrivi, carnali e sprezzanti, che alla fiorita eleganza inimitabile ed allo smalto finissimo dei vasi greci contrapposero, inaudita magia, il crudo colore dell'argilla e l'efficacia realistica dei loro tracotanti segnacci neri. Nelle sculture di terracotta, soprattutto, si vedono ancora, freschissime, le impronte impulsive e spicciative delle loro mani da mattonai.[49]

> [...workers both exceptional and mediocre, sensuous and disdainful, who, through a magic unheard of, set against the inimitable, flowery elegance and fine enamel of Greek vases the crude colour of clay and the realistic forcefulness of their arrogant, dark, scratched lines. In the *terracotta* sculptures, more than anywhere else, one can still see the impulsive and hurried imprints of those brickmakers' hands.]

The apparently negative lexical field of rough craftsmanship is transformed through the sheer strength — structural minimalism, down-to-earth solidity, powerful endurance — of Etruscan artistry. The materiality, the tangibility of their work, and by extension, the permanence of their spirit, is expressed through a metaphorical vision of fingerprints left, in a quasi-scientific perspective, on history. The diffuse feeling of tangible materiality is projected onto a mythical level where the Etruscan people are seen as the embodiment of an ancient legend, Vulcan-like figures shaping and breathing life into their own mythical existence.[50] As the link is finally established with modern Italian identity, the Etruscans are presented in a metaphor which collapses all levels of the historical reconstruction, rendering the Etruscan past as the mould which gives birth to twentieth-century Italy. Artistic ability, which made the Etruscan unique — thus different, differentiated and recognisable — becomes the metaphorical projection of the unicity, thus the recognisable identity, of the contemporary Italian nation:

> Oggi, di questo popolo misterioso e sopraffatto che siede alle origini della nostra civiltà, venuto non si sa da dove, dal mare forse, ma rivolto a monte, non ci rimane che lo stampo corrotto della sua immagine sulla terra, là dove s'è coricato morendo.[51]
>
> [Today, of this mysterious and defeated race seated at the origins of our civilisation, who arrived from who knows where, from the sea perhaps, yet turned towards the land, nothing is left but the corrupted mould of their image on the earth, where they lay dying.]

One notices here, incidentally, how the use of the term 'corrotto' [TN: potential significations range from immoral to dishonest, decomposed, rotten, altered, changed] projects a problematic and polemic dimension on the previously evoked *nationalistic* reading of contemporary Italian reality. We will indeed consider further on the degree to which such a nationalistic trend can be seen as being only one side of the literary structuring equation. What is relevant for the current observation is that the tracing of the symbolic sphere of Italian identity is here made through an historical dimension emphasising the presence of a continuous link between mould and moulded, creators and created.

Further, one notices how what has been considered as the Fascist fascination with historical symbolism, appears to mimic in a similar process the association between a *mythicised* past and the Italian present. Indeed, Mussolini's founding of twelve cities between 1928 and 1940[52] deliberately echoed the founding of twelve cities by the Etruscan League, a gesture in turn repeated by Cosimo de' Medici's founding of twelve cities on the symbolic boundary between Tuscany and the ancient 'Etruria' or Latium. Such a layering of historical resonance similarly echoed in the architectural choices made by the Regime for the new towns. A systematic favouring of the planimetric model, based on ancient Roman military encampments, together with a diffused use of medievally inspired towers set indeed Italian fascist architecture at odds with the contemporary predominant trends in European architecture.[53]

Returning to the literary example from Cardarelli's *Il Sole a Picco*, one notices how the historical circle of identity formation is closed by a reading of Italian contemporary reality through a pre-historical/quasi-mythological lens, unveiling how ancient Gods inhabit the day-to-day reality of the small island of Capri. Beyond traditional poetic conventions, Cardarelli's mythological world enters contemporary scenes to impress upon the reader the indissoluble link between glorious past and present times.

> Ecco qua il sole di Capri. Questo è positivamente Febo, di cui si discorre nell'Adone del cavalier Marino. Tutte le mattine si leva, puntuale, e va ad assidersi tranquillamente sul trono di Monte Solaro, senza nulla di epico. Di lassù scocca le sue frecce sottilissime, disperdendo in un baleno le argentee nebbioline che, favorite dallo scirocco, tenterebbero, poverette, di opporgersi al sorgere d'un tanto sole. Tiranno famigliare, vero Borbone del cielo che non teme disordini ne rivoluzioni nei suoi stati. Ma per noi è anche il sole dei lunari e delle luminarie di Piedigrotta, enormemente tondo, giallo, crinito di fiamme e regale come un'insegna da Albergo del Sole. Dio popolare del Mezzogiorno a cui si sacrificano in abbondanza cocomeri e poponi e sono anche dedicati nella stagione del solleone [...] gli spari notturni ed i fuochi d'artificio.[54]

[Here is the sun of Capri. This is indeed Febus, mentioned in Marino's Adonis. Every morning he wakes, on time, and quietly, with no epical drama, sits on his throne on Mount Solaro. From up there, he throws his thread-like arrows, dispersing in a flash the silvery fogs which, supported by the southern wind, would like to try, poor them, to oppose the rising of such a sun. Familiar tyrant, true Bourbon of the sky, who does not fear unrest or revolution in his lands. For us, however, he is also the sun of the lanterns and lights of Piedigrotta, hugely round, yellow, fleeced with flames and as regal as the *Albergo del Sole* banner. Popular god of the *Mezzogiorno*, to whom watermelons are sacrificed in numbers and to whom, in high summer, [...] night shootings and fireworks are dedicated.]

Yet, though ostensibly embodied by the apollonian figure, the cultural identity which is systematically framed in Cardarelli's work remains always strongly related to a close, intimate, *familiar* dimension. The poet underlines the lack of *epic* elements in his god-figure. The accent is set on a sketch which is close to popular representations and to a popular understanding of identity. Thus one notices how the insertion of a cultural reference to the Bourbon dynasty 'tiranno familiare, vero Borbone' allows for an immediate undermining of any potential scholarly resonance to the quoting of a mythical figure and allows for a referring to a historical-political figure which appears at once as *familiar* and as belonging to the informal sphere of the *family*. The tone is indeed that of a smiling, impertinent, celebration based on the un-ostentatious offer of 'cocomeri e poponi'.

Such a reduction/simplification of the cultural reference to a dimension which can appear as closest to the audience's understanding finds a strong echo in the reiterated use of the portrait in its most schematic embodiments. The shape, the form, the structure of Italian identity filters through the stylised use of *types,* which allows for a simplified tracing of identity boundaries and for the simultaneous referring to a communal past, the time of a portrait being, as noted by Francine Dugast-Portes, 'd'abord celui d'un héritage'[55] [first of all, [the time] of a legacy].

At the national level, the identity recognised by Cardarelli is thus first of all that of a humble, somewhat rural, working-class world, which apparently disconnects itself from a highly literary dimension. In *Appendice di Prosa* [Appendix of Prose], he notes:

> Dire che l'Italia è un paese popolare significa richiamarla alle sue origini antiche, ai suoi aspetti naturali, alla sua civiltà ereditaria. Significa ridarle il senso e la responsabilità della sua lunghissima, incomparabile storia.[56]
>
> [To say that Italy is a working-class country is to recall its ancient origins, its natural aspects, its hereditary civilisation. It means to give it back the meaning and the responsibility for its very long, unequalled history.]

Additionally, an evocation of the 'popolare' becomes the excuse for a rich gallery of portraits in which regional characteristics — and the apparently deep-seated differentiations between regional identities — are a paradoxical basis for the depiction of a coherent Italian identity based on internal cultural diversity. Unity in difference, in a sense, in a process which reinforces traditionally accepted national stereotypes, is what characterises Cardarelli's idealised nation:

> Giungono insieme 'gli aquilani', bella, umile, forte razza; chiusi nei loro mantelli turchini come tanti carabinieri di cui hanno anche il passo. Con la loro andatura e la pellegrina somigliano pure a San Rocco. E mangiano il polentone. Costoro sono gl'iloti e gli schiavi della terra.[57]

> [The inhabitants of Aquila arrive together, a beautiful, humble, strong race; wrapped in their turquoise mantles, like the *carabinieri* with whom they share the way of walking. With their stride and their coat they also look like Saint Rocco. And they eat *polentone*. They are the helots and the slaves of the earth.]
> [TN: *Carabinieri*: military corps with police functions. *Polenta*: dish made of maize flour.]

As noted by Charles Burdett, and as previously stated in relation to the constitution of Italian external identity, the figurations in Cardarelli's texts, and in other texts representative to an extent of the *strapaese* movement, founded their ideological significance on 'the logic of their binary oppositions'.[58] Aquilani vs Maremmani, Romani vs Toscani and yet all of them characterised by a unique founding identity which to a degree underplays internal boundaries to the advantage of external frontiers.

In parallel to the popular strata of differentiated identities runs a complex superstructure in which national identity becomes embedded in a thematic and stylistic register of high literary and artistic allusions. Italian identity is thus firmly established in the shadow of illustrious past artists and writers.[59] Such a heritage is reflected in the apparently popular types in a mixing of the *high* and *low* which becomes the embodiment of Giotto's celebrated 'creativa ignoranza' [creative ignorance]:

> Il mio vecchio padrone di casa, il sor Ettore, marito della Sora Nunziatina, era di professione scalpellino, e, naturalmente, uomo di poche lettere, ma parlava come un dio. Toscano di buona razza, si rappresentava i fatti e gli uomini della storia come se ci avesse vissuto in mezzo, con uno spirito, cioè, al tutto confidenziale. E niente di più lo dilettava quanto ragionare di arte e di storia. Aveva letto Macchiavelli, Guicciardini, il Vasari, il Varchi e le tragedie dell'Alfieri. Era naturalmente, come lo sono tutti i bravi popolani d'Italia, un classicista. Non per nulla si chiamava Ettore.[60]

> [My old landlord, Master Hector, Mistress Nunciatina's husband, was a stonecutter and, naturally enough, a man of basic education, yet he spoke like a god. Tuscan, from a good race, he thought about the facts and men of history as if he had lived among them, that is to say, with a spirit of confidentiality. Nothing delighted him more than to discuss art and history. He had read Macchiavelli, Guicciardini, Vasari, Varchi and the Alfieri's tragedies. Of course, like all of Italy's workmen, he was a classicist. He was not called Hector by chance.]

The poetic voice becomes here the expression of a double heritage which manifests itself in the mixed generic tones of the compositions. We will later focus on the extent to which traditional novelistic models were effectively undermined in Italian literary production of the 1920s and 1930s. In our present reflection, we will limit our analysis to the degree to which both literary and popular tones appear in the mixed ballad-like compositions characterising the texts that won literary prizes in the period.

Thus, in Cardarelli's *Santi del Mio Paese* [Saints from my Country], the popular — proverb-like — litany of Saints is inscribed within a much higher literary composition, mixing in a set of complex patterns not only poetry and prose but also popular language and high allusions, proverbs, nonsense and poetic rhetoric:

> Io non so se di me qualcuno ha cura,
> che nacqui all'ombra delle antiche mura.
> Vien San Martino che piove e c'è il sole,
> vedi le vecchie che fanno all'amore.
> Rustico è San Martino, prospero, antico,
> e dell'invidia natural nemico.[61]

> [I do not know if someone cares for me,
> I, who was born in the old walls' shadow,
> Saint Martin comes, with both sun and rain,
> See the old ones making love.
> Saint Martin is rustic, prosperous and ancient,
> And a natural enemy of envy.]

Similarly, Achille Campanile's choice for his title *Cantilena all'Angolo della Strada*, [Singsong on a Street Corner] winner of the 1933 *Viareggio* prize, is evocative of popular, repetitive songs, which he goes as far as echoing within his own lines, inserting a popular voice in the more refined context of his own prose: 'Brave reclute. Per ora sanno poche cose. Sanno che a navigar sul mare ci voglion barchette e a far l'amor di sera ci voglion ragazzette. E a far l'amor di sera ci voglion ragazzette.' [Good recruits. For now, they do not know much. They know that to sail you need a small boat and to make love at night you need a girl. And to make love at night you need a girl.][62]

Italian identity is thus constructed in terms of a complex patterning of cultural references blending the *popular* and the *cultured*, the *local* and the *national*, the *historical* and the *contemporary* in an idealised web where differences are absorbed in a stabilised and culturally validated conceptual construct, reflected in the winning works.

The granting of a literary prize to such works appears to rest on the acknowledgement that 'the work of differentiation and formation of intervals [...] has been concluded'.[63] Not only is the literary work itself recognised as an instance of the stabilisation of significance — in that completed aesthetic structure — but so is the cultural reorganisation of the symbolic sphere, which the work displays, understood as being both meaningful and successful. 'The 'distinctness' of the signs, as a synthesis of intelligible meanings and material substrates of expression, [is] completed'[64] in a context where the literary work becomes an instance of the degree to which the *cultural* signs are indeed seen as distinct — in that expression of a distinctive and distinguishable identity — and intelligible.

Thus the community uses the articulation of metaphorical boundaries — of the territory, of the historical evolution, of the *Italian* type — in order to construct its own identity. In such a view, the aesthetic act is not simply invested by an ideological dimension, 'rather, the aesthetic act is itself ideological, and the production of an aesthetic or narrative form is to be seen as an ideological act in its own right, with the function of inventing imaginary or formal solutions to unresolvable social contradictions'.[65]

Problematisation of identity-framing processes

In the case of Italy's literary prizes, we have so far considered the degree to which recurring patterns at the thematic level, interacting with an openly nationalistic cultural background, were aimed at providing a cognitive structure, serving as a basis for the construction of a renewed Italian identity, in a process similar to the one identified in the French case.

However, as will be shown in the subsequent parts of the study, *stylistic and generic* instabilities appear to undermine from within the formal dimension of winning literary productions, which, indeed, often hover between novel and poetry, journalistic prose and literary composition.

In parallel, Italy's symbolic boundaries and the construction of the Italian community appear to be systematically challenged through the *thematic* renegotiation of the country's structural frontiers. Such a renegotiation appears to be specifically embodied in the links tying the Italian cultural world to the practice and discussion of travel experiences. The references to travelling and, in itself, the very practice of travelling fracture the structural stability of the symbolic scene through the dialectic dimension which invests the concept of *boundary*.

Ultimately, the symbolic function played by the notion of *boundary* disrupts the closed binary relation tying subject to artistic object such as it is conceived in a *Weltanschauung* perspective, to the advantage of an apprehension of the dynamic and open-ended — self-*r*enegotiating — role of cultural institutions, such as literary prizes, in the landscape of identity production and validation.

In order to consider the ways in which the notion of *boundary* can be used to highlight the instability and dialectic negotiation, rather than the resolutive closure, characterising the social function of literary institutions on the Italian cultural scene of the 1920s and 1930s, however, it might be first necessary to momentarily focus once again on the theory of identity constitution.

Such a brief consideration aims specifically at assessing how, at the theoretical level, the notion of boundary acts as a disruptive element in the field of cognitive stabilisation. Such a consideration will in turn allow for the subsequent matching between the theoretical notion of boundary and the culturally specific examples of symbolic and structural boundaries emerging from the Italian context. Ultimately, such boundaries and their function in the identity-constructing process, characterising the case in Italy, will offer an instance of the ways in which — at the general level — the theoretical model for the assessment of the function of cultural institutions can be amended to illustrate the degree to which such a function is, at heart, a dynamic and ultimately a self-undermining and self-transforming one.

By extension, in such a perspective, the *Weltanschauung* deadlock tying cultural production and cultural identity is undermined. Indeed, when considering the verbal definition of *Frenchness* or *Italianity* as expressed in the context of nationalism, we have already referred to Manchester anthropologist Anthony P. Cohen's definition of the notion of *community* in terms of its oppositional character:

> A reasonable interpretation of the word's use would seem to imply two related suggestions: that the members of a group of people (a) have something in common with each other, which (b) distinguishes them in a significant way from the members of other putative groups. 'Community' thus seems to imply simultaneously both similarity and difference. The word thus expresses a relational idea: the opposition of one community to the other or to other social entities.[66]

Additionally, however, Cohen establishes the notion of *symbolic community* by relying on a theoretical differentiation between the idea of a *symbolic* sphere and that of a tangible, external, *structural* dimension of social reality. In other words, Cohen distinguishes the notion of symbolic community from that of structural community. Crucially, such a disconnection potentially engenders a situation in which the limits of the symbolic community and those of the structural community, far from corresponding to one another, are set in contrast to one another. In Fig. 9, the potential disconnection highlighted by Cohen is represented in the *partial* overlapping of structural and symbolic fields.

Such a model is complicated by the awareness that each instance of group identity which might form the ground for the establishment of a symbolic community is submitted to internally eroding forces. Indeed, as the multiple *individual* identities forming the texture of the wider group-identity — in turn giving form to the sub-group identities illustrated in the scheme — enter the dynamics of symbolic community-building, one notices how the setting-up of a stable symbolic dimension is ultimately internally undermined by individual drives towards differentiation. The same applies to the external pressures which, proceeding from the wider macro-groups dimensions potentially at work, similarly undermine the stability of the symbolic dimension and can go so far as interacting with the structural dimension itself.

Fundamentally, such a theoretical approach unveils how the formation of a community, either from a structural or symbolic perspective, ultimately rests on the capacity to negotiate stable physical and symbolic boundaries between what is held to be the familiar and the communal and what is held to be the external and the foreign. The notion of limit, the dynamics according to which lines are crossed and boundaries established, therefore enter the process of identity-building as founding elements. The negotiating process extends from the individual to the macro-group levels and turns back on the individual level in a constant dialectic exchange of symbolic framings and settings.

Crucially, such a dynamic between instances of identity-framing and instances of identity-undermining is similarly attributed to the individual's own sphere of cognition in Lacan's previously mentioned theory of identity-construction. Indeed, according to the psychiatrist, while images of wholeness give us an image of ourselves as distinct from the world, they never align with us perfectly. There is an inevitable, structural, gap between the truth of fragmentation (a body that constantly changes and transforms itself, a consciousness influenced by contrasting representations) and images of self-identity and wholeness.

Maurice Merleau-Ponty's analysis of the degree to which perception of the world — and the related perception of the self — are similarly characterised by an unresolved

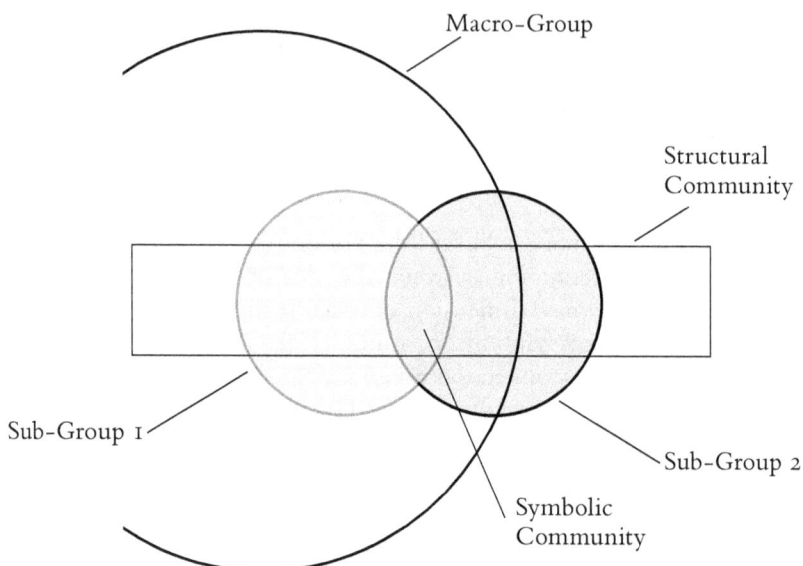

Fig. 2.2. Symbolic and structural Community

inner instability and an ever-present dynamic motion reveals the specific nature of such a gap. The dynamic, ever-active, ever-changing dimension of the identity-cognition process emerges as Merleau-Ponty underlines how the phenomenological world is not *pure being* understood in terms of an all-encompassing wholeness which reveals itself equally, instantaneously and completely to all subjectivities. In fact, the phenomenologist is at pains to stress how the existence of such a wholeness would intrinsically deny the very existence of individual subjectivities.

True, according to the critic, 'the world is always "already there" before reflection begins'.[67] Man is thus conceived of as being 'in the world',[68] as fused with the world-dimension and simultaneously as participating in the flux of universal signification which infuses everything. Man is thus set in a context in which 'the all-embracing synthesis [...] without which there would be no world'[69] entails a flowing of meaning which encompasses him.

However, the world is ultimately perceived 'as strange and paradoxical'[70] in that the disconnection that fundamentally characterises the relation between consciousness and the world, which causes the subject to be perceived as 'a condition of possibility distinct from [...] [the] experience'[71] of the world, also signifies that unity of consciousness cannot be realised simultaneously with the consciousness of the world.[72] As the world is conceived through analytical reflection in terms of an 'all-embracing synthesis'[73] 'without which there would be no world',[74] consciousness is placed in a position in which it can apprehend the world only through the very disconnection which makes the process of understanding itself ultimately incomplete — incomplete because intrinsically lacking the apprehending consciousness itself. In that sense, Merleau-Ponty's world cannot be but 'paradoxical' in that fundamentally incomplete. Indeed, the conceiving mind remains ultimately severed from such an all-encompassing flow and it is such severance which allows for the apprehending process.

What is relevant for the current study is that, as the critic undermines the possibility of *pure perception*, he affirms the understanding of the perceptive act in terms of an indeterminateness which runs parallel with his acknowledgement of the impossibility of an idealistic, all-embracing, pure perceptive act. Such an indeterminate dimension is actually celebrated as Merleau-Ponty affirms how 'we must recognize the indeterminate as a positive phenomenon [...] its meaning is an equivocal meaning'[75] and recognises how 'the perceived, by its nature, admits of the ambiguous, the shifting'.[76]

Following from this affirmation lies the understanding of both the perceiver and the perceived as fundamentally incomplete, in that *wholeness* has been defined as being unavailable to perception.[77] Thus perception is perception of *incompleteness*, of the very gap which stands at the basis of the relationship between the consciousness and the world. In that incompleteness, the perceptive process becomes immersed in a space-temporal dimension where absence plays a key role.

If perception of the world, in other words, of an external sphere, is apprehended through absence and incompleteness, the perception of the self is similarly understood in terms of a lack of all-encompassing wholeness which prevents a fusion between the individual and the communal, the object and the subject. Identity thus becomes ultimately defined through absence, lack and openness rather than through presence, wholeness and cognitive closure.

However, the very presence of Merleau-Ponty's 'world' does not allow for the reflection to be closed with the simple recognition of the existence of such a gap/absence. Indeed, how to account for what is *present, perceived* and *cognised* and for the understanding of the self which takes place in parallel with the apprehension of such a gap?

We have previously seen how the centrality of the notion of structure is fundamental in the phenomenological approach to significance. For, indeed, not only is it a 'key feature of all phenomenological enquiry that it understands consciousness — whether thinking, feeling, remembering, or otherwise — as "intentional", that is, directed towards an object'[78] but also that it understands that object to be always related to a distinguishable structure. In Merleau-Ponty's words,

> When Gestalt theory informs us that a figure on a background is the simplest sense-given available to us, we reply that this [...] is the very definition of the phenomenon of perception, that without which a phenomenon cannot be said to be perception at all. The perceptual 'something' is always in the middle of something else, it always forms part of a field.[79]

Should the *gap* be cancelled, the structural dimension, in losing its position against the *background* emphasised by Merleau-Ponty, would become the background itself, losing all identity and, indeed, existence. Thus meaning, understood as structure, is made to exist, according to Manfred Frank, precisely through the relation between the absence we have underlined[80] and the presence of the 'world'.[81]

From such positions, there emerges the central function played by the notion of *boundary* in the negotiation of signification and identity. The boundary indicates here not a closed and secured framework but an open frontier line, stretching to the end of cognitive perception yet ultimately unable to enclose it in a stabilised 'wish–landscape'[82] and defining *structure* not as a stable and self-standing cognised form but as 'an absent cause, since it is nowhere empirically present as an element, it is not part of the whole or one of the levels, but rather the entire system of relationships among those levels'.[83]

Challenging Boundaries

It is precisely the investigation of such a contradictory system of relationships which appears to characterise the Italian authors in the period under consideration. In a process echoed, as will be illustrated, in the thematic and stylistic dimension of the novels, literary prize-winning authors appear to be projected in a restless investigation of the very physical and symbolic limits of the structural community we have evoked in the context of Cohen's analysis. This leads, in turn, to the problematisation of the symbolic community itself. Ultimately, the very notions of community and individuality appear to be challenged in the Italian context.

Such a process indicates how Italian literary competitions, far from favouring the celebration of a specific cultural identity, predominantly appear to focus on the questioning and challenging of the very process through which identity is shaped and formed.

Writing of travel — writing as travel

We have mentioned the degree to which the blending of popular and high literary discourses characterises the thematic and stylistic choices in winning literary works of the period. Such a blending becomes particularly significant if read in the light of the deep transformations affecting the Italian literary world in the early decades of the twentieth century.

Between 1890 and 1915, journalism became an increasingly important player on the Italian cultural scene. The trend was initiated when, taking Anglo-Saxon professional journalism as a paradigm, Ancona-born journalist Luigi Albertini (1871–1941) shaped the *Corriere della Sera* according to new, international models,[84] transforming the Milanese newspaper into the most important Italian daily of the pre-war years.

As cultural figures such as Luigi Einaudi or Luigi Pirandello started to write for the *Corriere*, a new trend — which could be extended to the Italian journalistic scene as a whole — began to develop: an innovative writing style blended the traditional Italian emphasis on the literariness of cultural writing with the immediateness of newspaper pieces. Specifically, literary style enters journalistic writing through the use of acknowledged literary *authors* as occasional contributors.[85]

By extension, in the literary world, literary and journalistic prose became increasingly difficult to tell apart and was also rewarded in the context of literary competitions. Journalists often came to produce *literary* work which was, to an extent, disconnected from their professional activity.⁸⁶ As an example, one might mention Guelfo Civinini (1873–1974), 1937 *Viareggio* winner for *Trattoria di paese* [A Country Tavern], who worked more or less continuously for the *Corriere della Sera* between 1920 and 1942, and who alternated poetic production — *I sentieri e le nuvole* (1911) [Pathways and Clouds], *Stella confidente* (1918)⁸⁷ [Confidant Star] — with journalistic narratives of his travels in Africa — *Sotto le piogge equatoriali* (1930) [Under Equatorial Rains], *Ricordi di carovana* (1932) [Memories of a Convoy], *Un viaggio attraverso l'Abissinia sulle orme di Vittorio Bottego* (1930) [Travelling across Abyssinia on Vittorio Bottego's Steps].

The original blending of literary and non-literary writing is specifically embodied in the peculiar format of the emphatically cultural *terza pagina* [TN: page of a daily newspaper, dedicated to cultural themes]. Enrico Pea (1881–1958), 1938 *Viareggio* winner for *La Maremmana*, in his 1945–1953 *L'Arca di Noè* [Noa's Arch], significantly subtitled *Racconti, Memorie, Elzeviri* [Stories, Memories and Elzevirs], can proudly claim:

> Sono uno scrittore di 'terza pagina' da una venticinquina d'anni [...] L'esercizio dello scrivere in terza pagina giovò ad uno scrittore lento come sono io. La necessità del guadagno, la limitazione dello spazio, una certa puntualità di consegna, la doverosa chiarezza. E l'orgoglio di doversi sempre tener su: di non cadere tra un pezzo e l'altro. Mi hanno sveltito. Ho dovuto vigilare le oscurità, rimuovere gli idiotismi, tenendo presente gli italiani e non la regione.⁸⁸

> [I have been writing for the 'third page' (cultural page) for the past twenty-five years [...] The process of writing for the third page suited a slow writer, like me. The need to receive a wage, the limited space, a certain punctuality requested in the delivery of the piece, the necessary clarity. And the pride in always maintaining a good standard: of not falling between an article and the next. That kept me on my toes. I had to check for lack of clarity, remove stupid failures, think of Italian readers in general and not of any specific region in particular.]

A cultural page *par excellence*, a paradoxical journalistic feature conceived and realised in a country marked by one of the highest rates of illiteracy in Europe,⁸⁹ the *terza pagina* soon became the newspaper space in which literature took form and substance, in which literary projects were attempted and new voices made themselves heard.

It is, in particular, a space in which mixed or experimental generic forms emerge. Commenting on 1933 *Viareggio* winner Achille Campanile's (1899–1977) career as a humourist, theatrical author and journalist for *Corriere Italiano*, *Idea Nazionale* and *Tribuna di Roma*⁹⁰, critic Oreste del Buono notes how

> Giornalismo, teatro, narrativa sono classificazioni di comodo, ovvero divisioni, spartizioni, specializzazioni che Campanile usa per farsi intendere, e anche compensare, dagli altri nell'esercizio della sua professione di scrittore, ma in cui, in definitiva, non crede mai interamente. Così, dall'inizio alla fine, si sentirà sempre libero di travasare il suo materiale da un articolo a un testo di teatro e a un romanzo o viceversa, dando ininterrottamente e generosamente luogo ad altre composizioni, congiunzioni, conflagrazioni.⁹¹

> [Terms such as journalism, theatre, narrative prose are classifications of convenience, that is to say divisions, specialisations used by Campanile to make himself understood, and to be paid, by others in his profession as a writer. He, however, never wholly believed in them. From beginning to end, he did always feel free to transfer his material from an article to a theatrical text, to a novel or vice versa, endlessly and generously giving birth to new and different compositions, conjunctions and conflagrations.]

As a result, the prose work which emerges from such a cultural dimension is the fruit of a mixed breeding of both literary and non-literary prose. Carlo Emilio Gadda's (1893–1973) 1934 Bagutta winner *Il Castello di Udine* is, for instance, made up of a series of excerpts previously published in magazines such as *Solaria*, *L'Ambrosiano* and *Italia Letteraria*, mixed with diary fragments, the recounting of travel in the Mediterranean, a short historical sketch, and *La Fidanzata di Elio* [Elio's Girlfriend], the sole genuine fragment of prose fiction.[92]

Similarly, Tumiati's *I Tetti Rossi* [Red Roofs] — 1931 *Viareggio* Prize-winner — is the collection of a series of diary excerpts, memoirs, sketches and literary impressions collected between 1929 and 1931 and originally published in Piero Pancrazi's magazine *Pegaso*. The exception to the rule, Corrado Tumiati (1885–1967) was, when he won the *Viareggio*, a famous psychiatrist with more than twenty years' experience in psychiatric asylums and dozens of scientific publications to his name. The passage from scientific to journalistic prose and, finally, to literary prose is, though, indicative of the tendency for generic instability characterising the Italian literary scene in the late 1920s.[93]

From a strictly stylistic point of view, literary prose is transformed through the insertion of journalism-typical *elzeviri*. Originally defining the typographic character first designed by the Dutch Christoffel Van Dyck for the volumes published by the Elzevier family between the sixteenth and seventeenth centuries, the *elzeviro* can be described as

> [...] un compromesso bastardo del giornalismo italiano, mezzo articolo normale, mezzo racconto, mezza confessione, mezza invenzione, mezzo impegno e mezzo intrattenimento, mezza arte e mezza evasione. E' il componimento che apre la terza pagina, quella per così dire letteraria, ma che può allignare anche nei capicronaca e nei commenti di colore.[94]

> [...a bastard compromise of Italian journalism, in part a standard article, in part a narrative, in part a confession, in part an invention, in part a committed piece, in part entertainment, in part art and in part just fun. It is the piece that opens the 'third page', the literary one, but it can also appear in other parts of the news.]

Cardarelli's depiction of the Capri landscape is indicative of the style used in the *elzeviri* fragments. Sketching out the landscape, Cardarelli merges the metaphorical representation of the landscape as a culinary work of art with the ideologically marked association of Italy as a country of artists and — both culinary and non-culinary — masterpieces:

> Cesto di dovizie, galleggiante e fiorente sul mare, l'Isola di Capri è un composto di cose preziosissime in cui s'armonizzano elementi moreschi, greci e romani, sopra un fondo roccioso e naturale del più squisito barocco.[95]

[Basket of delicacies, floating and flourishing on the sea, the island of Capri is made of very precious things, an harmonic blending of Arab, Greek and Roman elements, against a rocky and natural background in the more delicious Baroque style].

The layered game of cultural allusions collapses references to Italian identity with the journalistic sketch of a culinary event, the reportage of a particularly attractive touristic spot, the ironic matching of high literary rhythms with the down-to-earth thematic background of the depiction:

> Corrono e s'affondano tortuose, in mezzo, le stradicciole di zucchero, in un nugolo di polvere al vento che infarina le viti e gli alberi sui bordi, tra i vecchi muri scrostati e scuri come il pane di casa, sui quali il sol d'agosto mette splendidi riflessi d'un rosso vinoso.[96]

[Small, contorted streets of sugar run and clash in their middle, in a windy cloud which covers with floor-like dust the vines and the border trees, between old walls, dark and crumbling like home-made bread, on which the August sun sets wonderful burgundy highlights.]

The exploration of the thematic and stylistic boundaries between literary and journalistic prose is to be read bearing in mind the development and success, sanctioned by literary competitions, of literary works derived from journalistic assignments abroad or from journalistic travels within the Italian territory. The physical exploration of the territory which runs parallel to the re-negotiation of aesthetic boundaries concurs in the problematisation of established cognitive frameworks.

Italian travel writing, whose origins have been traced to the eighteenth-century epic and picaresque narratives,[97] emerges from its very beginnings as a genre focusing on the concept of *border*, ranging from erotic escapes to pseudoscientific explorations, aimed, in its initial expressions, at exploring the limits between the *real* and the *fantastic*.

Between works such as Pietro Chiari's *Filosofessa italiana* [The Italian Philosopher] (1753), Ippolito Pindemonte's *Abaritte* [TN: First name of protagonist] (1790) or Zaccaria Seriman's *Viaggio di Enrico Wanton alle Terre Incognite australi ed ai Regni delle scimmie e dei Cinocefali* [Enrico Wanton's Travels to the Austral Lands and to the Monkeys' and Dog-Headed's Kingdoms] (1749) and Foscolo's *Ultime lettere di Jacopo Ortis* [Jacopo Ortis' Last Letters] (1802), however, there occurs a major turning-point away from the imaginary sphere towards a new, nineteenth-century perception of travel as a *real*, actual experience.[98]

If some elements of such an approach had been anticipated by the eighteenth-century attention to the details of everyday life[99] and, in particular, to the social assessment of the developing urban landscape, the nineteenth century not only saw the further development of such a thematic trend but also the broadening of the possibilities for undertaking *real* travel activities.[100] Italian literary travel writing became, as a consequence, centred on the physical exploration of territorial boundaries.

In parallel, in the light of the literary trends characterising Italian journalism, one sees how, following in the footsteps of some major nineteenth-century authors such as Edmondo de Amicis (1846–1908) for *La Nazione*, Giovanni Faldella (1846–1928) for *Gazzetta Piemontese* or Edoardo Scarfoglio (1860–1917) for *Il Mattino*, journalists of the 1920s and 1930s produced real travel reports displaying an increasingly *literary* cut.[101] As a result, the traveller/author is set at the symbolic boundary between different social identities and roles, investigating the limits of literary creation and documentary narration, while simultaneously negotiating the structural internal and external boundaries of the national territory.

Throughout the first three decades of the twentieth century, journalistic/literary travel narrative saw an enduring success. In 1932, Giovanni Comisso, winner of the first *Bagutta* prize in 1929, published the narration of his travels to the Far East under the title *Cina-Giappone* [China — Japan]. They inscribe themselves within a wider current that sees Mario Soldati (1906–1999) and Giuseppe Antonio Borgese (1882–1952) travelling to the United States in the 1930s or Bruno Barilli (1880–1952) visiting Africa as narrated in his 1931 *Il sole in trappola* [The Trapped Sun]. If Barilli's travels to Denmark, Sweden and Norway appear both in the fourth chapter of his *Il viaggiatore volante* [The Flying Traveller] (1946) and in a series of fifteen articles published in the *Gazzetta del Popolo*, Antonio Baldini's (1889–1962) Paris is illustrated in the 1934 *La vecchia del Bal Bullier* [The Old Woman from the Bullier Dancing]. Writing for the *Corriere della Sera*, Emilio Cecchi (1884–1966) established himself as perhaps the most important travel writer of the period between the two world wars, extensively reporting on his trips to the United States (*America Amara* [Bitter America] — 1940), Mexico (*Lettere dal Messico* [Letters from Mexico] — 1932), The Netherlands, and Greece (*Et in arcadia ego* — 1936).[102]

As briefly anticipated, the development of journalistic travel, far from being limited to the exploration of foreign territories, is also particularly interesting in that it often appears to be focused on the exploration of the internal Italian landscapes. One notices here the shift from the external to a depiction of the internal as *other* — as a reality yet to be discovered. Thus Riccardo Bacchelli's 1928 *La ruota del tempo* [The Wheel of Time] (*Bagutta* founder and 1936 *Viareggio* winner with *Il rabdomante* [The Water Diviner]) is based on descriptions of the Italian landscape. In 1939, Carlo Emilio Gadda — 1934 *Bagutta* prize winner — published a collection of articles he had written on travels within Italy, *Le meraviglie d'Italia* [Italy's Wonders].[103] Similarly, Alberto Savinio (1891–1952) collected a series of papers on his journeys through Milan and northern Italy which were published under the title of *Ascolta il tuo cuore, città* [Oh City, Listen to your Heart] in 1944.[104]

As Fascism first — and later the Second World War — sealed off the outer frontiers of the Italian peninsula, the focus on internal frontiers became increasingly symptomatic of a questioning and examining of the symbolic territorial boundaries of the country in relation to the question of cultural and literary identity. Even Silvio Negro (1897–1959) — 'maestro del 'vaticanismo' moderno' [master of modern Vatican studies][105] and 1936 *Bagutta* winner — depicts life in the Vatican in the form of an unorthodox travel book.[106]

Such an exploration of the internal frontier is also echoed in purely *literary* winning compositions. In Cardarelli's *Il sole a picco*, reaching the railway station means negotiating a network of personal, social and physical boundaries which mark the isolation of the small 'paese' [TN: in this context, village or small provincial town] from the external world. One notices how Cardarelli's use of the lexical field of enclosure secures the delimitation of the landscape while also expressing the sense of closure that characterises local reality.[107] Significantly enough, the cities evoked by Cardarelli are presented as the external, foreign *other*, in a process in which the poet evokes an old, medieval vision of an *Italia dei Comuni* [Italy of the cities] in which each city is a different territorial and political entity.

On the one hand, the railway is seen as a physical, material boundary, which marks the extreme edge of his own familiar territory. The lexical field of imprisonment marks the description of the landscape while the careful listing of each object in the picture reinforces the sense of framing, of delimitation which characterises the reality of the railway station for the young Cardarelli:

> Le pietre dei binari di prima e seconda linea, sporche d'olio, la ruggine e l'erba dei binari morti, i vagoni rossi della piccola velocità in giacenza e in attesa di essere caricati, i capannoni pieni di balle di paglia, il bugigattolo oscuro e sudicio del lampista, il disco, lo scambio, i cancelli, le staccionate, la ghiaia delle panchine, ecco tutto ciò che, per anni ed anni, ha costituito il divertimento dei miei occhi e il trastullo delle mie mani [...] Vita da galeotti, giù alla stazione.[108]

> [The stones of the first and second line tracks, dirty with oil, the rust and the grass of dead tracks, the red wagons used for slow convoys, waiting to be loaded, the barns filled with bales of hay, the lampman's dark and dirty recess, the signals, the railway points, the gates, the barriers, the stone benches, this is all that, for years and years, has provided entertainment for my eyes and hands [...] A prisoner's life, down at the station.]

On the other hand, the railway is the open door, the way to escape a 'paese' whose limits are nevertheless shifting and uncertain, as evoked in a manuscript from 1930 *Viareggio* winner Lorenzo Viani (1882–1936).

His sketch evokes the term 'paese' only to describe a space which is significantly defined as a border-line reality, marked by the presence not so much of inhabitants but of travellers — migrants who will never return to their homes and whose departure deeply fractures and lacerates both the landscape, abandoned, returned to wilderness, and the social fabric of Italian society.

> [...] Il mio paese è situato tra la montagna e il mare — tagliati da una grande via maestra che dalle altezze del Bracco, costeggiando il mare di Liguria e i suoi borghi si distende nel piano di Pisa per perdersi nella vasta solennità della Maremma. La mia prima ispirazione è stata la strada, l'antica patria nostra e gli uomini, che questa casa aperta sul silenzio dei cieli, non hanno voluto abbandonare mai, che portano sul volto i segni di fierezza e d'angoscia di melanconia e di ferocia insieme, i vagabondi, gli uomini liberi.[109]

> [... My country is located between the mountain and the sea — divided by a wide road which, descending from the heights of the *Bracco* (TN: mountain), running along the Ligurian sea and its hamlets, stretches along the plain of Pisa and finally loses itself in the vast solemnity of the *Maremma* (TN: lowlands

between Tuscany and Latium). The road — which is our ancient home — was my first inspiration together with the men who never wished to leave this home, open to the silence of the skies, who display on their faces their pride and their anxiety, a mix of melancholia and ferocity, the homeless, the free.]

Travel, displacement, and dislocation all characterise the literary production of those years. Actually, negotiating the symbolic issue of the *boundary* appears to be the predominant literary theme of prize winners in the 1920s and 1930s. Narrations become almost exclusively focused on travel narrative in a process which matches the professional travelling of journalists which we have previously evoked.

Significantly, between 1923 and 1928, Giovanni Comisso (1895–1969) writes the first *Bagutta* winner *Gente di mare* [People of the Sea], while recalling a personal experience of sailing along the Venetian coast in 1922.[110] If the narrative displays traces of the Romantic[111] emphasis on the journey/quest as return to the homeland 'in the perspective of initiation as a symbol of ultimate metaphysical belonging',[112] one notices how such a return appears to be indefinitely delayed, how the journey is protracted in a series of ever-repeated attempts at escaping — aimed, though, only at postponing an inevitably non-lasting return. The very sense of belonging is erased:

> Vi sono appena giunto che vorrei ripartire subito, partire di nuovo, col primo treno. [...] Dai luoghi in fuori, non mi è familiare quasi più nulla e nessuno. Ho perso il filo delle parentele e delle discendenze. Si sono annebbiati nella mia memoria i nomi delle casate; e delle loro vicende, morti, nascite, matrimoni, non so più nulla da tanti anni.[113]

> [I have just arrived and would like to leave immediately again, with the first train [...] Starting with the territory, nothing and no one is known to me anymore. I have lost the thread of relatives and their descendants. In my memory, the names of the families, their stories, deaths, births, marriages are lost in a fog; I have known nothing about any of them for many years now.]

Such a feeling of displacement is a diffuse one. Attempts are repeatedly made to map out an ever-shifting territory. In a fragment illustrating the ringing of bells throughout the Italian peninsula, Cardarelli uses the textual fragment to provide Italy with a centre, with a dominant identity, with a firm territorial point of reference. The predominance of the Florentine bells acts as a reminder of the necessity of recognising a focal point in Italian identity while also sketching out the degree to which such an identity, as symbolised by the never-ending echoes of similar bells throughout the country, is inherently undermined by the very proliferation of sounds filling the country's landscape.[114]

The intrinsically shifting nature of the landscape being portrayed, the ever-retreating boundaries of the symbolic 'Paese', spell out a problematic shift away from firm, clearly defined frames, to a problematised representation of the very concept of *boundary* itself. In Trinh T. Minh-ha's words,

> Every 'voyage' can be said to involve a re-siting of boundaries. The travelling self is here both the self that moves physically from one place to another, following 'public routes and beaten tracks' within a mapped movement, and the

> self that embarks on an undetermined journeying practice, having constantly to negotiate between home and abroad, native culture and adopted culture, or more creatively speaking, between a here, and a there, and an elsewhere.[115]

Thus, read at the level of the national dimension, the boundary invests powerfully the social discourse in that it embodies the systematic questioning which is enacted, at the social level, on the topic of the country's own material frontiers. Such a sense of dislocation, of the obsessive awareness of that space which is missing, absent, which never corresponds to the traveller's own ever-shifting space, strongly projects onto the Italian cultural scene a sense of place conceived within a utopian framework of impossible locations.

The boundaries of the community, understood as its external structural framework, are, however, not the only ones that appear to be challenged in the literary production of those years. Indeed, Cohen's model on the inner articulation of social sub-groups forming the wider symbolic community reveals, in fact, an ever-retreating pattern of social framing. In particular, it posits the problem of identifying precisely the boundaries of given cultural entities and defining the relationship between all social groups and their own internal sub-groups, at a given historical period.

The observation of the constant 'contamination' of the literary and journalistic fields in the context of Italian cultural politics expresses, in this context, the question of the definition of clearly delimited sub-groups within the broader symbolic community. As symbolic boundaries appear to echo the instability of structural outer boundaries, so boundaries between internal sub-groups seem, too, to be unstable and constantly shifting.

What appears to be underlined in the textual production of Italian literary competitions under examination is that any attempt at defining the boundaries of a symbolic community leads to the recognition of the fundamentally dynamic interplay at work between any sub-group forming part of the community under consideration and the wider social group as a whole. Consequently, delimiting the symbolic sphere to the associated perception of given specific groups can be considered as problematic in that any group focused on can potentially reveal itself to be made up of an endless series of sub-groups which, retreating down to the single individual, can neither encompass nor represent the community as a whole.

From artistic portrait to social criticism

Incidentally, the very definition of the individual becomes problematic. Such a dimension is highlighted, at the stylistic and thematic level, by the mixing of representational art — in particular expressionist painting — and literary writing which can be traced in the Italian literary competitions of the time. Indeed, the blending between the sub-groups of journalism and literature previously highlighted does not represent the only expression of generic mixing in the Italian literary prizes of the 1930s. The influence of painting on literature unveils, as will be argued, the degree to which the limits between the group and the self are evoked, analysed and challenged. In particular, the following analysis seeks to highlight how such a challenge is founded on an explicit consideration of the self-reflexive potential of representation and on the displaying of a reiterated concern with social types, social roles and individual — not to mention group — identity.

Earlier on, we considered how far aesthetic categories and artistic practices became blended in the Florentine reviews of the turn of the century. The development of the 1910s and 1920s *Cenacoli* in the Versilia region — home of the Premio *Viareggio* — provides another example of the mingling of authors and painters, philosophers, pseudo-politicians, visionaries, autodidacts and anarchists who operated on the Italian cultural scene of those years.[116] The example of the *Cenacolo* founded by the 1871 Genoa-born Ceccardo Roccatagliata Ceccardi (1871–1919) is significant of the intellectual background against which *Viareggio*-winning authors came to compose their works.

> 'La Repubblica di Apua', una specie di nuovo cenacolo fondato da Ceccardi nel primo decennio del '900, che constava di un 'manipolo' con funzioni di guida e si insigniva di un 'Libro d'Oro' per la memoria delle eroiche imprese, venne aperta a Lorenzo Viani che vi coprì la carica di 'Grande Aiutante'.[117]

> [The Republic of *Apua* is a sort of new cenacle, founded by Ceccardi in the first decade of the twentieth century, with a small group of leaders and a 'Golden Book' for the recording of heroic initiatives. It was opened to Lorenzo Viani who acted as 'Great Helper'].

In the proximity of the multi-disciplinary and somehow peculiar cultural context of the 'Repubblica di Apua', Lorenzo Viani, an author and 1929 *Viareggio* winner in his own right, became thus, for instance, responsible for illustrating the work of his friend and 1938 *Viareggio* winner Enrico Pea.[118] Literature and visual art, in the Viareggio and the Versilia contexts, became increasingly intermingled throughout the 1920s and 1930s.

A similar trend can be identified on the national scale. Not only do Futurist experiments with calligraphy and the representative potential of the semiotic dimension characterise the dialogue between the figurative and the literary. A *pictorial* emphasis can also be traced in the articulation of a more traditional descriptive dimension within the sphere of the literary. Echoing nostalgic Grand Tour landscapes, Italy is, for example, explicitly depicted through conventionally Romantic visual schemes in Cardarelli's *Il sole a picco*:

> Poi un acquedotto seicentesco che sparisce e riappare in mezzo ad una fuga di colli, l'immancabile cimitero alto sulla rupe, che pare una scena di Boecklin, le tombe etrusche, i grottini dell'acqua, le mille fosse e burroni e grotte naturali e sopra tutto, posata su due colline, la vecchia Tarquinia sepolta tra le ginestre, bianca e ventosa.[119]

> [And then you see a fifteenth-century aqueduct appearing and disappearing in the midst of rolling hills, the inevitable cemetery high on the cliff, like a scene from Boecklin, the Etruscan tombs, the water grottoes, a thousand ravines and natural caves and, on top of it all, leaning on two hills, the old town of Tarquinia, buried in gorse, all white and windy.]

In Cardarelli's typical fashion, techniques of pictorial representation are used to sketch a scene which appears to unfold gradually before the reader's eyes. In addition to the tracing of the landscape, one is also, though, faced with a *mise en abîme* in which the landscape itself is perceived in terms of the fictitiousness of its construction — as a work of art in terms of both its *artistry* and its *artificiality*: 'pare una scena di Boecklin.' The emphasis on the artificiality of representation is expressed through the proliferation, in Cardarelli's work, of allusions to the world of painting, to the value of the work of art and to the association between Italy, painted landscapes and works of art in general. All seems enumerated according to stereotyped artistic models 'l'immancabile cimitero', yet objects *appear* and *disappear*, literally *escape* ('fuga') the limits of the framed scene, proliferate beyond any possible representational capacity 'mille fosse e burroni e grotte naturali', undermining from within the representational act attempted by the author. The physical boundaries of the framed description are inherently challenged.

In a different passage, the *gingillo*, precious miniaturised object representing a self-contained microcosm, similarly becomes the embodiment of the contradiction between the representation of an artistic, ordered, objectified, landscape and the inner tensions inevitably undermining such an object from within:

> Minuscolo paese: un gingillo. Chiese, torri, campanili, case gentilizie, archi e logge, strade e piazze, ogni cosa corrisponde ad un leggiadro principio d'armonia, di civiltà e d'utilità pubblica. Dalle preziose cappellette romaniche erette per quattro devoti, con spreco di colonne enormi all'interno, fino alle abitazioni barocche e alle viuzze che portano impresso, dolcemente ricurve, il gusto del Seicento e del Settecento, tutto par fatto in questo paese, di epoca in epoca, con l'amore del piccolo, a solo scopo di portarvi in processione il Santissimo; e perché non avesse, in così poco spazio e senza spingersi oltre il cerchio delle mura, a mancare di nulla; neppure del senso e del decoro delle distanze, splendidamente create e conservate in virtù della varia fisionomia delle contrade e della distinzione netta fra il sacro ed il profano, il nobile e l'ignobile, il pubblico ed il privato.[120]

> [A tiny town: a trinket. Churches, towers, bell towers, noblemen's houses, arches and loggias, streets and squares, everything answers to a graceful principle of harmony, of civilisation and of public utility. From the precious Romanic chapels raised for a handful of faithful, with a waste of columns within, to the baroque buildings and the small streets, sweetly curved, which display the taste of the fifteenth and sixteenth centuries; everything seems to be created, in this small town, in every epoch, with a love for miniature, to bring the Blessed Sacrament in procession. It was also created so that, albeit in so little space and without leaving the enclosure of city walls, nothing is missing, not even the sense and order of distances, wonderfully created and maintained thanks to the varied physiognomy of districts and to the clear distinction between the sacred and the profane, the noble and the vile, the public and the private.]

Even in the apparently iron-clad, balanced inner structure of Cardarelli's *miniature*, the challenge to the perception of a stable symbolic landscape strongly emerges: the reiterated use of triadic, balanced, enumerations, the referring to the lexical field of spatial delimitation, the thematic emphasis on the miniature scale of the perceived clash with the inner disruptions which challenge the structural stability of the construct *'spreco di colonne enormi all'interno'* and with the impossible proliferation of architectonic styles which flood the sketched microcosm with multiform complexity. Once more, the notion of boundary, apparently firmly established through the reiteration of antithetical, clearly established differences — 'netta' — is in fact undermined by the impossible collapsing, within a single dimension, of the limited and the boundless, the micro- and macrocosm.

The specific challenging potential of *pictorial-like* representation with regard to the notion of boundary, emerges all the more in the interaction between visual art and the *typifying* trend discussed earlier in the context of Emilio Gadda's and Vincenzo Cardarelli's works. Representing characters as one would sketch a portrait of given types can be seen as a process of structural stabilisation through the objectification of the individual's identities. However, as stated by Dugast-Portes, by collapsing the spatial and the temporal dimensions, the use of the portrait embodies, in fact, an instance of the problematisation of the notion of boundary:

> On pourrait constater de même que, dans ces œuvres très proches de nous, les portraits qui effacent les étapes du temps effacent en partie aussi les limites dans l'espace. [...] Le portrait, fondant l'être et le monde, devient élément d'une réalité ductile, évanescente.[121]

> [Similarly, one could point out that, in works very close to us, portraits which erase the time also erase, in part, spatial limits [...] The portrait, by fusing the being and the world, becomes part of a reality which is ductile and evanescent.]

Considering the Italian cultural context we have described, the choice of referring to the thematic and stylistic sphere of the portrait is therefore not a casual or — indeed — a rare one. By undermining such a process of objectification, winners of literary prizes underline the ethical problems that the classification of the individuals according to pre-established models can entail and challenge the schematic classification practices of the Regime and its production of artificial masculine and feminine cultural models.[122]

While Lorenzo Viani favours, in both his pictorial and literary representations, 'fisionomie di dolore: volti emaciati e tesi, facce terree o allucinate o assorte'[123] [faces in pain, worn out and tense, ashen or crazed or absorbed] of hunger-driven migrants, beggars or corpse-like destitutes, a world away from Fascist representations of the new Italian *ideal*, Cardarelli's biting gallery of grotesques[124] unveils the tragic seclusion of characters enclosed within inescapable social roles and stereotypes. Thus the dry, dictionary-like accurateness of the definition of the hierarchically inferior position of the 'contadino' [labourer] unveils the hopelessness of his social status: 'Colono, egli è colui che abita e lavora la terra ma, non la possiede'[125] [settler, he is the person who lives on the land and works the land but does not possess it]. The essentially inescapable nature of belonging to a determined character/type is similarly highlighted, for instance, in Re Tarquinio's picture.[126] The character, at first glance, appears to be characterised by physical and psychological excess, an excess which, seemingly, is self-consciously celebrated: 'alto quasi due metri', 'aitante', 'spavaldo', 'colossali', 'grosse'. However, physical and psychological boundaries enclose him on multiple levels, his movements are limited, his appearance appears faked, his body is damaged: 'costretto', 'in maniera da non poterne uscire più', 'fino al ginocchio', 'incerettati', 'tinti', 'martoriata'. As imprisoned in a complex network of social stereotypes ('antico sergente di cavalleria', 'pavoneggiarsi agli occhi di tutte le belle del paese') as he is bound by the material restrictions of tight clothes and economic destitution ('un rasoio che non rade', 'qualche ombreggiatura e ditata di nero alla radice dei baffi e dei capelli',) Re Tarquinio expresses the impossibility of escaping the process which ultimately transforms him into a grotesque and deformed object of curiosity, good only for the 'museo anatomico'.

A similar use of the portrait emerges in the work of Lorenzo Viani. Born in Viareggio on 1 November 1882 into an extremely poor family, Viani affirms himself both as a painter and novelist, drawing as early as 1923 a famous gallery of popular *types* — Gli Ubriachi [The Drunk], and exhibiting his work in Paris in 1925. Specifically, these are the self-same types of marginals, anarchists and emigrants of his 1930 *Viareggio*-winning novel Ritorno alla Patria [Return to the Homeland]. The protagonist of the novel, strongly echoing in his experiences Viani's own past as an anarchist, meets in America a gallery of desperate characters sketched so as to echo the strong expressionist lines of Viani's own visual portraits. As in other authors, the use of the *type* approach is certainly not aimed at celebrating the Fascist vision of the Italian identity. In Viani's expressionist approach, as further illustrated through the predominantly autobiographic emphasis of its narrative, it is the *common* characteristics shared by human beings that are explored and highlighted.

A similar approach to characterisation is perhaps even more evident in Corrado Tumiati's Tetti Rossi: Ricordi di Manicomio [Red Roofs: Memories from an Asylum]. Framed within a complex spatial-temporal narrative progression, Tumiati's asylum is constructed on the juxtaposed snapshots of interns and doctors and ultimately rests on a series of figures which reveal themselves as the central focus of the narrative. Thus sections such as La figlia, La sposa, La madre, Monache, Primetta, Il fabbro, Pazzo morale, Il negriero filantropo, Colleghi, Il signor Pilade, Ritratto di infermiere, Cronici tranquilli, Sfinge, L'agitata, Mirì, Il ladro, Cappellai, Poveri al dispensario, L'Elvira, Visitatori, Un risanato [The Daughter, The Bride, The Mother, Nuns, Primetta, The Ironmonger, The Moral Madman, The Philanthropic Slaver, Colleagues, Mr. Pilade, Nurses' Portrait, Quiet Chronic Cases, Sphynx, The Agitated, Mirì, The Thief, Hatters, Poor at the Dispensary, Elvira, Visitors, The Cured] follow one another in a process where attention to the pictorial is highlighted by a discrete yet ever-present use of the art-related thematic references 'Interno', 'ritratto'[127] [An Interior, Portrait] and where the spectator contemplates the presented figures as he would, strolling down an exhibition corridor, observe a gallery of drawn likenesses. The sentence structure is light, with brief brushstrokes sketching the outline of the characters' social role, psychology and physical appearance:

> Il Signor Pilade è il segretario dell'ufficio medico. Il suo passo è silenzioso, lungo e quasi elastico. Non parla quasi mai, sorride talvolta [...] Alle prime rose lo vedi apparire con un abito a coda sul quale infila da vent'anni un soprabitino

color tortora ornato d'un bavero di velluto marrone. E in capo regge guardingo
una mondanissima bombetta bigia.[128]

[Mr Pilade is the medical office secretary. He proceeds with silent, long and
almost elastic steps. He speaks rarely, and smiles occasionally [...] You can seem
him appear at dawn, wearing — as he has done for the past twenty years —
morning dress and a dove coloured coat with a brown velvet collar. On his
head, cautiously perched, rests a fashionable, grey, bowler hat.]

The seriousness of the narrative tone, the inherent pathos of the represented figures, the tragic dimension of the ordinary men and women which are presented forbids any ironic or humorous interpretation.

As in Viani's work, one of the most significant features of *Tetti Rossi* is the denounced impossibility faced by the doctor/narrator of inserting within a specific *bureaucratic* category the patients whom he meets in his daily dispensary. Metaphorically mapping out a territory of exclusion, of non-existence from a social perspective, he simultaneously emphasises the recognition of the impossibility of representing the *human* in its inherent complexity and unfathomable depth. In the following example, the depicted character escapes all social categories and is represented only indirectly, through a series of negative sentences:

A lei non posso dare denaro perché non è mai stata in ospedale, né posso
ricoverarla perché, secondo la Legge, non è 'pericolosa'; a lei è precluso il
carcere perché quel darsi e quel questuare clandestino non bastano a un reato;
a lei sono ormai vietati i 'pii istituti' per l'età matura...[129]

[I cannot give her money, since she has never been in the hospital. Neither can
I admit her to the hospital since, according to the Law, she is not dangerous.
The jail is closed for her, since her clandestine begging and selling herself do
not amount to a crime. Because of her advanced age, religious hospices are
forbidden.]

Such a reflection is inserted through a formal opposition between the solidity of the narrative structure — the carefully closed and constructed spatial and temporal progression displayed in the text — and the narrator's open avowal of the impossibility of reaching a comprehensive and satisfactory depiction of the characters appearing in the text. The chronological structure is given by the gradual representation of all the steps of human age, from infancy to the degeneration of old age and death. The progression is opened by the arrival in the asylum of a young girl, significantly described as she crosses the external limits of the garden — 'La donna è giovane, bella, di una bellezza agreste, ma solida e regolare'[130] [the woman is young, beautiful, a beauty of a rural type yet solid and well-formed] — and the quasi-simultaneous arrival of a young child in the second fragment: 'Un infermiere porta il loro nato sul lettuccio d'esame. Un grosso cranio senza pensieri, un volto deforme senza sorriso, una svogliata malsicura animalità'[131] [A nurse brings their newborn and lays him down on the examination bed. A large head without thoughts, a deformed face without a smile, an uncertain, listless animal dimension]. The narrative then moves smoothly through the main steps of both chronological and social life: the married woman, 'vecchia, alta, pallida, assente'[132] [old, tall, pale and absent], the mother, the father 'irrigidito'[133] [rigid] all the way to old age and death.

Such a progression is matched by a spatial movement which goes from the external world at the edge of the hospital, to the internal, enclosed, secure chambers of the 'agitati' — the dangerous patients who cannot be cured. A sense of growing enclosure is therefore inserted between the depiction of a suicide attempt taking place, significantly, on the *external* wall of the psychiatric structure — 'La ragazza s'inginocchia sulle mura, cala i piedi dall'altra parte, sul precipizio del fossato, scivola lentamente il ventre e il petto sulle vecchie pietre e rimane appesa con otto dita al culmine della muraglia'[134] [the girl kneels on the walls, lowers her feet on the other side, on the precipice overlooking the moat, lets her belly and breasts slid slowly on the old stones and remains hanging by eight fingers from the top of the wall] — and the scenes of imprisonment in the *inner* sections of the hospital, as the epidemic of 'vaiolo emorragico' [hemorrhagic smallpox] forces doctors and patients in a shared and common space of imprisonment. The masks applied to the terminally ill are evocative of the loss of identity occurring in the internal sphere of the hospital as all relation with the external world is forbidden and interrupted. Yet they are also expressive of the ultimate imprisonment of the characters within ever more claustrophobic physical boundaries.

Significantly, the greater the growing enclosure, the greater is the difficulty, for the narrator, of actually framing and describing the characters he seeks to present and define. Deliberately, in the innermost 'agitati' section, the entire structural universe is undermined as limits themselves are called into question and the symbolic setting of borders and order is deeply dramatised:

> Veramente se entri in quella camera, hai l'impressione che l'universo barcolli e ti vien fatto d'appoggiarti agli stipiti tanto il tremito e l'affanno di chi vi s'aggira sembra trasmettersi alle cose che egli guarda e tocca.[135]
>
> [Truly, if you enter that room, you have the impression that the universe is teetering and you feel as if you need to lean on the doorframe. So strong are the trembling and the grief of those walking in that room that it seems they are transmitted to the objects touched and seen by the inmates.]

As the sense of enclosure culminates, one notices how description becomes impossible, how the un-representable nature of the human in its more extreme manifestations — in its questioning of the limits of the very notion of *human nature* — is highlighted. The patient is transformed into a sphinx-like figure which, in its mythical dimension, transcends the very limits of what can be represented:

> E di colpo si è slanciato contro un uomo che non guardava. E l'avrebbe strozzato, se non lo riconducevano sul letto. Poi qualcuno gli ha sorriso — invisibile — e si è voltato a ringraziare con la cauta grazia di un cortigiano. E ha pianto, alla fine, di sotto al lenzuolo d'un pianto gelido, senza dolore. E non siamo stati capaci — in quattro — di scoprirgli il volto tanto tenacemente lo copriva. Sfinge. O simbolo mostruoso dell'insondabile irragionevolezza di tante condotte umane.[136]
>
> [Suddenly, he threw himself against a man who was not looking. He would

> have throttled him if he had not been taken back to his bed. Then somebody — invisible — smiled at him and he turned and thanked him with the cautious grace of a courtier. At the end, he cried, under the sheet, icy, painless tears. He hid himself with such strength that we did not manage — the four of us together — to uncover his face. Sphinx. Horrific symbol of the unreasonableness of so much human conduct.]

Crucially, the doctor acknowledges the limits of both literary depiction and his own intellectual capacity of framing the individual, of giving shape and form to the *human*: 'Debbo volgere il capo altrove e non guardarti perché in te troppe cose sono distrutte [...] Non posso descriverti'[137] [I must turn my head and look away because too many things are destroyed in you. [...] I cannot describe you].

As the return towards the external dimension is guaranteed at the end of the book however, one notices that such a refusal to represent the non-human is echoed by an awareness that any attempt at representation inevitably reduces, simplifies, objectifies the person who is depicted. Significantly, the healed patient sketched in 'un risanato' appears only through the poetic metaphor of an ever-changing sea:

> Perché lo spettacolo d'una mente risanata non ha l'eguale nel mondo. E io non odo la sua risposta e dimentico la pena sofferta, l'orgoglio della prova raggiunta, il fragile caduco destino che ci affratella, per guardare il suo volto come si guarda, cessato il turbine, risplendere ancora il mare.[138]

> [The vision of a healed mind has no comparison in the world. I do not hear his answer, I forget the suffering, the pride of having overcome the challenge, even the fragility of our shared destiny to contemplate his face as one watches, after the storm, the shining sea.]

The flowing, potentially endless sea is thus compared to the multiform dimension of human nature in a process which openly undermines any attempt at typifying which might have been attempted in the initial parts of the book:

> Non esiste il tipo d'una sola cosa. Tutti siamo tipi di tutto. Come, stando alle più recenti teorie della medicina, ognuno di noi ha in sé i germi di tutti i mali, così abbiamo in noi in varia misura l'essenza di tutti i caratteri. Il tipo dell'avaro può essere anche il tipo del fanfarone, o dell'invidioso, o d'altro, o di molte cose insieme. Persino, il tipo dell'avaro può anche essere il tipo del prodigo dentro di sé. Chi può sapere? La cosa è meno semplice di quel che pare.[139]

> [There is no single type of a single thing. We are all types of everything. Just as, according to the latest medical theories, each one of us carries in himself the potential for all illnesses, so we carry in ourselves, to varying degrees, the essence of all personalities. A tightfisted man can also be a braggart, an envious man, or something else or many things all together. A mean man can even hide a generous streak. Who knows? Things are not so simple as they appear.]

Autobiographical trends: from the other to the self

In this context, one notices therefore how a shift is enacted away from the drive to the objectification of an Italian dimension through stereotyped models towards the representation of humanity as an expression of a universal yet multiform condition.

Ultimately, the systematic deconstruction of a framing and structuring process leads to the acknowledgement that the objectified representation of being is not achievable.

The theoretical implications of such attention to the process of portrait-drawing are evoked by A. Ablamowicz. Commenting upon the uses of the literary portrait, the critic notices how such a procedure entails

> au moins deux visions ou, si l'on veut, deux manières de décrire, toutes les deux passant cependant par une technique propre au portrait littéraire lui-même:
> — une manière horizontale, qui représente le réel comme une surface, divisée selon les relations de ressemblance ou de différence (sexe, classe sociale, milieu, territoire psychologique, professionnel, etc.),
> — une manière verticale, où l'invention l'emporte sur l'intention reproductrice et c'est là, à juste titre, qu'on verra des personnages absorbés par la quête de 'l'être' derrière le 'paraître'.[140]
>
> [at least two visions or, if you wish, two ways of describing, which nonetheless share the same technique, proper to the literary portrait:
> — a horizontal approach, representing the real like a surface, divided according to relations of resemblance or differentiation (sex, social class, milieu, psychological territory, professional dimension, etc.),
> — A vertical approach, where invention overcomes the intention of reproduction and this is where one sees characters absorbed by the search for 'being' behind 'appearances.']

In this view, the process of identity formation in the context of literary expression is to be perceived through a dialectic between what little can be somehow established in the *horizontal / spatial* dimension and what remains in the sphere of the unformed and belongs to the *vertical / temporal* sphere. In a particularly significant fragment from *Tetti Rossi*, the utopian projection of a dreamed, impossible, city becomes the illustration of the individual's own inner dreamed — restored, transformed, redeemed — nature:

> Se mi piacesse sognare ad occhi aperti la mia Città del Sole, ne sognerei soltanto le fondamenta. Che sarebbero psicologiche. E composte di tre rare bontà: buon senso, buon gusto e buon cuore.[141]
>
> [If I were to imagine my *Città del Sole*, I would only consider its foundations. And they would be psychological ones. They would consist in three rare forms of goodness: good sense, good taste and a good heart.]

Significantly enough, the name Città del Sole refers here to the ideal city illustrated in the 1602 work on utopia by Tommaso Campanella.

The idealised space and the idealised individual merge in Tumiati's dream in a process which, however, because of the very utopian nature of the reflection, denies any closure or objectification to the construction of the individual. As the 'fondamenta' represent the initial step for architectural construction, Tumiati's sentence echoes the Blochean attention on the yet-to-be-realised, opening the representation of the individual's consciousness to the dynamism of a *potential* and undefined dimension.

By extension, the problematisation of the individual's representation leads literary prize winners' attention away from the drive towards representing the *other* to the questioning of the possible representation of the speaking self. Beyond the apparent ideological construction of one's own community, one notices how 1930s Italian narratives embrace, in fact, the problematic and challenging questioning of the authors' capacity of articulating their own identities. As opposed to the structuring of the group, it is the very construction of the self which is ultimately called into question.

In this light, the importance of both the biographical and autobiographical trends within the winning narratives can hardly be challenged. Indeed, the works of Campanile, Bellonci, Cardarelli,[142] Gadda, Comisso, and to an extent Viani and Pea, are all either openly autobiographical or display a strong biographical cut.

From the perspective of biographical narrations, one notices an undermining of stereotyped representations aimed at promoting a much more *realistic* attempt at psychological analysis, as displayed in Gadda's down-to-earth, intimate asides in *Il Castello di Udine* [The Castle of Udine]:

> L'umile fante, come il poverello d'Assisi e i marron glacés, sono adattissimi per il boudoir di certe signore. Io rispetto e venero il Gran Santo ma, essendo io un retore, dico che la miseria a me mi fa paura.[143]

> [The humble foot-soldier, just like the poor of Assisi [TN: Saint Francis of Assisi] and chestnut candies, are perfect for ladies' sitting rooms. I respect and venerate the Great Saint but, being a rhetorician, I say plainly that poverty scares me.]

In Maria Bellonci's (1902–1986) case — 1939 *Viareggio* prize-winner and founder with husband Goffredo Bellonci of the *Strega* literary prize — the importance given to the accuracy of historical reconstruction sustains the attempt to capture, in the proliferation of minute details, a *genuine* historical dimension, which is held to be missing from official representations. One thus notices how the portrait of Lucrezia Borgia in Bellonci's eponymous novel is built on a careful blending of the novelistic and the historically documented.[144] A brief excerpt describing Lucrezia's leaving of Rome in order to marry her third husband in Ferrara is expressive of the blending of facts and subjective impressions breathing life into Bellonci's *novelistic biographies*:

> Risaliva ora verso il nord, lei adoratrice del sole, dei giardini, delle gaie feste fiorite; lei che non conosceva l'odore della nebbia, lasciava l'oro maturo del sole di Roma per il grigio tutto pause metafisiche del cielo di Ferrara. Nel silenzio nevoso le voci cadevano senza sonorità a terra, e pareva inutile cercare di sollevarle in un accento di trionfo. La città dolce e torbida, opulenta e miserevole, taceva, era ferma, taceva, non veniva a salutarla, non aveva nemmeno più il volto che ella conosceva, si rifiutava alle sue domande e al suo sguardo con il pudore ostile delle cose contro chi le abbandona. Quella che passava non era più la figlia del papa, Lucrezia Borgia, ma la duchessa di Ferrara, sconosciuta nata ora, straniera, che si doveva guardare senza rivelarle nulla, chiudendo nei muri perfino le connessure dei mattoni. Già Roma e Lucrezia non si riconoscevano più.[145]

[Now was the time for her to go north, she who adored the sun, the gardens, the happy flowered parties, she who did not know the smell of fog. She left the ripe golden sun of Rome for the grey metaphysical pauses of the Ferrara sky. In the snowy silence, voices fell soundlessly to the ground and could not be raised with a triumphant accent. The sweet and murky city, at once opulent and miserable, was silent, remained motionless, did not come to say goodbye. She did not recognise its face, it did not answer her questions, it escaped her gaze with that hostile reserve that things have for those who abandon them. She who was passing wasn't the Pope's daughter anymore, Lucrezia Borgia, but the Duchess of Ferrara, a newly born foreigner, unknown, whom one should watch without revealing anything, closing down within walls even the joints of the bricks. Rome and Lucrezia did not recognise each other anymore.]

In Gadda's novel, too, a portrait of Pope Innocenzo II — Gregorio Papareschi (1130–1143) — similarly unveils an interest for subjective emotions, expressed through the use of free indirect style, and novelistic fictitious descriptions of the historical context:

Fu, nel sole giocondo e splendido, un monello di via in Piscinula: fra pendule brache tacitamente apparso, fulvo contro al nitore de lenzuoli e sotto alle pergole delle camicie in gloria. Inseguito dalla cagnara avversa svoltava come la saetta a piè nudi entro l'ombre di Torre Anguillara o, rifugiatosi in vicolo della Paglia, lo avevano tra i piedi e gli zoccoli, anelante ancora, fermo d'un subito, gli stallieri e i cavalli. Ignaro del pettine, quando il caso dava, polemizzava a sassate con i borghigiani di Castello: e chi cerca trova.[146]

[He started as a street urchin, under a playful and splendid sun, a street kid in Piscinula: he silently appeared from under loose knickers, red hair flaming against white sheets and suspended rows of resplendent shirts. Running from rival gangs he escaped lightning-fast, bare-footed, in the shadows of the Torre Anguillara or, seeking refuge in the Vicolo della Paglia, tumbled to a halt, still panting, under horses hooves and footmen's legs. Disheveled, when needed, he relied on stone-throws to bicker with the Castello inhabitants: seek and ye shall find. (TN: Torre Anguillara, Vicolo della Paglia, Piscinula, Castello — areas of Rome.)]

In such narratives, the limit between fiction and history is dramatised, as is the reflection on the (im)possibility of ever reaching a true representation of objects and subjects. The reader is left in doubt as to the origin of the narrative act: fiction or history? Once more, one notices how thematic concerns regarding the impossibility of obtaining a stable representation are matched by the stylistic choice of playing with generic distinctions in order to highlight the inherent instability of the narrative act. The attempt to provide an order to the unfolding of life events, an attempt which is actually inherently undermined by the very narrative act which should sustain it,[147] is indeed further challenged by the blending of generic styles as sketches, portraits, memoirs and confessions are fused and confused. Taking Gadda's example, the mixing of genuine autobiographical moments with pure fiction and journalistic narrative illustrates the intrinsic instability of the biographical/autobiographical genre as it appears in the context of Italian narratives in the 1920s and 1930s.

For instance, one notices how, in Cardarelli's case, there is a strong thematic link between the landscapes evoked in the poetic compositions and those traced in the prose fragments, in a process whereby both the poet's and the narrator's voice blend and mix in order to give shape to Cardarelli's own intimate reflections on his own memories and his own life.[148] His vision of the autumnal lake in *Lago*[149] strongly echoes a similar autumnal vision in *Ottobre* [October] as the poet recalls his holidays by the lake, a vision which will furthermore appear in his evoking of a lost love in a similar lake setting in *Astrid*.[150]

The use of the autobiographical genre is considered as typical of the period we are analysing,[151] in particular in the context of the Vociani movement [TN: group of authors experimenting with new literary themes and styles at the beginning of the twentieth century, close to the literary review *La Voce*]. Interestingly, how Charles Burdett's reading of the preference for the autobiographical mode does not take into account the thematic and stylistic trends we have emphasised so far, pointing instead to the use of autobiography as a tool for establishing a Nietzschean control over the individual.[152] Yet a consideration of the autobiographical emphasis in the light of the previous analysis points instead to the dramatisation and problematisation of the attempt at controlling the self rather than a celebration of such a process. Indeed, as underlined by Philippe Lejeune, 'autobiography is [...] one moment of a dialectical enquiry, a moment of vertigo and metamorphosis'[153] rather than a moment of masterly self-affirmation.

The tracing of a portrait or self-portrait thus evokes a dramatisation of the attempt to frame a specific identity. In fact, presented as forever displaced in the temporal and spatial dimensions they inhabit, the (auto-)diegetic narrators appear as being ever threatened by annihilation.

Melancholia,[154] visions of decay,[155] the lexical field of death[156] dominate both travel narratives and temporal overviews of the authors' past: 'Con tutto ciò, lasciatemi rivedere la mia terra, lasciatemi andare una notte a dormire con i morti'[157] [Having said that, let me see my land once more, let me sleep one night with my dead].

The return to the past is often presented as impossible; lost identities cannot be recuperated or reconstructed and the individual is projected onto a dimension in which the absence of identity is deeply and tragically exposed.

> Ecco, fu in questo breve ripiano che mio padre colse l'erba medicamentosa per fasciarmi il dito tagliato dal falcetto [...] ma io non troverò mai più l'erba, ed è inutile che ne scriva qui il nome perché nessuno lo capirebbe.[158]
>
> [In this small patch, my father found the medicinal herb which he used to bandage my cut finger [...] but I will never find that herb again and it is pointless to write its name here since no one would understand it.]

The literary language itself appears to escape — and inherently undermine — the authorial descriptive/creative act. Indeed, in parallel with the challenging of social stereotypes, linguistic stereotypes are foregrounded. A telling example, anticipating much later thematic and stylistic explorations of the literary and theatrical *absurd*, is provided by Campanile's evocation of the imagined figure of the 'Uomo Nero' [black man/man in black], a figure traditionally evoked in popular culture to scare young children. Transformed by Campanile's ironic lines, the 'Uomo Nero' gains a life of his own, is inserted in the context of narration on the same level as the other *real* characters:[159]

> Questo essere terribile e misterioso — che, d'altronde, è di una cortesia esemplare verso chi lo chiama — non ha altro a cui pensare che i ragazzini? [...] Vero è che l'Uomo Nero, persona evidentemente seria, spesso chiamato, non si presenta mai. Resta quasi sempre dietro la porta; al massimo, qualche volta, si spinge fino a far sentire la sua voce...[160]

> [Has this terrible and mysterious being — who, by the way, displays an exemplary courtesy towards those who call him — really nothing else to think of than children? [...] In fact, the Black Man, obviously a serious person, though often called, never appears. He remains almost every time behind the door. At best, sometimes, he can make himself heard...]

The descriptive sphere is undermined when its socio-linguistic dimension is highlighted, in a process which unveils the constructed, framed, artificial nature of verbal expression:

> E le rondini, povere rondini. In quale misero stato le hanno ridotte i poeti a furia di dir: rondini, rondini! Non ne resta che una parola. Quell'uccello, che suole arrivare a primavera, è fuggito, spaventato dalla retorica, e nel cielo della poesia corrente resta a svolazzare pesantemente il suo nome. Somiglia più a un pipistrello che a una rondine: parole, parole, che intrecciano voli nel cielo della sera. Parole che passano per la strada, parole nei prati. Il mondo è un intrico di parole.[161]

> [And the swallows, poor swallows. What a miserable state they have been reduced to by poets, those poets who keep repeating: swallows, swallows! A word is all that is left. The bird coming in spring has run away, frightened by rhetoric and, in the sky of contemporary poetry, only its name is left to fly heavily about. It looks more like a bat than a swallow: words, words interweaving flights in the evening sky. Words passing in the street, words in the fields. The world is a net of words.]

In Carlo Emilio Gadda's mixing of proverbial expressions and literary prose, such a process anticipates much later deconstructive investigations of the text: 'Crescerà ne' vecchi muri l'urtica: e l'erba sopra la lassitudine mia. E l'erba che sarà cresciuta, la mangerà il cavallo, che campato sarà'[162] [Nettle will grow on the old walls and grass will grow over my lassitude. And the grass will be eaten by the horse, who will have survived. (TN: reference to an Italian proverbial expression indicating pointless and long waiting, like a horse waiting for the grass to grow)]. Stylistic and thematic self-consciousness, and a sustained reference to meta-fictional concerns, project the biographical/autobiographical references we have previously highlighted into a dimension where not only personal identity is problematised but the very act of artistic creation intended as a cognitively constituting process is inherently undermined. Indeed, as the observer is presented as being incapable of providing a stabilised framing to either the other or the self, it is the relation between the self and the structuring drive which is called into question and projected on to a plane where instances of construction and instances of formal, thematic and stylistic dissolution give birth to one another.

The Author in Time

As a result of such an identity-undermining drive and in the light of such a movement of Derridean deconstruction, the problem is posed with regard to the sustainability of the thesis that the literary prize institution enforces a specific idea of a community's symbolic identity. In other words, is the cognitively stabilised idea of a community to be considered as a sustainable, founding element in the understanding of the identity-articulating function of Italian — and by extension all — literary prizes?

Indeed, the symbolic landscape we have evoked, far from being based on a stable and clearly defined social structure, seems to rest on a shifting pattern of dynamic relations displaying a fundamentally 'inner dialectical quality'.[163]

The micro-group, such as it is understood in the context of the social community, can only be defined by contrast and through its constant inter-relation with the *ensemble* of other sub-groups, micro-groups and individuals, an inter-relation which has been defined in terms of an 'evaluative accent'.[164] A consideration of the endlessly retreating nature of the internal and external boundaries of the community and of its individual micro-constituents thus posits ultimately the problem of the very existence of such a community. It also questions the degree to which an acknowledgement of the shifting nature of symbolic boundaries runs against the matter of fact recognition of the undeniable subsistence of a coherent and — to an extent — stabilised dimension of shared symbolic and structural organisations. Just as a sign, though inherently lacking in an internal essence, can ultimately be distinguished from juxtaposed signs, so does the concept of community, though inherently undermined by its semiotic dimension, find a concrete embodiment in human structural constructions, social groups, political and territorial associations. In the specifics of the current example, it can hardly be denied that the 'Italy' community, undermined though it may be in the context of the literary production under examination, did and does certainly exist in specific geo-political and cultural forms.

To such an objection the current study hopes to answer by positing the distinction, made explicit by Anthony Cohen, between *the symbolic nature of the idea of community* and the *symbolic constituents of a community's consciousness*.

On the one hand, the acknowledgement of the fundamentally *symbolic nature of the idea of community* entails an understanding of the community in terms of a commonly perceived semiotic representation. It is such an aspect which has so far predominantly influenced the assessment of the connection between literary prizes and nationalism. Because of nationalism's own objectification of the image of a community's identity, literary prizes have been understood as tools enforcing and simultaneously emerging from such an objectifying trend. Should only such a perspective be considered, the Humboldtian view of the links between cultural specificity and cultural production would be confirmed as being the interpretive key to literary prizes' social and cultural function. But we have underlined how — because of the specific functioning of the human cognitive system — the Humboldtian view emerges as problematic, based on an essentially static approach to what is, in fact, a dynamic process. The apprehension of the notion of 'gap' in the cognitive process, exemplified, in the Italian case, by the relentless questioning of physical and symbolic boundaries, leads to the problematisation of cognition and, by extension, of identitary constructions.

The *symbolic constituents of the community's consciousness*, the above-mentioned boundaries, functioning as semiotic instances which run parallel to the symbolic idea of community itself, reveal themselves as a network of interconnected cultural elements, constructed on the dynamic expression of a dialectic rather than on the fixed structuring of a closed cognitive form. In this context, the idea of community itself becomes 'essentially enshrined in the concept of boundary',[165] as the symbolic constituents can ultimately only be apprehended through instances of ever-retreating semiotic 'différance'. The symbolic sphere expressed in literary competitions *dramatises* the interactions occurring at the symbolic level within the community itself rather than reflecting uncritically the community's self-constructed symbolic identity. In this perspective, one sees how the link between literary competitions and nationalism is but a partial view of a phenomenon which transcends, in its multiple embodiments, the nationalist identity-building perspective.

In the context of the previously mentioned dynamics between the symbolic components of the community's consciousness, narrating subject and narrative object exist within a dialectic relation and the notion of identity is projected on a constantly changing and self-shaping dimension[166] whereby 'writing changes us'. We do 'not write according to what we are' but 'are according to what we write'[167] in the awareness that the writing act, and the identity deriving from such a writing act, is always inherently threatened by *exhaustion*, the Jamesonian *nothingness*[168] which characterises the essence of the symbolic element.

'Discours limite, placés sur une limite et traitant de la limite'[169] [borderline discourse, set on a limit and considering the limit], the literary act, such as it emerges from the Italian context, is not, however, a destructive act. On the contrary, the dialogue between instances of articulation and instances of *absence* leads to the perception of the artistic work as the 'figuration/manifestation des potentialités utopiques dans l'espace créateur' [representation/expression of the utopian potential within the creative space], 'potentialités' which encompass the longed-for stabilisation of identity.

As a 'figuration anticipatrice' [representation which anticipates][170] of being, such utopian potential, such a cognised structure, is projected on the scene of common cognition and is socially recognised and commonly acknowledged through the embodied social structure of literary competitions. It is validated and endowed with universal significance through the act of aesthetic selection.

The 'utopian' as structural construct, such as it was presented in the initial part of the study must therefore be understood in terms of a partial redefinition. In the following part, the utopian potential will be re-framed in the light of the capacity of the literary institution of investing, through its aesthetic choice, the external world with a dynamic expression of what Bloch defines as 'the subject as intention'.[171] In other words, in the context of literary competitions, art is understood to participate in the structuring drive taking place at the cognitive level not by providing a closed aesthetic construct but by *being* a social phenomenon, by enacting a dynamic articulation of the symbolic field, in a process which renders the cognitive stabilisation, previously defined as the utopian, an ever-deferred process. Indeed, as noted by Arno Münster:

> En tant qu'anticipations d'un non-encore-devenu et figures caractérisées par un important 'excédent utopique', les œuvres font partie d'un réel inachevé, d'un monde processuel en mouvance permanente, toujours à la recherche de soi-même, de son identité authentique.[172]
>
> [As anticipations of something which is not-yet-become and as figures characterised by a major 'utopian excess', works belong to a real which is not yet finalised, they belong to an ever-processing, ever-moving world, always seeking itself, seeking its authentic identity.]

Art, in this context, does not consist in the closing of a boundary, but rather consists in the apprehension of 'a possibility in ourselves which is discovered and affirmed'.[173] Such a possibility consists in the drive towards the hoped-for framing of a stable identity. This is the 'utopian' space conceived in the Blochean perspective, the hypothetical sum of all existing possibilities,[174] which is utopian precisely in that, as previously displayed in the description of Merleau-Ponty's analysis, it is not ultimately reachable.

Such an understanding of the structuring drive is ultimately based, as in Bergson and Merleau-Ponty, on a reintroduction of the temporal dimension in the cognitive sphere. As, in Bloch, time is conceived predominantly in terms of the possible, of the yet-unrealised future, the utopian dimension of the literary work as it emerges from literary competitions is just as much the potentially realisable identification of a stable cognised structure as the potentially unrealisable projection of such a structure within a process of identity definition.

The question is therefore posed of the ways in which such a tension between objectification and the displacement of structural stability is specifically *negotiated* through the social formula of literary competitions and of the degree to which such a negotiation encloses the stabilising drives discussed in Chapter One while also encompassing the destabilising drives highlighted in this chapter.

In the following sections, such a process of negotiation will be discussed in the light of its defining elements.

The process of negotiation appears to rest on an act of 'labelling', namely on the transferral of the selected work within the category of 'art'. Inherent in such a process of 'labelling' is the disconnection of the novel/aesthetic object from its contextual — temporally and spatially bound — origin and the projection of the winning object within an 'a-temporal' cognitive sphere.

At this stage, a paradoxical dimension is unveiled. Indeed, the stabilising and identity-structuring function which the competitions fulfil can be sustained only so long as the interaction between subject, object and context triggers the mirror effect mechanism evoked in the context of the Lacanian analysis and is not submitted to temporal change.

On the other hand, temporal change being a constant, any attempt at transcending such a dimension would be impossible to conceive or implement. In order to preserve the identity-building potential of the literary institution, while also managing the temporal factor, the process of negotiation, far from being limited to the production of an aesthetic object, simultaneously and in parallel appears to trigger the shaping of a social persona: the author (see Fig. 10). Indeed, mediating between the assessing/reading subject and the contextual dimension, the authorial figure becomes the specular correspondent of the aesthetic object in that filter through which the contextual dimension is embodied in metaphorical form for the benefit of the subject.

The context of Italian literary prizes has illustrated the degree to which the authorial function can be self-consciously perceived — and self-consciously evoked — in terms of its boundary-negotiating potential. In fact, though not always emerging at the self-conscious level, the boundary-negotiating function of the authorial figure appears to be a *constant* symbolic element in the field of communal consciousness.

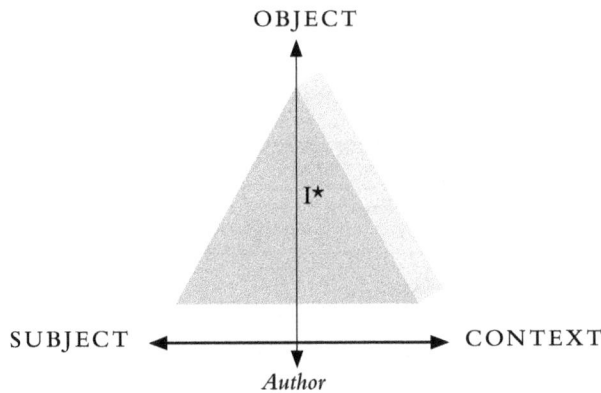

FIG. 2.3. The author (★ Literary Prize)

Focusing on the specifics of the relationship tying authorial persona and aesthetic object, one notices how the former is projected within a temporal dynamism which the aesthetic object lacks and which allows for the necessary mediation on the cognitive and symbolic sphere between instances of stability and instances of change.

Such a process of mediation is in turn embodied in the functioning of literary competitions in terms of a yearly — or otherwise temporally-defined — renewal. Ultimately, then, the authorial function, in that characterised by a temporal dimension, allows for the balancing of the objectifying trends enacted by the cultural institution with regard to the aesthetic object.

This, in turn, lends to the cultural institution a role in the process of identity-articulation since, far from being tied to the aesthetic object's momentary relevance, the cultural institution, through its temporal projection, caters to the identity-articulating needs of the ever-changing historical landscape.

Instability of the symbolic sphere

In order to clarify the function played, in this context, by the authorial figure, we will start by considering, as anticipated, the process of labelling undergone by the selected aesthetic object. In order to do so, we will briefly refer to Roland Barthes's semiotic ladder.

The French critic's definition of the semiotic ladder relies on the Saussurean understanding of the semiotic dimension in terms of an articulated system where each semiotic instance is defined through its relationship with — and distinction from — parallel semiotic instances. Based on the relation between the auditive image and the visual trace, the signified and the signifier, the Saussurean sign, understood as emerging from the relation between the former and the latter, is also simultaneously to be understood in terms of its potential as counterpart to other signs within the linguistic system. However, since the linguistic system operates on a multidimensional, diachronic, socially influenced and evolving dimension, one notices how a sign can be at once signified and signifier, depending on the 'value' temporarily attributed to it in the context of the overall semiotic and semantic network of binary relations.

Ultimately, the higher we go in Barthes's scale of signification, the greater the instability linking *signifier* and *signified*. The community's need to find a common agreement on how to establish signification would therefore appear to increase exponentially with each level of Barthes's scheme.

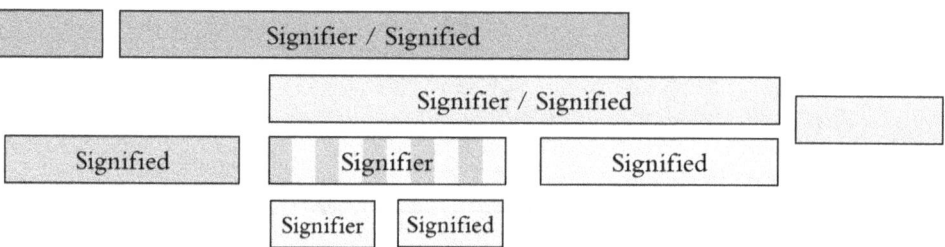

FIG. 2.4. Roland Bartes's semiotic ladder

Applied to the current analysis, the theoretical scheme can be interpreted as follows (see Fig. 2.5). At the initial level, the visual trace and the acoustic trace combine to form the basic sign — the single word. Taken in combination, the single words-signs lead to the formulation of the novel-sign in a process which consists in a one-step upward shift in the semiotic ladder progression.

As considered in the initial part of the study, the novel-sign acts in turn as a potential *signifier* to the *signified* context, allowing for the projection of an identity-related cognitive process which, in its multiple potential verbal objectifications — self-definitions, descriptions, social articulations — can be held, in turn, to possess or participate in a semiotic dimension at a higher level in the semiotic ladder.

Turning back to the level of the novel-sign, when considered in the context of an aesthetic assessment, such as the one taking place in the context of literary competitions, one notices, however, how the novel-sign simultaneously acts as a signifier for the context-signified and for a second dimension of signification, namely that of art/literariness.

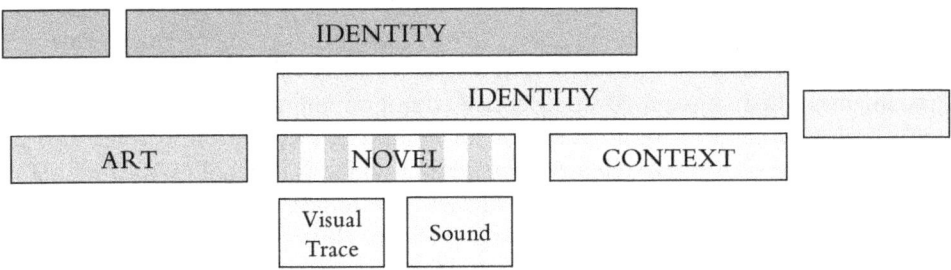

FIG. 2.5. An interpretation of the semiotic ladder

In the case of literary competitions, the signification of the label *art/literary work* can only be temporarily stabilised through its relation with a single novel/signifier. The process of stabilisation of the cognitive structure thus reaches its culminating point through the isolation of a *closed,* potentially whole, expression of the social cognitive sphere and its sanctioning of this expression as an element of social *value*.

As the selected novel is assigned a distinct, social signified, that of *art/literature*, it is also, however, to an extent, disconnected from the metaphorical/exemplificatory relation which ties it to the cognitive dimension. Indeed, seen as an object of aesthetic selection, the signifier/novel is projected on to a dimension in which it appears to simultaneously refer to two signifieds — that of the contextual dimension it exemplifies and that of the *art/aesthetic category* it metaphorically embodies.

On both levels, the relation is not sustainable for long. With regard to the external dimension, the dynamics of life render all attempts at structuration at best only momentarily relevant. In terms of the aesthetic categorisation process, as the symbolic relation between instances of signification is maintained purely through social agreement rather than on an exemplificatory basis, the link between the two semiotic instances is highly unstable and lasts only so long as the cultural agreement is made to last. Thus the selection process aimed at ensuring an adjustment of the metaphorical/exemplificatory relation of the work to the changing cognitive structure must be repeated at regular intervals. In the case of a large number of literary prizes, the process occurs on a yearly basis. One notices therefore how the process through which the winning literary work is isolated and marked out as significant, both in relation to the external dimension and in relation to the aesthetic judgement, is always inherently threatened by the instability of the semiotic discourse.

Between the precise moment in which the aesthetic judgement highlights the link between work and context — triggering the process for potential identity articulation and stabilisation — and the yearly rotation of literary successes, there occurs an important temporal shift. In this temporal framework, the constitution of the *authorial* figure — in other words, the transformation of the writer into a publicly acknowledged social persona — takes place.

In the following two sections, I will argue that the belonging of the authorial figure to a temporal dimension fundamentally changes the theoretical framework outlined so far. Through the author/figure, the essence and value of art are not simply limited to the cognitive stabilisation it offers, but are simultaneously linked to 'the dynamic and developing experiential activity through which they are created and perceived'.[175] In turn, such a dynamism is valuable in that it fulfils a fundamental role in the process of identity cognition and articulation. Thus, if the work is chosen in terms of its potential for cognitive stabilisation, it must also be understood in terms of the dynamic articulation which is enacted by the artist (and *through* the artist) in order to reach a conclusive — if temporary — structure. As will be seen, the temporal dimension plays a key role in this context.

The author as embodiment of the boundary

In the case of Italian literary works, we have considered the degree to which instances of estrangement and spatial dislocation permeate the thematic production of the 1920s and 1930s. Restless travelling, anguished journeying in search of lost homes and fictitious identities drive the authors in the pursuit of an imaginary 'paese' whose value appears to reside in its ultimately *unreal* and *unrealised* dimension.[176] The author finds himself in a position whereby 'mon lieu n'est pas mon lieu, où que je sois, je ne suis jamais à ma place' [my place is not my place, wherever I am, I am never home]. In other words, 'la paratopie spatiale est celle de tous les exils' [The paratopia of space is one of exile].[177]

In fact, as further illustrated by a brief overview of the history of the concept of *authorship* itself, the *author* as social figure, regardless of the self-conscious or self-referential dimension which his/her writings might possess, appears to be *essentially* endowed with a boundary-related symbolic potential. This is particularly important if the analytical framework sketched in the current work is to be considered beyond the context of early twentieth-century Italian literary competitions. Specifically, being defined *as* author triggers the inscription of the writer figure in a double perspective, whereby the author is seen as expressive of an *original* utterance and simultaneously representative of a socially acknowledgeable and *communally* recognisable cultural dimension, thus being symbolically established at the border-line between the individual and the communal, the familiar and the foreign, the self and the other.

The history of the concept of *author* itself is, as mentioned, in this context, significant. As the first signatures appear on cultural and artistic productions in Greece as early as the 6th century BC,[178] the authorial figure emerges within the symbolic sphere by differentiating itself from the anonymous figure of the craftsman.

With regard to the specific figure of the literary *poiêtês*, it appears to have been linked to the religious origins of poetic composition which saw the gradual emerging of a distinction between the figure of the seer — *mantis* — acting as a direct spokesman for the gods and that of the *prophētē'* who acted, in turn, as the seer's own spokesman before the community and 'was involved in the poetic formalisation of the prophecy'.[179] The secular figure of the *poiêtês* (poet) has its roots in the religious role of the *prophētēs*, and the social assessment of the ways in which the poetic utterance is given *form*[180] appears to have been marked ever since by its early association with the sense of authority, with the specificity granted to non-ordinary expressions characterising the religious dimension in which the poet/prophet's utterance originated. As a midway figure between the divine sphere and the social dimension, the artist presented himself as only partly connected to the everyday world of external reality. His link with the religious sphere framed the artistic figure within a symbolic space marked by the timelessness of the gods' eternity and the intrinsically indecipherable nature of the divine utterance. As the *prophētēs'* reproduction of the gods' words was replaced, in the compositions of the early rhapsodes, by the poet's representation of mythical events, 'the speaker who [framed] the myth [...] [was] an "author" so long as he or she [spoke] with the authority of myth, which is supposedly timeless and unchanging'.[181]

Born as a translator, a favoured interpreter, a producer of artificial narrative space and time for what intrinsically lacks a temporal or spatial structure — the divine dimension — the poet subsequently becomes a figure whose rhetorical presentation often favours his uncommon participation in the sphere of the divine.[182] The author/creator is thus set at the border of the intelligible and the expressible.

Moreover, through its Latin expression, *auctor*, the notion of authorship is endowed with the connotation of the specific value which the verb *augeo*, understood as augmenting, embodies. The author contributes a plus-value, a specific and unparalleled dimension to the work which renders it unique and transforms him into an *auctoritas*, the personification of a symbolic jurisdiction — authority — over his chosen field.

From the perspective of the authorial connection with the community — embodied in the social acknowledgement of the writer *as* author which started to take place during the earliest artistic competitions in Ancient Greece — it is the *communal* recognition of authorship which is significant. As the mythical narration is given a publicly acknowledged form, a conceptual object the community can recognise and shape itself against, the process through which the social group recognises the authorial position of pre-eminence takes place. Crucially, 'the concept of mimesis, in conveying a re-enactment of myth, is a concept of authority so long as society assents to the genuineness of the values contained by the framework of myth'.[183] As myths are themselves born within the community which gives voice to the artistic production, one notices how the author is inscribed into a circular process in which the author's voice, the communal assessment of the 'genuineness of the values' and the social endorsement of authorship reciprocally sustain and reinforce one another. The *auctoritas* granted by the community becomes a recognition of the individual utterance as both ostensibly original yet endowed with great potential social resonance and reflective or expressive of commonly shared conceptual frameworks.

In this context, the literary prize can be understood in the light of a ritual process of socialisation in which the writer is granted by the community the *auctoritas* which marks his/her new status as an *author*. Such authority embodies an aesthetic jurisdiction on the literary 'paratopie', an instance of intrinsic authorial liminarity:

'les milieux littéraires sont en effet des frontières'[184] [literary environments are indeed frontiers].

Indeed, placed on the symbolic limit between the community and the isolation of creativity and individualism, the author is at once inscribed within the social dimension through a communal endorsement and distinguished from the group by the very individuality which is granted through the status of *auctoritas*. In opposition to the objectified dimension of the static literary object, the authorial figure is endowed with a dynamism in that negotiator of the communal boundaries — spatial and temporal — of the cognitive process.

Why temporal? Let us briefly turn back to the Italian case. Not only does the authorial figure move *physically* on the territorial landscape, seeking to establish his community's own *structural* boundaries. Not only does the author symbolically *travel* on the cultural scene, moving between professional categories (journalist, poet, painter, writer). The process of displacement *links* the spatial to the temporal dimensions. The notion of boundary conflates into a single concept notions of time and space. Spatial concept, the passing of the boundary also creates a temporal shift, a distinction between the *before* and *after* which expresses the temporal dimension.

The very notion of space can ultimately be challenged: in line with Merleau-Ponty, space is not to be understood as

> the setting (real or logical) in which things are arranged, but the means whereby the position of things becomes possible [...] we must think of it as the universal power enabling them to be connected.[185]

This entails that the process through which 'structure' is perceived is a dynamic rather than a static motion and that one must 'pass from spatialized space to spatializing space'[186] in order to conceive of the dynamic articulation of cognition enacted through the authorial figure and by extension, of both personal and communal identity.

Author in time: durée and novelty

The artist is therefore the socially acknowledged *filter* through which a utopian (in the Blochean sense) cognitive stability can be obtained and control over the dynamic evolution of the external real can be gained. Such a view finds an echo in several critical positions.

According to Bergson, the artist is the one individual able to transcend the linguistic and spatial limits of the psychological framework, to reach the inner flowing, temporal consciousness, which is the ultimate expression of man's uniqueness and, thus, of his individuality. In contrast with the common perception which is founded on the recognition of the spatial frame, of the classificatory dimension of superficial consciousness, artists are able to suggest that which language is not made to express. In opposition to the intellectual grasp of the conceivable, the artist is able to follow the intuitive perception of the inconceivable: in Bergsonian logic, consciousness itself.[187] In this light, the ultimate object of artistic expression becomes the wholeness of consciousness.

Ultimately, such a discourse gives the artist the capacity to provide an all-encompassing stabilised structure which captures the dynamic flow and overcomes the gap-effect previously discussed: 'the essence of art would then be this: the truth of being setting itself to work.'[188] The completed artistic work, acting as a stabilising mechanism in the process of identity-shaping, 'is not to be understood as the reproduction of some particular entity that happens to be at hand at any given time; it is, on the contrary, the reproduction of a thing's general essence'.[189]

Such a stabilising function is, by extension, projected onto the author of such a work. The structuring capacity of the artist reaches here its highest expression in that it transcends the normal limits of cognitive possibility. Absolute form, which appears to echo the Kantian 'form of the purposiveness or finality of an object, insofar as it is perceived in it without any representation of a purpose or an end',[190] is similarly theorised by Clive Bell as he states how 'the emotion that the artist felt in his moment of inspiration he [felt] for objects seen as pure forms.'[191]

In the light of such an idealised view, art becomes an imposition of form on the dynamic articulation of external reality, a 'significant form'[192] which allows for the establishment of a direct link between the cognition of a significance in the structure of the work and the cognition of a significance in the mirrored structure of reality.[193] Thus, John Dewey notes how

> that which distinguishes an experience as aesthetic is conversion of resistance and tensions, of excitations that in themselves are temptations to diversion, into a movement toward and inclusive and fulfilling close.[194]

Once celebrated by the literary competition through which his social identity *as* literary *author* is sanctioned, the artist therefore becomes the significant spokesman of the *essence* of the community and he is shown to undertake 'his artistic labour not as a personal effort on his own private behalf, but as a public labour on behalf of the community to which he belongs'.[195] Thus Collingwood underlines that 'it is not merely artists, but the whole community, of which they are part, that comes to self-knowledge in their work',[196] while Ernst Bloch highlights how 'we search for the creator who allows us to confront ourselves in a pure form, who allows us to encounter ourselves'.[197] This is a view echoed in Sartre's perception of the writer as a figure expressing a 'une totalité émergeant du monde dans le vide et refermant en elle toutes ces structures dans l'unité indissoluble'[198] [a wholeness emerging from the world into emptiness and enclosing within itself all these structures in an indissoluble unity].

Thus, emerging in times when the cognitive structure is animated by strong destabilising drives, the institution of literary prizes displays an alternation of *two* complementary processes: a tension towards stabilisation and a drive towards change. Both allow the articulation of the tensions characterising the social context. As a consequence, defining the institution in terms of the cognitive stabilisation embodied by the authorial figure is to highlight only one aspect of its dynamic mechanisms, namely that of formal stabilisation. The authorial figure, immersed in a temporal dimension, transcends in fact the objectifying boundaries of cognitive stabilisation and embodies the Heideggerian awareness of the impossibility of forming 'a static structure'.[199] However, if only for a short time, the author is able to condense and express the dynamism of life within a publicly acknowledged cognitive framework, fulfilling a social function and answering a social need. Crucially, this happens only for a determined duration. Indeed, the writer, chosen as winner, is — through the very functioning of the prizes — transient by definition; present one year, gone the next. All stabilisation is a relative one.

From the perspective of a political/social reading, such an approach amounts to considering the degree to which the literary institution, emerging in a context of cognitive destabilisation amounting to a crisis of the social identity of a cultural group, acts as the provider of both cognitive stability and social identity through the celebration of a given metaphorical representation. At the same time, the literary institution challenges such a stabilisation and questions the very identity being displayed through the experiential dynamism embodied by the authorial figures that are being celebrated yet also systematically discarded.

Notes to Chapter 2

1. Leach (1976), p. 51.
2. Merleau-Ponty (2005), p. 20.
3. Ibid., p. xxiii.
4. Bloch (1988), p. 38.
5. Immanuel Kant, 'Critique of Aesthetic Judgment', in *The Critique of Judgment* [1790], trans. by James Creed Meredith (Oxford: Clarendon Press, 1982), p. 144.
6. Donald W. Crawford, in Gaut & McIver Lopes (2005), p. 59.
7. Louis van Delft, *Littérature et anthropologie* [Literature and Anthropology] (Paris: Presses Universitaires de France, 1993), p. 3.
8. Van Delft (1993), p. 3: '[...] pour faire court: une 'vision du monde', une **imago mundis** — et la manière dont cet esprit, en la forgeant, a procédé: le modus operandi, la forma mentis' [... in short, a vision of the world, an image of the world — and the way in which the mind has proceeded in order to forge it: its way of operating, the form of the mindset.]
9. Epicurus, 'Letter to Herodotus', www.epicurus.net, <http://www.epicurus.net/en/herodotus.html> [accessed 1 July 2017] (para. 45–46 of 54).
10. George A. Kennedy, in 'Classical Criticism', *The Cambridge History of Literary Criticism*, ed. by George A. Kennedy (Cambridge: Cambridge University Press, 1989), I, p. 214.
11. Nicola Ubaldo, *Antologia illustrata di filosofia* [Philosophy: An Illustrated Anthology] (Firenze: Demetra, 2002), p. 274.
12. Martin Manchester, *The Philosophical Foundations of Humboldt's Linguistic Doctrines* (Amsterdam: John Benjamins, 1985), p. 52.
13. Ibid., p. 60. The critic points here to the ambiguity surrounding Humboldt's conception of the initial formation of linguistic utterances. Underlining the difficulty of establishing in a definite manner Humboldt's preference for either an 'arbitrary' or a 'non-arbitrary' original conception, Manchester underlines how 'once some concept-word units are established (whether arbitrarily or not) further word-formation will develop in a non-arbitrary "motivated" fashion by retaining and employing these previously established sound-concept associations'.
14. Ibid., p. 99.
15. Ibid., p. 150.
16. Ibid., p. 107.
17. Timothy Clark, *Martin Heidegger* (London: Routledge, 2002), p. 65.
18. Anthony Cohen, *The Symbolic Construction of Community* (London: Tavistock, 1985), p. 118.
19. Ted Cohen, in *On Metaphor*, ed. by Sheldon Sacks (Chicago: The University of Chicago Press, 1978), p. 7.

20. Merleau-Ponty (2005), p. xxii.
21. Ibid., p. xxii.
22. Donald Crawford, in Gaut and McIver Lopes (2005), p. 59.
23. Francesco Perfetti, *Il nazionalismo italiano dalle origini alla fusione col Fascismo* [Italian Nationalism: From its Origins to the Fusion with Fascism] (Bologna: Cappelli Editore, 1977), p. 24.
24. Anna Cento Bull, in *The Cambridge Companion to Modern Italian Culture*, ed. by Zygmunt G. Barański and Rebecca J. West (Cambridge: Cambridge University Press, 2001), p. 41.
25. Perfetti (1977), p. 13.
26. Cento Bull (2001), p. 46.
27. Charles Burdett, *Vincenzo Cardarelli and his Contemporaries* (Oxford: Clarendon Press, 1999), p. 18.
28. Ibid., p. 18.
29. Perfetti (1977), p. 19.
30. Burdett (1999), p. 20.
31. Perfetti (1977), p. 26.
32. Burdett (1999), p. 19.
33. Perfetti (1977), p. 26.
34. Orio Vergani, 'Bagutta', in *Alfabeto del XX secolo* [Alphabet of the Twentieth Century] (Milano: Baldini & Castoldi, 2000), pp. 38–39.
35. Leonida Répaci, in 'Premio Viareggio', *Wikipedia*, <http://it.wikipedia.org/wiki/Premio_Viareggio> [accessed 1 July 2017] (quotation). See also <www.premioletterarioviareggiorepaci.it/>.
36. Marjorie Perloff, *The Futurist Moment* (Chicago: The University of Chicago Press, 1986), p. xix.
37. Burdett (1999), p. 135.
38. Ibid. p. 151. In particular, Solaria sought to: '[...] encourage a high level of debate about a whole range of European authors including Gide, Valéry, and Joyce. The informed debate concerning European literature, while it encouraged a level of censure from the pro-Fascist press, attracted the interest of many of the more innovative writers of the period. Although **Solaria** did not publish poetry after 1931, Giuseppe Ungaretti, Eugenio Montale and Salvatore Quasimodo all wrote for the review.'
39. Cohen (1985), p. 58.
40. Vincenzo Cardarelli, *Opere* [Works], rev. by Clelia Martignoni (Milano: Arnoldo Mondatori Editore, 1981), p. 447.
41. Peter Wollen, in *Travellers' Tales*, ed. by George Robertson et al. (London York: Routledge, 1998), p. 192.
42. Rita Baldassarri, *Lorenzo Viani* (Firenze: La Nuova Italia, 1982), p. 15.
43. Ibid. p. 15.
44. Carlo Emilio Gadda, *Il Castello di Udine* [The Castle of Udine], [1934], intro. by Guido Lucchini (Milano: Garzanti, 1989), p. 92.
45. Ibid., p. 102.
46. Perfetti (1977), p. 20.
47. Cohen (1985), p. 81.
48. Ibid., p. 15.
49. Cardarelli (1981), p. 382.
50. Ibid., p. 392. 'La materia da cui più la loro cruda fantasia rimase tocca e che lavorarono con miglior gusto fu l'argilla. E praticando, insieme, con la morte, una famigliarità del tutto incompunta, immaginandosi l'Ade orgiasticamente come un perpetuo saturnale, questa razza di bonificatori ma non georgici (cavatori, scultori, vasai) che prosperò un giorno, obliosa, sulle vulcaniche terre del centro d'Italia, portò a cottura il mito dell'inferno e creò, forse, dei suoi giganteschi numi, i più infuocati e rossi.' [Clay was the material they preferred to use and which touched more than any other their raw imagination. Sharing with death a painless familiarity, imagining the Underworld like an orgiastic, incessant saturnalia, this race of land workers — though not georgic (cave workers, sculptors, pot makers) — who, one day, flourished on central Italy volcanic lands, fired the myth of hell and created, perhaps, of all of its gigantic gods, the most red and burning.]

51. Ibid., p. 392.
52. Diane Ghirardo and Kurt Forster, 'Insediamenti e Territorio' [Settlements and Territory], in *Storia d'Italia* [History of Italy], ed. by Cesare De Seta, Annali 8 (Torino: Giulio Einaudi Editore, 1985), p. 629.

Mussolinia 1928	Aprilia 1936
Littoria 1932	Arsia 1937
Sabaudia 1934	Carbonia 1938
Pontinia 1935	Torviscosa 1938
Guidonia 1935	Pomezia 1938
Fertilia 1936	Pozzo Littorio 1940

53. Ibid., p.642.
54. Cardarelli (1981), p. 452.
55. Francine Dugast-Portes, in *Le Portrait Littéraire* [The Literary Portrait], ed. by Kazimierz Kuspisz et al. (Lyon: Presses Universitaires de Lyon, 1989), p. 236.
56. Cardarelli (1981), p. 980.
57. Cardarelli (1981), p. 400.
58. Burdett (1999), p. 142.
59. Cardarelli (1981), p. 336. 'Quello che io intendo per italiano è un carattere o piuttosto un estro di razza, tutto naturale ed eroico, perciò antichissimo e pieno di storia, sempre identico e riconoscibile in qualunque espressione del nostro genio. Consiste esso, più che altro, in uno stile o maniera di vivere, in una parlata e in un modo di ragionare. Lo si ritrova nel giudizio e nella fantasia di Tacito, in Dante, in Macchiavelli, in Leonardo, in Leopardi, nella letteratura del Cinquecento e nella famigliarità principesca di quel tempo; ed è qualche cosa di incomparabile con qualunque altra facoltà di razza barbara o civile, come la bellezza ariosa o proporzionata del nostro Appennino, dov'è nata la pittura e la favola di Giotto pastore, simbolo della nostra gloriosa e creativa ignoranza.' [What I mean by *Italian* is a character or rather a race type, wholly natural and heroic, very ancient and full of history, always identical and recognisable in all the expressions of our genius. It consists, more than any other, in a style or a way of living, in a way of speaking and of reasoning. You can find it in Tacito's judgment and imagination, in Dante, in Macchiavelli, in Leonardo, in Leopardi, in the literature of the sixteenth century and in the aristocratic familiarity of that time; and it is something which cannot be compared with any other faculty of any other race, either barbaric or civilised, like the airy and proportionate beauty of our Appennino, where the art of painting and the fable of Giotto the shepherd, the symbol of our glorious and creative ignorance, was born.] [TN: *Appennino*: mountain chain].
60. Ibid., p. 446.
61. Ibid., p. 82.
62. Oreste Del Buono, *Achille Campanile: opere, romanzi e racconti 1924–1933* [Achille Campanile: Works, Novels and Essays 1924-1933] (Milano: Classici Bompiani, 1989), p. 1375.
63. Manfred Frank, in *Manfred Frank: The Subject and the Text: Essays on Literary Theory and Philosophy*, ed. by Andrew Bowie (Cambridge: Cambridge University Press, 1997), p. 4.
64. Ibid., p. 4.
65. Frederick Jameson, *The Political Unconscious: Narrative as a Socially Symbolic Act* (Methuen: Cornell University Press, 1981), p. 79.
66. Cohen (1985), p. 12.
67. Merleau-Ponty (2005), p. vii.
68. Ibid., p. vii.
69. Ibid., p. x.
70. Ibid., p. xv.
71. Ibid., p. x.
72. Ibid., p. x.
73. Ibid., p. x.
74. Ibid., p. x.
75. Ibid., p. 7.
76. Ibid., p. 13.

77. Ibid., p. 71. Significantly, Merleau-Ponty notes how only 'if a universal constituting consciousness were possible, the opacity of the fact would disappear'. Thus 'the thinking EGO can never abolish its inherence in an individual subject, which knows all things in a particular perspective'.
78. Adrienne Dengerink Chaplin, in Gaut and McIver Lopes (2005), p. 160.
79. Merleau-Ponty (2005), p. 4.
80. Manfred Frank, in Bowie (1997), p. 4: 'Within the framework of a structure the only things that are visible, objective, significant, and are also capable of being replicated and generalised, are the signs and their relationships with one another (the mass of the codifiable). The gap as such evades the eye of knowledge, although it is precisely the gap that installed the positive terms in their functions as signs, i.e. as units of expression of meaning.'
81. Ibid., pp. 5–6: 'Thus the meaning that is to be understood is not based on a continuum entirely made up of meaning like itself, but on something which is itself not meaningful. The immediate transparency of the meaning is already clouded in its very origin, and if one were to call meaning the sayable, one would have to call its origin 'silence' as does Mallarmé.'
82. Bloch (1988), p. 71.
83. Jameson (1981), p. 36.
84. Alberto Asor Rosa, 'Intellettuali e Potere', in *Storia d'Italia*, ed. by Corrado Vivanti, Annali 4 (Torino: Giulio Einaudi Editore, 1981), p. 1239.
85. Ibid., pp. 1241–42.
86. Ibid., pp. 1241–42.
87. Maria Francesca Petrocchi, *Esperienze e scritture di viaggio* [Travel Writings and Experiences] (Viterbo: Settecittà, 2003), p. 20.
88. Enrico Pea, *L'Arca di Noè: racconti, memorie, elzeviri, 1945–1953* [Noa's Arch: Stories, Memories and Elzevirs], rev. by Enrico Lorenzetti (Viareggio, Lucca: Mario Baroni Editore, 1997), p. 11.
89. Alberto Asor Rosa, in Vivanti (1981), pp. 1241–42.
90. Del Buono (1989), p. viii.
91. Ibid., p. xii.
92. Guido Lucchini, in Gadda (1988), p. 7.
93. Cesare de Michelis, in Corrado Tumiati, *Tetti rossi: ricordi di manicomio* [Red Roofs: Asylum Memories], [1931] (Venezia: Marsilio Editore, 1987), p. 158.
94. Del Buono (1989), p. xxiv).
95. Cardarelli (1981), p. 453.
96. Ibid., p. 453.
97. Elvio Guagnini, *Viaggi d'inchiostro* [Ink Travels] (Pasian di Prato: Campanotto Editore, 2000), p. 11.
98. Ibid., p. 18.
99. Ibid., p. 29.
100. Ibid., p. 105.
101. Ibid., p. 107.
102. Burdett (1999), p. 184.
103. Ibid., p. 185.
104. Ibid., p. 185.
105. L. Furno interviewed by L. Accantoli, in *Filippo Sacchi e Silvio Negro scrittori-giornalisti vicentini del Novecento* [Filippo Sacchi and Silvio Negro Twentieth Century Journalist-Writers from Vicenza], ed. by Adriana Chemello (Venezia: Marsilio Editore, 2001), p. 70.
106. Ibid., p. 58.
107. Cardarelli (1981), p. 428. 'Andare alla stazione, tanto valeva per lui quanto mettersi in viaggio e rivedere quelle città dell'Italia centrale, come Livorno, Lucca, Siena, Modena, Piacenza, città ricche d'ogni ben di Dio....' [Going to the station was, for him, like travelling and seeing once more those central Italy towns, like Livorno, Lucca, Siena, Modena, Piacenza, cities filled with all sorts of wealth...]
108. Ibid., pp. 430–31.
109. Baldassarri (1982), p. 50.

110. Rossana Esposito, *Invito alla lettura di Giovanni Comisso* [An Invitation to a Reading of Giovanni Comisso] (Milano: Mursia, 1990), p. 82.
111. Paul Gifford, in *Literature and Quest*, ed. by Christine Arkinstall (Amsterdam: Rodopi, 1993), p. 17.
112. Ibid., p. 19.
113. Cardarelli (1981), p. 384.
114. Ibid., p. 450.
115. Trinh T. Minh-ha in Robertson et al. (1998), p. 9.
116. Baldassarri (1982), p. 12.
117. Ibid., p. 12.
118. Antonia Arslan and Patrizia Zambon, *Enrico Pea* (Firenze: La Nuova Italia, 1983), p. 9.
119. Cardarelli (1981), p. 375.
120. Ibid., p. 377.
121. Francine Dugast-Portes, in Kuspisz et al. (1988), p. 246.
122. Patrizia Dogliani, *Il fascismo degli italiani* [The Fascism of Italians] (Novara: De Agostini S.p.A., 2014).
123. Baldassarri (1982), p. 10.
124. Cardarelli (1981), p. 405.
125. Ibid., p. 399.
126. Ibid., p. 400. 'Chi sia re Tarquinio lo potete desumere dal fisico. Vi basti sapere che il direttore d'un museo anatomico gli voleva comprare lo scheletro. Immaginate un pezzo d'uomo alto quasi due metri, costretto in certi abiti lisi, corti, attillati, abbottonatissimi, in maniera da non poterne più uscire. Con tanto di stivali che gli arrivano fine al ginocchio e un cappelluzzo da cacciatore delle Alpi, posato con mirabile equilibrio sopra una testa che, da qualunque parte la si guardi, è un capolavoro di strinatura; una voce orrida; due piccoli mustacchi all'insù, incerettati e nerissimi, tinti al nerofumo, sopra una faccia martoriata da un rasoio che non rade, ma porta via la pelle ed il pelo, di un' epidermide più dura del cuoio e rossa come una bistecca cruda, sempre con qualche ombreggiatura e ditata di nero alla radice dei baffi e dei capelli; tutto un personale aitante e spavaldo da antico sergente di cavalleria abituato a pavoneggiarsi, da quarant'anni, agli occhi di tutte le belle del paese e luoghi circonvicini, munito d'un paio di mani grosse e tozze che escono dai polsini male inamidati e dalle maniche sfuggite, come due pinne colossali. Questi è re Tarquinio.' [You can understand who King Tarquinio is just by looking at him. You should know that the director of a museum of anatomy wanted to buy his skeleton. Imagine a robust man, nearly two metres tall, squeezed into threadbare, short, tight, fully buttoned clothes, looking as though he will never be able to escape from them. With high boots reaching his knees and a little hat, like those worn by hunters in the Alps, remarkably balanced on a head which, no matter from where you look at it, appears like a burned work of art; he possesses a horrid voice, two small, high-pointed moustaches, waxed and carbon-blackened, set on a face martyrised by a blunt razor which takes away both hair and skin, his epidermis harder than leather and as red as a raw steak, always displaying some shadow or dark smudge at the roots of both moustache and hair. He is a robust, cocky character, like a cavalry sergeant of old, used to swaggering, for the past forty years, before all the village beauties — and the ladies from the neighbouring places — endowed with a pair of big, rough hands emerging from some badly starched cuffs and attempting to escape the sleeves, like two colossal fins. This is King Tarquinio.]
127. Cesare de Michelis in Tumiati (1987), p. 161.
128. Tumiati (1987), p. 81.
129. Ibid., p. 130.
130. Ibid., p. 15.
131. Ibid., p. 18.
132. Ibid., p. 24.
133. Ibid., p. 30.
134. Ibid., p. 42.
135. Tumiati (1987), p. 50.

136. Ibid., p. 106.
137. Ibid., p. 107.
138. Ibid., p. 153.
139. Del Buono (1989), p. 1316.
140. Aleksander Ablamowicz, in Kuspisz et al. (1988), p. 227.
141. Tumiati (1987), p. 101.
142. Cardarelli (1981), p. 417.
143. Gadda (1988), p. 42.
144. *Maria Bellonci: opere* [Maria Bellonci: Works], ed. by Ernesto Ferrero (Milano: Arnoldo Mondatori Editore, 1994), p. xxvi.
145. Ibid., p. 291.
146. Gadda (1988), p. 161.
147. Ibid., p. 70. Inevitably the autobiographer also experiences, at least for the narrative of childhood, a certain difficulty in respecting this order [chronological order]: his memories are poorly dated, and he is afraid of confusing periods of time; his memory plays tricks on him — the forgetfulness, the memory that returns after the fact, the document that is found later and contradicts the memory, and so on...
148. Ibid., p. 42.
149. Ibid., p. 458.
150. Ibid., p. 43.
151. Burdett (1999), p. 56.
152. Ibid., p. 59.
153. Philippe Lejeune, *On Autobiography* (Minneapolis: University of Minnesota Press, 1989), p. 74.
154. Cardarelli (1981), p. 374.
155. Ibid., p. 374.
156. Del Buono (1989), p. 1317.
157. Cardarelli (1981), p. 384.
158. Chemello (2001), p. xviii.
159. Del Buono (1989), p. 1130.
160. Ibid., p. 1328.
161. Ibid., p. 1370.
162. Gadda (1988), p. 26.
163. Barker (2003), p. 94.
164. Ibid., p. 94.
165. Cohen (1985), p. 14.
166. Turner and Bruner (1986), pp. 300–01.
167. Maurice Blanchot, *The Space of Literature*, [1955], trans. by Ann Smock (Lincoln: University of Nebraska Press, 1982), p. 90.
168. Jameson (1981).
169. Maingueneau (2004), p. 48.
170. Münster (1985), p. 150.
171. Ernst Bloch, *A Philosophy of the Future*, trans. by John Camming (New York: Herder and Herder, 1970), p. 77.
172. Münster (1985), p. 149.
173. Blanchot (1982), p. 90.
174. Münster (1985), p. 73.
175. Richard Shusterman, in Gaut and McIver Lopes (2005), p. 128.
176. Cardarelli (1981), p. 383.
177. Maingueneau (2004), p. 87.
178. Aron et al. (2002), p. 33.
179. Gregory Nagy in Kennedy (1989), p. 26.
180. Stéphanie Champeau, *La Notion d'artiste chez les Goncourt* [The Notion of Artist According to the Goncourt Brothers] (Paris: Honoré Champion Editeur, 2000), p. 13.
181. Gregory Nagy in Kennedy (1989), p. 48.

182. Talon-Hugon (2004), p. 22.
183. Ibid., p. 48.
184. Maingueneau (2004), p. 72.
185. Merleau-Ponty (2005), p. 284.
186. Ibid., p. 284.
187. Henri Bergson, *Le Rire* [The Laugh] [1900], 23rd edn (Paris: Editions Alcan, 1924).
188. Martin Heidegger, in Farrell Krell (1993), p. 162.
189. Ibid., p. 162.
190. Donald W. Crawford, in Gaut and McIver Lopes (2005), p. 59.
191. Clive Bell, *Art* (Oxford: Oxford University Press, 1987), p. 44.
192. Ibid., p. 54.
193. Ibid., p. 54.
194. Gaut and McIver Lopes (2005), p. 260.
195. Collingwood (1938), pp. 314–15.
196. Gordon Graham, in Gaut and McIver Lopes (2005), p. 140.
197. Bloch (1988), p. 100.
198. Sartre (1948), p. 193.
199. Thomas E. Wartenberg, in Gaut and McIver Lopes (2005), p. 154.

CHAPTER 3

Spain 1950–1975: Utopia and Dystopia

The tension between the construction of identity and the challenging of constructed identities, together with the specific interaction which relates such a tension to the figure of the author, similarly emerge in the novels having won literary prizes in the context of Francoist Spain, in the period spanning from 1938 to ca. 1975.

Specifically, in the Spanish novels, a reiterated ambiguity appears to blur and dissolve, at the thematic level, the distinction between authorial and narratorial figures, collapsing *real* external authors and *fictitious* internal narrators within a unique metafictional dimension. Such a process repeatedly culminates in the portrayal of a series of unreliable, unstable and ultimately self-destructive figures of authors/narrators.

Such a dimension significantly develops in parallel to the progressive thematic and stylistic dissolution of a *realist* perspective, expressed through the projection of a self-unravelling and self-undermining universe of fiction onto the external sphere. Structural, symbolic and narrative boundaries are undermined. Ontological dissolution is highlighted. The progressive affirmation of metafictional narrative aesthetics takes centre stage.

Read in the light of the Francoist discourse on the pre-eminence of *culture* as identity shaping tool — as expressed, in particular, by the political and governmental emphasis placed on education in those years — the aesthetic selection enacted by Spanish literary institutions appears paradoxical.

Indeed, on the one hand, the Francoist myth of the ontological potential of culture can easily be connected to the Blochean utopian belief in the capacity of culture of being 'creative'.[1] In this context, literary prizes can indeed be seen as cultural institutions which, as illustrated in the preceding chapters, by validating cultural objects on the social scene, intervene in the process of identity creation and ontological constitution.

On the other hand, however, through the aesthetic choices made, the studied prizes validate a social discourse which can be seen as being in opposition to the Francoist emphasis on the constructive function allegedly played by the *cultural dimension* in the processes shaping Spanish identity. In particular, one notices how, as artificiality and fictitiousness destroy and overcome all attempts at defining genuine — whole — beings, *fiction* — turning to *artificiality* if not *falseness* — defines in a negative perspective the thematic and stylistic content of the winning novels.

Once more, the analysis of literary competitions reveals a contradictory relation. On the one hand, the cultural institution is understood to operate as a tool within an ideological governmental framework. On the other hand, through its operations, that self-same institution challenges the system within which it operates.

In order to analyse such a contradiction, this work will rely on the third dynamic relation — understood to be at the basis of the functioning of the cultural institution — as analysed in the theoretical framework, namely the relationship between the process of aesthetic selection and the contextual dimension.

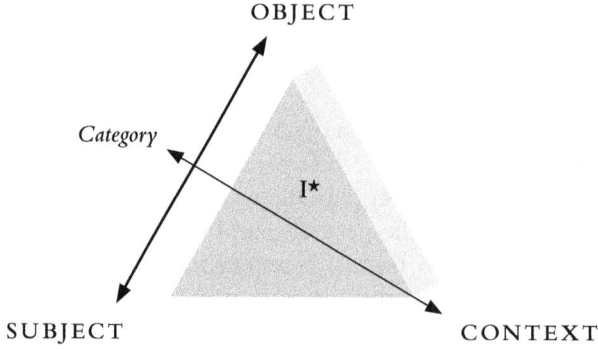

FIG. 3.1. Categorisation as social action (★ Literary Prize)

Indeed, having considered the relation tying *metaphorical* construct and **SUBJECT** constitution and having analysed the relation between the construction of the aesthetic **OBJECT** and the shaping of an *authorial* subject, the focus is now on the consideration of the action arising from the relation between assessing **SUBJECT** and aesthetic **OBJECT**, which is understood to be embodied in a process of *categorisation*.

The process of categorisation has been previously briefly discussed in terms of an act of *labelling*, whereby the winning novel is inscribed within the sphere of LITERATURE/ART. The specific term of *categorisation* is, though, particularly useful as it has been defined according to two distinct approaches, the latter of which throws a specific light on the Spanish case.

On the one hand, according to the definition of *linguistic* categorisation,

> just about all words, as well as grammatical and phonological structures, are categories. A sentence such as 'the cat sat on the mat' can be analysed for how all of its words categorize objects, events, time, definiteness and spatial location, and how grammar puts them all together in a categorized description of the world.[2]

On the other hand, the notion of *propositional* categorisation embodies a different approach to the phenomenon of categorisation whereby, in the forms 'dogs are animals' or 'Socrates is mortal', 'a named entity is explicitly placed into a named category'.[3] Through such a view, according to Derek Edwards, it is possible to understand the process of categorisation as a means to accomplish social actions rather than as an expression of automatic 'representations of pre-formed cognitions'.[4]

It is indeed such an approach which can be held to occur in the context of literary prizes since, through the social ritual of aesthetic selection, the art/object is inserted within a number of symbolic and linguistic categories such as ART, LITERATURE, BESTSELLER, WINNER, etc... Crucially, categorisation involves not simply the deploying of 'categories prototypically, but [makes] typicality the topic of talk and makes it problematical'[5]. The conscious selection and celebration of given literary works is, in other words, the key to the unsettling potential of the categorisation act. By underlining the self-conscious, metafictional dimension arising from Spanish competition-winners, one highlights the explicit act of challenge which the institution responsible for the winning, hence the categorising act itself, actually promotes. In such a perspective, the potential social impact of the literary/cultural institution and its functioning as an identity formulating tool, far from being endorsed and celebrated in an unproblematic perspective, appears as being inherently challenged and self-consciously critically perceived.

Embodying Franco's Cultural Ideal

The paradoxical relationship between aesthetic choices and social function of the institution is best apprehended, as mentioned, if one first takes into consideration the degree to which the exponential development of Spanish literary competitions in the period from the 1940s to the early 1970s appears to embody the Francoist drive towards the use of culture as a tool for the shaping of identity.

As illustrated by Franco's programme of cultural development, the governmental strategy aimed at ensuring ideological, political and cultural unity in a country that was internally divided and internationally isolated relied on an understanding of culture as the privileged medium to blend *form* of the State and *form* of the individual.

Through the aesthetic selection enacted by literary competitions, an aesthetic selection realised *via* an act of categorisation, Franco's politics of cultural fashioning appeared to take a concrete embodiment. Indeed, considering the act of categorisation as a practice which constructively intervenes in the social sphere through the organisation of experience entails an understanding of the social function of literary competitions in terms of how far they embody an utopian belief in the potential for a fashioning of the mental — and by extension the social — order.

Spanish literary prizes

As noted by José María Martínez Cachero, the proliferation of literary prizes in Spain throughout the Francoist period is truly remarkable and can be traced back to the desire for cultural re-birth which immediately followed the end of the civil war[6] and which led, in addition, to the creation of literary competitions, to the proliferation of literary publications (*Escorial* (1940), *El Español* (1942), *La Estafeta Literaria* (1944), *Fantasía* (1945)), to the founding of the *Escuela Oficial de Periodismo* [TN: school of journalism founded in 1941 by Juan Aparicio, journalist and politician] and to the development of cultural institutions such as *Editora Nacional* [TN: Publishing house founded by the Francoist authorities during the civil war].

The phenomenon of literary competitions in Spain, in the Francoist period, reached such a dimension that the rapid development of this type of institution in the 1940s can be paradoxically assessed as a relatively slow beginning[7] if considered in the light of the exponential growth which followed.

Very quickly, the political endorsement of existing literary competitions,[8] soon giving way to the constitution of new (literary and non-literary) ones[9], favoured the establishment of the 1940 *Premio Miguel de Unamuno* by the *Patria Hispana* publishing house in Madrid-Barcelona, the *Premio Lecturas* by the *Ediciones Hymsa* in 1942, the *Premio Fastenrath* by the German hispanist Juan Fastenrath in 1943, the 1943 *Premio José Antonio Primo de Rivera*, the 1947 *Premio Internacional de Primera Novela* by the editor José Janés, the 1949 *Premio Miguel de Cervantes* and fellow official prize *Enrique Larreta* in 1950, as well as the *Valencia* in 1950 and the *Don Quijote* in 1951. By the end of the decade, the competitions landscape encompassed a varied network of

> premios académicos, oficiales o estatales, editoriales o comerciales, de un ocasional mecenas [...] con dotación cuantiosas o modesta, [...] con jurados fijos o con jurados variables; para novelas inéditas o para novelas publicadas; con destino exclusivo o primordial para jóvenes y noveles escritores o, más bien, para galardonar dedicaciones al género muy contrastadas ya; premios de reciente creación, de una sola convocatoria inclusiva, y premios que vienen de la anteguerra.[10]

> [academic prizes, either official or state-sponsored, commercial, promoted by publishers or by an occasional sponsor, [...] with either generous or modest endowments [...] with either fixed or changing juries; [those aimed at] either unpublished or published novels, targeting exclusively or principally young and new writers or celebrating controversial contributions to the novelistic genre; prizes recently created, some of them with just one edition and prizes from the pre-war years.]

Focusing solely on the decade of the 1950s, one could mention the emergence of the *Don Quijote*, with a prize of 100,000 pesetas, the Spanish *Femina*, with a prize of 50,000 pesetas, of the *Menorca*, with a prize of 200,000 pesetas, of the *Fundación March*, with a prize of 300,000 pesetas, not to mention the official *Miguel de Cervantes*, granted since 1949 by the *Ministerio de Información y Turismo* [Ministry of Information and Tourism].

Two of the main prizes emerging during the Francoist period, which will be considered for the purposes of the current analysis, are the *Premio Nadal* and the *Premio Planeta*.

The *Premio Nadal* (the *Premio Eugenio Nadal*, in full) was conceived in 1944 and promoted by the *Destino* weekly magazine in Barcelona in memory of Eugenio Nadal Gaya (1917–1944), chief editor, teacher of literature and author of *Ciudades en España* [Cities in Spain], who died when he was just twenty-seven years old. The first *Nadal* prize was awarded on 6 January 1945 at a dinner in the *Café Suizo*, on the Barcelona *Ramblas*, by a group of friends of the departed. Among others, Ignacio Agustí (journalist and writer 1913–1974), Joan Teixidor (poet 1913–1992) and Juan Ramón Masoliver (art critic 1910–1997) presented the first *Nadal* to Carmen Laforet's *Nada*, which beat (by three votes to two) *En el pueblo hay caras nuevas* [There are New Faces in the Village] by José Maria Alvarez Blázquez and *La terraza de los Palau* [The Palau's Terrace] by César González Ruano.

The success of the first winning novel significantly contributed to the subsequent growth on the social scene of the prize itself. If just 26 novels had been submitted in 1945, by 1947 more than 100 novels were entered into the *Nadal* competition, a number that would reach 200 by the 1950s. The growing importance of the prize led the competition to move from the *Café Suizo* to the *Café Glaciar* in 1949, to the *Hotel Oriente* in 1950 and to the Ritz Hotel in Barcelona in 1958.

The importance of the prize and the degree to which *Nadal* authors have concretely marked the literary landscape in twentieth-century Spanish fiction can easily be considered through a short overview of its most notable winners in the period under examination: *Un hombre* [A Man] by José María Gironella (1946), *La sombra del ciprés es alargada* [The Shadow of the Cypress is Extended] by Miguel Delibes (1947), *Las últimas horas* [The Last Hours] by José Suárez Carreño (1949), *La noria* [The Ferris Wheel] by Luis Romero (1951), *El Jarama* [The River] by Rafael Sánchez Ferlosio (1955), *La Frontera de Dios* [God's Frontier] by José Luis Martín Descalzo (1956), *Entre visillos* [Behind the Curtains] by Carmen Martín Gaite (1957), *Primera Memoria* [Awakening][11] by Ana María Matute (1959), *El día señalado* [The Announced Day] by Manuel Mejía Vallejo (1963) and *El buen salvaje* [The Noble Savage] by Eduardo Caballero Calderón (1965).

The *Premio Planeta* was founded by José Manuel Lara (1915–2003) in 1952 with the aim of supporting Spanish authors. Initially endowed with 40,000 pesetas, the prize, as early as 1953, reached a sum of 100,000 pesetas, increased to 200,000 pesetas in 1959 and to 2,000,000 pesetas in 1973.

The first jury was composed, among others, of Bartolomé Soler (author, playwright 1894–1975), César González Ruano (journalist 1903–1965), and José Manuel Lara himself. Promoted by the Editorial Planeta, also sponsoring the *Premio De Novela Fernando Lara*, the *Premio Azorín*, the *Premi de les Lletres Catalanes Ramon Llull*, and the *Premi Série Negra*, the prize is, after the Nobel Prize, the richest literary prize at the international level with a funding of €601,000. The *Premio Planeta* is annually awarded on 15 October, in honour of St Theresa (the name of José Manuel Lara's wife), and though current editions have not been immune from bitter criticism and polemic,[12] the prize has been a major player in the twentieth-century Spanish literary landscape.

First presented on 12 October 1952 to *En la noche no hay caminos* [There are no Roads in the Night] by Juan José Mira, the *Premio Planeta* was to be subsequently awarded to authors such as Ana María Matute for *Pequeño teatro* [Little Theatre] (1954), Tomás Salvador for *El atentado* [The Assault] (1960), Torcuato Luca de Tena for *La mujer de otro* [The Neighbour's Wife] (1961), Luis Romero for *El cacique* [The Chief] (1963), Jamón José Sender for *En la vida de Ignacio Morel* [In Ignacio Morel's Life] (1969), as well as to Mercedes Salisachs, José María Gironella and Carlos Rojas.

The meanings of culture

The exponential growth and long-standing success of literary competitions in Francoist Spain can be related to the regime's emphasis on the constitutive function of art[13] and on the Francoist understanding of the social potential of culture as ontological tool. Indeed, the view of literature as 'una literatura que [...] al valor estético agregue lo humano'[14] [literature adding, to the aesthetic value, the human dimension] can be traced to the regime's belief in the ability of culture to shape a new communal identity for Spanish society which emerged, torn and divided, from the civil war. As expressed by José Antonio Girón de Velasco, *Ministro de Trabajo* [Minister for Employment] under Franco:

> Sólo una fuerza es capaz de fundir las paredes aislantes y crear el clima común en que la Paz social pueda servir de base a la Justicia social. Esta fuerza es la Cultura de universal patrimonio. Creo que cuando se habla de diferencia de clases, se habla en realidad de diferencia de culturas. Más aún, cuando se habla de luta de clases, ¿no se quiere, más bien, hablar de una lucha de culturas?[15]

> [There is only one force, able to undermine the isolating walls and to create a common dimension in which social peace can be the building ground for social justice. This force is that of a universally shared asset such as Culture. I believe that when people talk about class differences, they are really talking about cultural differences. Moreover, when people talk about class struggle are they not, in fact, really talking about a confrontation of cultures?]

Indeed, as underlined by Gustavo Bueno in his 1996 *El mito del la cultura*[16] [The Myth of Culture], culture can be understood as a factor playing an increasingly central role on the political and social scenes of the Western world, driving, throughout the nineteenth and twentieth centuries, both ethical and esthetical behaviours and perceptions.

In Francoist Spain, the 'myth of culture' went so far as to replace (according to Leoncio González Hevia)[17] the '*mito de la Raza*' [the myth of race] and radically influenced Francoist social policies. The critic is indeed at pains to point out the frequent references to cultural politics in public speeches of the Francoist period, the governmental commitment to education and training, the emphasis on the re-organisation of cultural life through the shaping of the University system, the promotion of specific anti-modernist ethic and aesthetic values, and the widespread use of censure and control.

However, as noted by Luis de Llera, compared with the cultural background of Italian Fascism, Spanish Francoism is not striking for its 'cultural pretensions'. Indeed, having pointed out the degree to which the army remained, throughout, Franco's most trusted tool for the enforcement of the *régime*, the critic stresses how, with regard to the cultural dimension, Franco

> en el major de los casos apreciaba un nuevo regeneracionismo cultural, capaz de revalorizar el proyecto de una España unida que considerase como ideal el imitar la tradición gloriosa del los tiempos mejores de nuestra historia.[18]

> [in the majority of cases, [Franco] set great store by a new cultural regeneration, able to grant new value to the project of a united Spain, which would consider

the imitation of the glorious tradition of the best years of our history as an ideal approach.]

Thus any assessment of the function of the cultural dimension in the context of Francoist Spain must take into account both the Francoist interest for the cultural dimension and the limits to which such an interest was subjected.

What both critics agree upon, though, is the idea of culture as an ontological tool for the constitution of a renewed, albeit broadly fictitious, Spanish identity. According to such a reading, culture was perceived by the Francoist government as a tool to counter revolutionary chaos, as an instance of the manufacturing and objectification of a linear and unproblematic Spanish identity. In other words, culture, in the Francoist understanding, can be understood as expressing that process through which a 'socially shared cognitive organisation'[19] can be enforced.

We have already partly highlighted, in the second chapter, the limits inherent in such a static view of identity enforcement. By applying the challenging potential inherent in the act of categorisation to the analysis of Spanish literary competitions, one analyses once more — albeit from a different perspective — the phenomenon of cultural production in terms of the limits to which the enforcement of such a 'socially shared cognitive organisation' can be confronted.

In order to highlight such limits, it can be useful to reverse the 'culture' *equal* 'shared cognitive organisation' equation, modifying, by the same token, the understanding of the term of 'culture' itself.

On the one hand, we have indeed seen, in the analysis of the metaphorical relationship between the art object and the external context, how the cultural object is tied in a reciprocal bond with the cognitive sphere of the subject. Such a relation is apprehended in the reading of the cultural object in terms of the cognitive organisation it can enforce.

On the other hand, should one read the 'culture' *equal* 'shared cognitive organisation' in reverse — in the sense that obtaining a hoped-for 'shared cognitive organisation' is to be understood as the driving 'culture' of the regime — it becomes clear that the term 'culture' comes to express the degree to which the Francoist regime sought to uphold the ideal of a uniform Spanish identity.

On the one hand, one is therefore faced with the possible uses of 'culture', while, on the other hand, it is the 'culture' of the regime itself which is called into question.

Such a distinction is useful in the light of the paradoxical thematic and stylistic content displayed by the novels having won literary competitions in the Francoist period, which will be analysed in the following sections of this work.

If the success of the phenomenon of literary competitions appears to uphold *the use of culture made* by the Francoist regime, its embracing of the utopian potential of the cultural act, the potentially critical content of the novels selected by those self-same competitions appears designed to undermine *the culture of* the regime, indeed, its belief in the possible implementation of a homogenous cultural model.

Criticism vs. creation

This challenging potential can be related to a further peculiar characteristic displayed by literary competitions: the capacity of such institutions to function ostensibly in the absence of an explicit and public critical approach to the literary work.

Indeed, paradoxically enough for an institution anchored in an act of judgement, the (often secret) assessment process takes place away from the public scene and no report of the critical consideration of the novels under scrutiny needs to be produced. In contexts marked by censorship, such a dimension suggests one of the reasons for the sustained success — in potentially difficult cultural and political conditions — of the social phenomenon under examination. In this context, one notices indeed how the literary prize body adapts to a context of censorship through the re-negotiation and transformation of its own cultural origins.

In the eighteenth century, art competitions belonged to the new institutional conditions of art appreciation, which found their principal embodiment in the *Académies* and *salons* displaying works of those who, originally seen as craftsmen, were increasingly being considered as artists.[20] In such a context, together with a new understanding of the notion of art, there emerged two other social and cultural phenomena which have characterised the history of art from the Enlightenment onwards, namely the notions of 'public' and the figure of the 'critic'.

Crucially, as — against rational investigation, against discursive and conceptual thought — the work of art was increasingly associated with a process of awareness based on intuitive knowledge, art and criticism became increasingly separated into distinct cultural embodiments.[21] As noted by Carole Talon-Hugon, such a perspective rests on the incompatibility of art and criticism and while the latter focuses on the conditions of knowledge, it is the former which is understood to embody the fundamentals of being.[22] Additionally:

> Les nouvelles conditions institutionnelles de l'art [...], jointes à la nouvelle vision hédoniste de l'art (si le but est de plaire, 'tous les hommes doivent être en position de donner leur propre suffrage quand il s'agit de décider si les poèmes ou les tableaux font l'effet qu'ils doivent faire' écrit l'abbé Du Bos dans ses *Réfléxions critiques sur la poésie et la peinture*), contribuent à l'émergence de la notion neuve de public.[23]

> [The new institutional conditions of art [...], added to the new hedonistic vision of art (if the point of art is to please, 'all should be in the position of expressing their choice when the time comes to decide if poems or paintings have the intended effect' writes the abbot Du Bos in his *Critical Reflections on Poetry and Paintings*), contribute to the birth of a new notion: the public.]

Thus public and critics were both faced with the exposed, manifested, work of art and challenged to interact with the aesthetic object in a new perspective, where the notion of taste came to dominate the cultural discourse.

In the context of literary competitions, such as they appear to function in the Francoist period, such a triad — critic, public, art object — is undermined through the exclusion of the 'critic' figure from the cultural dimension. Indeed, if, 'a su manera, un jurado hace crítica y dirige el gusto del público lector'[24] [in its own way, a jury makes criticism and influences the taste of the general reader], it is the notion of 'público' which ought to be understood as providing the basis for the social function of the literary competition under Francoist rule.[25]

In Pedro de Lorenzo's article *La creación como patriotismo* [Creation as Patriotism] published on 14 February 1943 in *Arriba*, the break between art and criticism is read in the light of a patriotic celebration of the creation of essence in opposition to the nihilism which is understood to characterise the critical endeavour:

> Crear es un deber patriótico, urgido ahora por la especial idiosincrasia del momento español; crear equivale a construir, cosa que no sempre se ha hecho si se toma como instrumento la crítica, operación más vocada al pesimismo y a la esterilidad.[26]

> [The act of creation is a patriotic duty, rendered more urgent today by the specific nature of the current Spanish situation; to create means to build, and this is not what happens when critical tools are used, criticism being an operation turned towards pessimism and sterility.]

The literary competition thus presents to the wider audience a winner in line with the above-mentioned 'patriotic duty'. Yet as the thematic and stylistic content of the winning novels appears to challenge Francoist ideology, the critical act, apparently missing from the judgment process, emerges as actually leading the choices of the literary institutions and as being turned against the very *régime* which supports the functioning of the institution itself. Aesthetic criticism becomes ideological and political criticism and the social action inherent in the process of categorisation is revealed as the opposite of the social action expected from the institution.

The Political Function of Realism

The paradoxical position of literary competitions in the context of Francoist Spain emerges, in the first instance, when considering the number of *realist* novels which found widespread approval and cultural acknowledgement within the context of literary competitions.

Indeed, according to Geneviève Champeau, not only was the objective recalling of facts and details aimed at undermining the barrier posited by censure and at bypassing the rigid controls imposed by the regime on cultural production, but realism was also essentially developed in a context of political protest and of attempted resistance against the *mythologising* and *fictionalising* discourses of Francoism:

> [...] la propagande du régime est perçue comme pure fiction, une machine à illusion, de sorte que, selon une formule de J. Goytisolo, pour les romanciers espagnols de l'époque, la réalité était leur unique évasion. Le réalisme n'apparaît plus alors comme un anachronisme, mais comme une nécessité conjoncturelle...[27]

> [The régime's propaganda is perceived as pure fiction, a machine creating illusions. As a result, according to J. Goytisolo, for the novelists of that time, reality was their only evasion. Realism is therefore not an anachronism but a conjunctural necessity.]

In particular, the critic notes the degree to which the *realist* approach allows for an undermining of the figure of the narrator — embodiment of the *tyrannical* tendencies of Francoist Spanish society — through the hiding of the narratorial figure under the veil of an ostensible narrative neutrality.

Realism appears, however, to slowly make way for a more self-conscious approach to fictional narratives well before the end of the Francoist period. It is precisely through the highlighting of narratorial figures and the foregrounding of the narrative action itself that literary prizes might — the conditional tense being here, as will be further argued, necessary — appear to abandon their support to resisting political discourses and embrace 'une fonction sociale de la literature'[28] [a social function of literature] in line with the utopian Francoist emphasis on art and literature's creative potential.

Forms of realism in winning Spanish narratives

Realism emerges as the dominant aesthetic trend as early as the 1940s. According to José María Martínez Cachero, the realist novel becomes 'la novela-tipo'[29] [the novel-type] and 'es a una tradición de realismo a la que la mayoría de nuestros novelistas actuantes, recién llegados o mayores, parecen adscribirse...'[30] [most of our novelists, whether newcomers or confirmed authors, seem to follow a tradition of realism].

To take the example of Luis Romero's short descriptive passage, taken from his 1963 novel *El cacique* [The Chief], one notices indeed a marked attention to the relation between chosen narrative topics and the events of everyday life, matched by the specific favouring of a realist mode of representation:

> La madre vuelve de la cocina con la plancia que acaba de retirar de la lumbre. Se humedece los dedos con la punta de la lengua y roza la superficie pulimentada y caliente; pequeñas burbujas de saliva se evaporan crepitando.[31]
>
> [The mother returns from the kitchen with the iron she just removed from the fire. She moistens her fingers with the tip of the tongue and touches lightly the polished and hot surface; small bubbles of saliva crackle and evaporate.]

Focusing on the latter and referring to Roland Barthes's realist codes, 'statements which appeal to the background knowledge [of the audience] and which [...] assume that the reader will recognise and assent to them',[32] one notices how the author creates an effect of realism by emphasising spatial movements which can be recognised as *familiar* by his readership 'vuelve de la cocina', by pointing to textures and sensations which enhance a sense of tangible materiality 'humedece', 'caliente', by underlining the detailed immediacy of actions and reactions 'se humedece', 'se evaporan', highlighted by the recurrent use of the present tense.

Luis Romero relies on physical manifestations and spatio-temporal references to plunge his readers into a tangible universe of, at times, even trivial details,[33] carefully setting a layering of apparently *au fait* references to the landscape — 'las casas del pueblo, del color de la tierra, se arraciman alrededor de la iglesia, cuyo campanario, **según dicen**, es el más elevado de los contornos'[34] (my emphasis) [the village houses, coloured like the earth, are clustered around the church, whose steeple, they say, is the highest of the neighbourhood] — and adding the illusion of possessing an insider's knowledge to the detailed sketching of the geographical and territorial layout: '**desde aquí** se ve el llano, los campos, los caminos, el río, las huertas, la fábrica de electricidad, el puente junto al cementerio...' [from here, one sees the plain, the fields, the roads, the river, the orchards, the electrical factory, the bridge next to the cemetery ...], '...**después de la última curva** comienza a divisarse el campanario'[35] (my emphasis) [... after the last curve, one begins to glimpse the bell-tower].

Authors such as José Semprún or Eduardo Caballero Calderón, additionally favour what Roland Barthes defines as realist operators, 'signalling to the viewer that it is the *real* which is being described'.[36] Thus, for instance, the notion of *fictitiousness* is introduced — '... toda la historia de Angustias resultaba como una novela del siglo pasado'[37] [Angustias's whole story seemed to be taken from a novel from the last century] — only to be inherently undermined through the contrast established between the ostensibly *real* narration and the fabricated, untrue nature of intra-diegetic novelistic events. By highlighting the potential connection between the ongoing *récit* and the hypothetical novel to which it could be somehow related or associated — 'si estuvieras en una novella...'[38] [if you were in a novel] — and most importantly, by undermining such a connection, the author strengthens the realistic effect, exorcising the reader's potential viewing of the text in terms of fiction and reinforcing the *veridicity* of narrated events. Jorge Semprún goes as far as pointing to the potential defects and deficiencies of the *true* narration, as opposed to the inner balance and tight structure of the hypothetical fictional story, in order to further reinforce the *realistic* effect of his main narrative. An imperfect text thus becomes authentic, genuine, verified, thanks to the very imperfections which render it difficult to accept by a readership used to balanced schemes of fiction:

> [...] si fueras un personaje novelesco, seguro que ahora te acordarías, mirando a Dolores Ibárruri, de otro encuentros con ella. En las novelas hábilmente construidas, las iluminaciones de la memoria quedan muy bien, resultan muy vistosas. Además, permiten dar al relato una densidad que no consigue con un desarrollo narrativo meramente lineal.[39]

> [... if you were a fictional character, surely you would now remember, looking at Dolores Ibarruri, other, previous meetings with her. In the cleverly constructed novels, the illuminations of memory play a very visible and successful role. They also endow the story with a density not achieved with a purely linear narrative development.]

The carefully constructed tension between the 'mera superchería'[40] [mere trickery] of the concept of fiction and the analysed texts is further enhanced by the emphasis accorded to accurate historical reconstructions. Roland Barthes's 'proliferation of realistic details'[41] can be expanded to encompass precise and accurate references to historical facts and to specific, easily verifiable, dates:[42] 'El local fue clausurado en septiembre de 1950, cuando el gobierno francés prohibió las actividades del partido español en Francia y puso fuera de la ley vuestras organizaciones'[43] [The place was closed in September 1950, when the French government banned the activities of the Spanish party in France and outlawed your organisations]. History is thus seen as retrievable and depictable, in a process in which 'language (narration) serves as an adequate vehicle for conveying the truth about such events'.[44]

Always with regard to the manipulation of the temporal dimension — though situated at the opposite end from the emphasis on historical accuracy we have discussed — one notices an extreme attention to an unthinking, instantaneous, disclosing of the action, which offers the illusion of being somehow contemporary to the act of reading itself. One might perhaps here consider such an effect in terms of *enhanced authenticity* rather than technical *realism*. Its result is nevertheless that of powerfully contributing to the overall *realistic* effect we have evoked. Thus, a direct address to the reader allows for an impression of greater immediacy, as the novelist's audience is directly involved in the unfolding events: 'Ves perfectamente que sólo ha escrito unas pocas líneas, con su letra grande y desgarbada, en la cuartilla que se dispone a leeros'[45] [You can see very well that he has only written a few lines, with his large and awkward script, on the sheet of paper from which he is about to read to you]. Under the eyes of the reader, the present tense favoured by numerous authors emphasises the simultaneity of gestures, decisions and emotions: 'De la calle entra un ruido desacostumbrado; ante la puerta pasa un automóvil pintado de verde. Los vecinos se asoman, y el tío Raposo y el Voluntario también salen a la calle'[46] [An unusual noise enters from the street; a green painted car drives in front of the door. Neighbours look out, and both the Uncle Raposo and Voluntario go out too].

Of the multiple forms in which such a realist trend appears to have embodied itself, the *objectivist* one is perhaps one of the most widely referred to. Specifically supported by the *Nadal* competition, a generation of young authors, strongly influenced by the Sartrean ideal of the committed author,[47] sees literary production as a tool to overcome censorship and communicate to the Spanish audience information about the social, cultural and political reality which the government-influenced press is unwilling and/or unable to express.[48] As famously stated by Juan Goytisolo,

> los novelistas españoles — por el hecho que su público no dispone de medios de información veraces respecto a los problemas con que se enfrenta el país — responden a esta carencia de sus lectores trazando un cuadro lo más justo y equitativo posible de la realidad que contemplan. De este modo, la novela cumple en España una función testimonial que en Francia y los demás paises de Europa corresponde a la prensa, y el futuro historiador de la sociedad española deberá apelar a ella si quiere reconstruir la vida cotidiana del país a través de la espesa cortina de humo y silencio de nuestros diarios.[49]

> [Spanish novelists — because their audience has no real access to accurate and true information on the problems facing the country — address this lack of information by drawing a picture of reality as fair and as unbiased as possible. Thus, in Spain, the novel has a testimonial function, which in France and other European countries belongs to the press, and the future historian of Spanish society must keep this function in mind if he wishes to reconstruct the daily life of the country despite the thick curtain of smoke and silence drawn by our daily newspapers.]

Embodying such a trend stands, perhaps more than any other novel of the period, Rafael Sánchez Ferlosio's 1955 Nadal winner *El Jarama* [The River], a novel which Martínez Cachero defines, not casually, as 'un apreciable documento lingüístico'[50] [a significant linguistic document].

Through the dispassionate observation of a group of friends throughout a day of rest in the countryside, the author displays an approach to the real which rests on the systematic tracing of gestures, expressions, words, movements and actions and on the downplaying of the psychological in favour of the observable external dimension. The position is that of the neutral photographic camera which takes in, with documentary precision, conditions and events and feeds back an a-temporal framing of everyday life.

One notices moreover how the favouring of short, fragmentary sentences, of a scene by scene approach, appears to be strongly influenced — in addition to the Sartrean production — by the *neorealist* cultural (and in particular cinematographic) wave arriving from Italy to Spain in the early 1950s, a trend culminating in the series of *neorealist* films shown at the Institute of Italian Culture of Madrid in 1951. Indeed, according to Randolph D. Pope, the effect was immediate on both film directors and literary writers alike: many saw or heard about Antonioni's 'Chronicle of Love' (1950), De Sica's 'Bicycle Thief' (1948) and 'Miracle in Milan' (1951), and Rossellini's 'Open City' (1945) and 'Paisà' (1946).[51]

In considering the cinematographic and cultural influence of Italian neo-realism, one also notices how Spanish novels of the period express a tendency towards what could perhaps be defined as *neo-naturalism*, a trend based on stylistic and thematic references to naturalist nineteenth-century novels which had similarly appeared, for instance, in the early Viscontian *La Terra Trema* [The Earth Trembles].

Luchino Visconti's reproduction of Giuseppe Verga's *I Malavoglia* in *La Terra Trema* (1948) — in particular, a scene on the beach in which the fishermen and their women watch the stormy sea as it engulfs a sinking ship — is directly echoed in Ramiro Pinilla's 1960 *Las Ciegas Hormigas* [The Blind Ants]:

> Estaba junto al padre, mirando el barco de cinco mil toneladas que sabíamos se hundiría irremediablmente. [...] Parecía como si todas las tormentas anteriores, desde que el mar fue creado, no consisterón más que en ensayos previos para ofrecernos ahora aquella apoteosis de ruido, poder y espuma.[52]

> [He stood by his father, looking at the five thousand ton boat which we knew was irremediably doomed to sinking. [...] It seemed as if all previous storms, since the sea was created, were no more than rehearsals aimed at offering us, now, that apotheosis of noise, power and foam.]

Not casually does, in this perspective, Martínez Cachero define Ferlosio's novel in terms of 'casi un frío inventario naturalista'[53] [almost a cold naturalist inventory]. The *naturalist* trend of Ramiro Pinilla's novel is further enhanced by the sustained *animalisation* of the characters, a process strongly emphasised from the initial title onwards, in the parallel established between the small group of protagonists — Sabas, Ismael, Cosme, Bruno, Nerea, Fermín, Josefa, Abuela, Pedro, Berta — and the insect world of ants.

The authorial emphasis on animalisation, repeatedly underlined, as in the episode which associates Josefa with a cow successfully bought by her husband Sabas,[54] is matched by a strong emphasis on topics such as the inevitability of destiny, doomed occurrences and fatal successions of accidents, which often typify, at the thematic level, traditional nineteenth-century naturalistic novels.[55] Giuseppe Verga's *Provvidenza* [Providence] is here substituted by Ramiro Pinilla's characters' ambiguous reluctance/incapacity/impossibility of altering the course of events. The desperate gathering of the coal stolen from the sinking ship is to be pursued regardless of the tragedies befalling the family, the hostility of the village, the threat of illness, imprisonment, social isolation and death.[56]

Again, neo-naturalist echoes can be traced in the thematic focus of novels which have been defined as being expressive of a social realist perspective. Armando López Salinas's *La Mina* [The Mine], finalist in the 1959 Nadal competition, together with novels such as *Central Eléctrica* (1958) [The Electric Power Plant] by Jésus López Pacheco, *La Piqueta* (1959) [The Axe] by Antonio Ferres or *La Zanza* (1961) [The Lance] by Alfonso Grosso[57] were intended to oppose the allegedly escapist literature of the preceding decades.[58]

However, the acknowledgement of the critical potential of the novels mentioned has often entailed a contrasting of the *realist* production, not only with the novels which precede it, but also with the increasingly *non-realist* novels which allegedly follow it. Thus, while pointing to the traditional realism of works such as *Nada* (1945) by Carmen Laforet, *La Sombra del Ciprés es Alargada* [The Shadow of the Cypress is Extended] (1948) by Miguel Delibes, *Las Últimas Horas* [The Last Hours] (1950) by José Súarez Carreño, *La Colmena* (1951) [The Beehive] by Camilo José Cela, *El Furor y la Sangre* (1954) [The Blood and the Fury] by Ignacio Aldecoa, *Los Bravos* (1954) [The Brave] by Jesús Fernández Santos or *El Jarama* [The River] (1956) by Juan García Hortelano,[59] critics have often underlined the presence of a subsequent shift towards self-consciousness, metafiction and an openly postmodern[60] understanding of the relation between the text and the world.

According to such an approach, 'sometimes during the 1960s, the mirror breaks for Spanish narrative'.[61] Thus, works such as Luis Martín Santos's *Tiempo de Silencio* (1962) [The Time of Silence], Juan Goytisolo's *Señas de Identitad* (1966) [Identity Signs], Miguel Delibes's *Cinco Horas con Mario* (1966) [Five Hours with Mario], José María Guelbenzu's *El Mercurio* (1968), Camilo José Cela's *Vísperas, Festividad y Octava de San Camilo del año 1936 en Madrid*, (1969) [Vespers, Feast and Octave of St. Camillus in the year 1936 in Madrid] 'wreak havoc on the reality, idea and ideal of realism'.[62]

The text becomes visible

The challenge to realism emerges, in the first instance, through the undermining of the transparency and neutrality of the text. It becomes *visible as* an object in itself and ceases to be a see-through medium allegedly allowing for the unmediated apprehension of the external dimension. The sheer materiality of the text as artefact is repeatedly underlined through its being presented as an artificially constructed medium of communication, and, in particular, as one amongst many possible verbal expressions.

Thus one notices how traditional novelistic fiction is interrupted by a series of alternative dramatic modes of expression — cinematographic montage or theatrical scenes — which emphasise at once the *fictitious* nature of the written text and the dynamic articulation of fictitious events by the dramatised authorial/narratorial figure. For instance, Jorge Semprún testifies to his own activity as a dramatist, inserting the theme of textual construction within a first layer of fictional narrative:

> Al calor de ese entusiasmo escribí una pieza dramática, durante los meses siguientes. Una obra de teatro en tres actos, que se titulaba 'Soledad', y que escribí en francés, a pesar de lo que el título pueda hacer suponer.[63]

> [In the heat of that enthusiasm I wrote a dramatic piece, over the following months. A play in three acts, which was titled 'Soledad' and which I wrote in French, despite what the title can reasonably lead us to expect.]

Eduardo Caballero Caldéron goes one step further in inserting a full segment of theatrical drama written by his auto-diegetic narrator within the matrix narrative:

> Primer cuadro: Rincón de café en la plaza de Saint-Germain des Prés. Un camarero viejo entra por el foro, cuya puerta se supone comunica con el restaurante. Trae en la mano una bandeja con unas copas, una botella de Ricard, una botella de agua Perrier.[64]

> [First frame: coffee at the corner of the *Place Saint-Germain des Prés*. An old waiter goes through a door which supposedly leads to the restaurant. He brings in a tray with glasses, a bottle of Ricard, a bottle of Perrier water.]

Such a process is repeatedly reproduced as, for instance, he projects a cinematographic sequence within the novel:

> Secuencia: Un automóvil avanza lentamente por una carretera helada y resbalosa.
> Secuencia: Paisaje visto desde el interior del automóvil.
> Secuencia: Ruedas del automóvil patinando en una colcha de nieve[65]

> [Sequence: a car moves slowly down an icy and slippery road.
> Sequence: landscape seen from the inside of the car.
> Sequence: sliding car wheels on a quilt of snow]

and which is echoed by the insertion of the 'theatre' model sequence in *Nada*:

> GLORIA — ¿Dice eso Román?
> ABUELA — Sí; la otra noche, cuando yo buscaba mis tijeras... era ya muy tarde y todos estabais durmiendo, se abrió la puerta despacio y apareció Román. Venía a darme un beso [...]
> GLORIA — Román antes me quería mucho. Y esto es un secreto grande, Andrea, pero estuvo enamorado de mí.[66]

> [GLORIA — Is that what Roman says?
> GRANDMA — Yes; the other night when I was looking for my scissors... it was very late and you were all sleeping, the door slowly opened and Roman appeared. He came to kiss me [...]

GLORIA — Roman used to like me very much. And this is a big secret, Andrea, but he was in love with me.]

Ramón J. Sender's protagonist's exclamation — 'Al Diablo la verosimilitud. Todo es un juego. Lo que pasa es que llevamos milenios tratando de descubrir las leyes de ese juego sin conseguirlo. Y los poetas son los llamados a tacerlo'[67] [To hell with verisimilitude. Everything is a game. What happens is that, for the past thousands of years, we have tried to discover the laws of the game, but failed. And the poets are sworn to silence] — testifies to the dramatised perception of the *artistic* act as an instance of the *artificial*.

The playful dimension of such a dramatisation emerges rarely yet effectively as expressed in the stylistic alternation of *real* chapters of the novel and fake *internal chapters* of the fictitious novel written by the protagonists in *La Muchacha de las Bragas de Oro* [Golden Girl]. Indeed, from chapter twelve onwards, they increasingly merge to fuse in a unique narrative text. Thus chapter 12 becomes chapter XXIII in a process where both dimensions are collapsed onto a unique ontological level.[68]

The playfulness we have evoked similarly emerges in the much earlier *El Buen Salvaje* as the role — both social and literary — of the author/ narrator is highlighted by the *mise en abîme* in which the auto-diegetic narrator presents itself as incarnating an hetero-diegetic narrator who hopes to see his *authorial* status socially recognised in the context of a literary competition: 'Para hacer lo mismo que los ganadores de premios literarios de París, me he puesto a escribir sobre la mesa del bistrot, ante un vaso de cerveza que huele a agrio y pierde la espuma rápidamente'[69] [To do the same as the winners of literary prizes in Paris, I started writing at the *bistro* table before a glass of beer that smells sour and quickly loses its foam].

The narrator becomes visible

With regard to the specific issue of narratorial figures, Jorge Semprún's interrogation '¿no se había decidido eliminar de una vez a Narrador y Personaje, devolvendo el lenguaje a su exacta función de desvelamiento de las cosas entorno?'[70] [Had it not been decided to eliminate both the Character and the Narrator for good, giving back language to its exact function of unveiling the context?] gains an ironical dimension if considered in the light of the degree to which *author* figure and *narrator* figure merge, in a process in which the act of narration is not only deprived of its neutrality but projected at the very heart of the narrative process itself.

The highlighting of the authorial role displayed in the notes to the sixth edition of *El Jarama* [The River] is but one of multiple instances of meta-narrative reflection. In the specific example, the accent is set on the difficulty of establishing the notion of *authorship*, in a context in which words belonging to one author are mistakenly attributed to another.[71]

In Jorge Semprún's *Autobiografía de Federico Sánchez*, the link is similarly established between a reflection on authorship and a reflection on narration as the *real* author — Semprún — narrating *his* own life, gives voice to a complex system of second-person address by textually interacting with his alter ego, Federico Sánchez, the name he was given while acting in secret in the context of the Communist Party.

Thus external author, overt internal narrator and narratee are but one and the same person, dramatised under a series of different names.

The shift from author to narrator reaches full circle in *El Buen Salvaje* as the protagonist and narrator is presented and dramatised *as* an author:

> La idea que se me había perdido y que acabo de encontrar es que yo construiré mi novela con materiales puramente imaginarios, pues la imaginación es mucho más fuerte y convincente que la realidad: la prefigura, la condiciona, la determina, la predispone y la impone como una necesidad interior.[72]

> [The idea that I had lost and just found again is that I will build my novel with purely imaginary materials, because the imagination is much stronger and more convincing than reality: it foreshadows reality, conditions reality, determines reality, prepares it and imposes it as an inner need.]

In many of the winning novels, first person narration[73] emphasises and dramatises the central thematic function of the authorial figure by reinforcing the effect of a fusion between author and narrator: 'Yo nací en Ávila, la vieja ciudad de las murallas, y creo que el silencio y el recogimiento casi místico de esta ciudad se me metieron el alma nada más nacer'[74] [I was born in Avila, the old enclosed city, and I think the silence and the almost mystical concentration of this city entered my soul at birth].

Moreover, not only do the novels analysed display a presence of auto-diegetic, internally focalised, narrators but they also dramatise at the thematic level the figure of the narrator by a procedure of *mise en abîme* in which narratorial/authorial figures proliferate:

> Pero lo que más nos atraía a nosotros de aquel enjambre inquieto, aureolado de una polvareda espesa y maloliente, eran los narradores de crímenes. De entre todos, la Bruna disfrutaba de nuestras preferencias, ya que, al interés avasallador de sus relatos unía el mérito de recitarlos cantando y acompañada por las notas agrias y desafinadas de la guitarra de su marido ciego.[75]

> [But what attracted us most about that restless swarm, haloed by thick, foul-smelling dust, were the narrators of crimes. Of them all, the Bruna was our favourite, since she added to the overwhelming interest of her stories the merit of reciting them with a song, accompanied by the sour and off-key notes of her blind husband's guitar.]

A series of minor *narrating* characters emerges from the pages of the winning narratives, characters whose mysterious nature enhances all the more the purely functional role played as thematic underlining of the central role of the narrative concept itself: 'Un hombre tatuado y rubicondo que escupía tabaco y bebía orujo, que le habló de una islas maravillosas y lejanas, cuyos mares circundantes guardaban fortunas en las entrañas'[76] [A ruddy, tattooed man, spitting snuff and drinking pomace brandy, who spoke of wonderful and distant islands, surrounded by seas hiding fortunes in their depths].

As a result, one notices how echoes of narrating figures are projected on one another as the narrating process itself is framed in a continuous *mise en abîme* in which characters openly reflect on the unstable status of their own words — 'Si todo eso constituye una historia, probablemente empezó a mediados de junio de 1976, una noche que Mariana Monteys escribió a una amiga que estudiaba en Londres'[77] [If all this makes up a story, it probably began in mid-June 1976, one night when Mariana Monteys wrote to a friend studying in London] — and on the uncertainty of their own affirmations:

> Se le atribuía a la Bruna una fecundidad asombrosa. Había quien afirmaba que la Bruna había llenado de hijos las cunetas de todas la carreteras de España. Nunca le preocupaba el momento. Traía el hijo por sus propios medios allí donde la sorprendía el trance. La criatura, con el cordón umbilical colgando, era adoptada sempre en el pueblo más próximo al lugar del parto. De esta sencilla manera la Bruna no había perdido aún su libertad, y su voz cascada podía seguir soñando por los ámbitos del mundo entero.[78]

> [The Bruna was credited with amazing fertility. There were those who claimed that Bruna had filled the ditches of all the roads in Spain with children. She never worried about the time of delivery. She gave birth on her own wherever labour surprised her. The creature, with the umbilical cord still hanging, was always adopted in the village nearest to the place of delivery. With this simple method, the Bruna had not yet lost her freedom, and her cracked voice could keep sustaining dreams all over the world.]

Thus they play with suspense and the audience's expectations — both intra-diegetic and extra-diegetic — in a process which echoes the *A Thousand and One Nights* style of narration, with its deferred fragments and interrupted narrative flow:

> 'Bien ¿Qué ora tenemos, sobrina?'
> 'Temprano. ¿Qué pasó luego?'
> 'Otro día te lo cuento. Puedo adelantarte que la enfermedad de tu tío no era esta vez una gripe, a las que siempre fue propensa. Y fin de capítulo. Necesito poner en orden los recuerdos...'[79]

> ['Well, what time is it, niece?'
> 'Early. What happened then?'
> 'I'll tell you another day. I can anticipate that, this time, your uncle's illness was not a flu, to which he was always prone. End of the chapter. I need to sort out the memories ...']

The act of creating narrations, of producing fiction, is therefore projected at the heart of the thematic concern of the novels in a process in which 'historias completas, apenas iniciadas e hinchadas ya como una vieja madera a la intemperie [...] historias demasiados oscuras'[80] [complete stories, histories just started yet already swollen like an old weathered piece of wood, stories which are too dark] are foregrounded and emphasised.

The process of storytelling controls the narrative scene so powerfully that, not only do the intra-diegetic narrators focus on past or current happenings, but they also invest the future course of events by anticipating actions and reactions, by projecting the story-telling process into a future dimension and by expanding the temporal frame to encompass quasi-prophetic control of the whole temporal spectrum: '[...] por esta puerta entrará algún día el niño como un torbellino a la vuelta de la escuela. Y entrará Jane también, cargada de paquetes, al regresar de sus compras'[81] [... some day, like a whirlwind, after school, the child will come in through the door. And Jane will also come in, loaded with packages, returning from shopping].

The Political Function of Metafiction

The emerging of meta-fictional thematic and stylistic instances posits, however, the notion of the social stance adopted by the literary works chosen in the context of Spanish literary competitions, not to mention that of the self-same literary competitions choosing the works evoked.

In her analysis of realism, Geneviève Champeau makes a case for the slow and gradual transformation of the so-called *realist* mode, evolving from what she defines as the *social realism* of the early years, to an intermediate step in which self-consciousness gains an increasingly central role in the structure of narration,[82] to a final moment in which works by Rafael Sánchez Ferlosio, Juan García Hortelano, Juan Goytisolo, Camilo Josè Cela and others display and highlight the impossibility of an absolute *reality* or truth: 'aux systèmes clos qui prétendent embrasser le réel se substituent des structures ouvertes et centrifuges. [...] L'accent est constamment mis sur un procès...'[83] [open and centrifugal structures replace the closed systems that claim to embrace the real [...] The emphasis is continually placed on an ongoing process ...].

In this perspective, in Spanish narrative an early attempt at undermining the ideological and political structures carried out through thematic choices is subsequently substituted by an attempt to transfer the intellectual *struggle* against preconceived forms and models on a stylistic plane: 'ce sont alors les pratiques textuelles qui constituent en elles-mêmes la proposition alternative faite au lecteur'[84] [it is then the textual practices which constitute in themselves the alternative proposal made to the reader].

However, such an evolution is simultaneously presented in terms of the disillusionment it displays with the possibility of having literature playing a central social function.[85] In particular, with the decline of the realist stance, there allegedly occurs a decline in the resistance to governmental rhetoric. José Semprun's 1977 *Autobiografía de Federico Sánchez*, for instance, goes as far as undermining the role of the committed intellectual[86] in a context in which the ideological apparatus of the left is displayed as being possessed of the same *mythologising* and *unrealistic* features of the right-wing *régime* ideology allegedly under accusation: 'No pienso que sea fácil encontrar en los escritos de los dirigentes políticos que se proclaman marxistas, un texto tan irreal o surreal como éste, tan enchido de deseo irrealizable y de frustrada ensoñación'[87] [I do not think it is easy to find, in the writings of the political leaders who proclaim themselves to be Marxists, a text as unreal or surreal as this one, so filled with frustrated desire and unattainable dreams].

My contention is, though, that the dramatisation of the poetics of narration displayed in winning narratives of the late 1950s to the 1970s displays a constant challenging dimension — be it with regard to Francoist leadership or to anti-Francoist ideological positions — which, in contrast to Champeau's disillusionment argument, is not undermined.

Thematically and stylistically, not only is the figure of the narrator foregrounded, but the limits of the credibility of any narrative are underlined, as displayed through the highlighting of the arbitrariness which the narrative form intrinsically implies. As a result, one notices a drive toward the problematisation of instances of representation and a related highlighting of the degree to which the undermining of coherent dialogic exchange radically challenges the ideas of cognitive community and communal identity.

In this perspective, the aesthetic choices enacted by literary competitions appear to wholly oppose contemporary political discourses highlighting the identity-shaping value of cultural — understood as *artificial, non-natural* — production and, far from ensuring the ontological stabilisation of the communal cognitive construct, literary competitions appear to run counter to the very cultural tendencies from which they, as social institutions, allegedly have their origin.

Dissolving the real

Actually, the distinction between initial realism and later meta-fiction might be less clear than traditionally argued. Indeed, even within allegedly realist narratives, one notices an emerging of the thematic and stylistic elements which dominate the later Francoist period.

For instance, Geneviève Champeau argues that *resisting realist* narratives are to be considered as challenges to the dominance of Francoist rhetoric. Yet in those same *realist* texts, one notices the disconnection between *appearance* and *reality* — indeed, the deconstruction of the notion of the *real* through the underlining of the tenuousness and shiftiness of *appearance*. The *real*, far from being favoured, is actually displayed as a dissolving and shifting instance, often related to individual perception.

As the potential signification of objects for an observer is foregrounded, they are invested with a signifying potential which highlights their inherently semiotic nature and downplays their *concrete* and tangible dimension. In *Pequeño Teatro* [Little Theatre], Kepa's much desired pearl comes thus to express a shift in symbolism from a representation of wealth, success and seemingly unobtainable well-being, to the expression of personal loneliness, failure and the bitterness of lost hopes and dreams:

> Un día, al fin, cuando ya era el gran Kepa alto y grueso, el majestuoso y temido Kepa, se permitió la banalidad de comprarse una perla, en homenaje. Como un símbolo, se juró llevarla sempre prendila en su corbata. Una vez en su poder, al esaminarla de cerca, decubrió que no era del todo esférica, ni del todo blanca, ni del todo brillante. Y le pareció aún menos valiosa de lo que había imaginado.[88]
>
> [One day, at last, when he had become the great Kepa, Kepa the tall, heavy, the imposing and feared Kepa, he allowed himself the banality of buying a pearl, as a tribute. Like a symbol, he vowed always to carry it pinned on his tie. When

it was in his power, upon examining the pearl closely, he discovered that it was not quite spherical, or entirely white or wholly shining. And it seemed even less valuable than he had imagined.]

What is striking in such an example is the underlining of the incoherence of personal representations, of the shifting, unstable nature of the *real* and of personal understanding and belief of what is, or will become, *true*. As with Kepa's pearl, the *real* is mingled with the *imagined* sphere in a process which will recur throughout the period. From utter excitement to abject despair, the characters of the novel do not seem ever to gain a firm grasp on either *reality*, which is forever displaced and dislocated, or on their dreams and ambitions. In *Pequeño Teatro* [Little Theatre], as in other texts of the period, characters are repeatedly presented as uncertainly hovering between *real* and *unreal*, in a process which clouds actions and events in a shifting mist of uncertainty and ambiguity.

True, in some cases, dreams — although omnipresent and widespread — can still be disconnected from reality. It happens, for instance, in the case of 'señora Gurrea', who 'soña',[89] [dreams] of surprising, with the strength of her imagination, the young Miguel. It also happens in the case of Miguel Delibes's evoking of tortured dreams[90] and twisted, deformed visions or in the case of the protagonist of the early *La Noria*, who re-lives the events which have shaken the foundations of her family, in particular the suspected relationship between Gloria and her brother-in-law, Román, in her dreams:

> Aquella noche tuvo un sueño clarísimo en que se repetía una vieja y obsesionante imagen: Gloria, apoyada en el hombro de Juan, lloraba... Poco a poco, Juan sufrió curiosas transformaciones. Le vi enorme y oscuro con la fisonomía enigmática del dios Xochipilli. La cara pálida de Gloria empezó a animarse y a revivir; Xochipilli sonreía también. Bruscamente su sonrisa me fue conocida: era la blanca y un poco salvaje sonrisa de Román.[91]
>
> [That night, I had a very clear dream in which an old, haunting vision presented itself again: Gloria, leaning on Juan's shoulder, was crying... Slowly, Juan underwent some curious transformations. He appeared as huge and dark with the enigmatic face of the god Xochipilli. Gloria's pale face became animated and seemed to come to life; Xochipilli too was smiling. Suddenly I recognised his smile: it was Roman's white and somewhat wild smile.]

One notices, however, the characters' often reiterated difficulty in distinguishing the texture of dreams from that of the external world: 'Entre sueños, algunas noches me parecía que el jeroglífico de mi inquietud se trasladaba al negro tablero y allí se combinaban las letras y los números de un enredo semimatemático preñado de incógnitas'[92] [In between dreams, some nights, it seemed that the hieroglyph of my concern was projected onto the blackboard and, there, letters and numbers were combined in a semi-mathematical tangle, fraught with unknown factors]. Similarly, Ana María Matute's Señorita Mirentxu, unable to distinguish the world of fantasy from that of the *real*, openly admits her confusion. In fact, in a fragment which significantly highlights a strong concern with the lexical field of sight, she displays a marked hesitation in the process of defining and framing a face by which she was struck.

Interestingly, such evocations of the world of dreams, although frequently repeated, tend to be a minority if compared to instances in which an ontological confusion of the spheres of the *real* and the *unreal* becomes wholly predominant. The simple-minded Illé is not the only character to succumb to such an ambiguity, as he sees fantastic beings emerging from the stormy waves.[93] Juan Marsé's protagonist also sees his life as 'espectral' [spectral], characterised by 'la irrealidad del intorno y la provisionalidad de las cosas'[94] [the unreality of the environment and the provisional nature of things]. Similarly, Josep María Gironella's main character's 'extraña[s] alucinación[es]'[95] [strange hallucinations] are expanded to encompass — during a night-time stroll taken by the young protagonists — the whole of a *fantastic*, moonlight landscape of mysterious lights and seductive shadows in which what was previously considered 'real' is unveiled as 'mentiras' [lies]:

> ... esta visita se nos antojaba como un puente que nos llevaba de la cumbre de la fantasía a la de la realidad, en la cual podíamos palpar y sobar a nuestro gusto todas las estremecedoras mentiras que habíamos saboreado anteriormente en letras de molde.[96]
>
> [... This visit seemed to be like a bridge that took us from the top of the fantasy to the heights of reality. From the latter, we could touch and feel to our liking all the shocking lies that we had previously tasted in print.]

As personal perceptions become predominant in the process of assessment and understanding of the relationship between *internal* and *external* dimensions, one notices a strong link with Merleau-Ponty's analysis of the thin limits underscoring the relationship between the *real* and the *perceived*, especially when *real* and *unreal* representations are characterised by a similar methodological rigour, strength of construction and apparent solidity of existence:

> If the reality of my perception were based solely on the intrinsic coherence of 'representations', it ought to be forever hesitant and, being wrapped up in my conjectures on probabilities, I ought to be ceaselessly taking apart misleading syntheses, and reinstating in reality stray phenomena which I had excluded in the first place.[97]

Such hesitancy is resolved in a confusion and fusion of both dimensions in a process which recalls Wittgenstein's observation of how 'it is obvious that an imagined world, however different it may be from the real one, must have something — a form — in common with it'.[98] It is precisely the indistinguishability of the *form* of the real from the form of the unreal which emerges in these novels.

Such a process reaches its paroxysm as the *real* and the *imagined* (which is in fact, as we will consider further on, the *narrated*) merge in a process in which ontological levels can no longer be distinguished or successfully disconnected. Thus Juan Marsé's *La Muchacha de las Bragas de Oro* [Golden Girl] displays a confusion of ontological levels as the dog invented by the small child strolling on the beach, whose existence, whose 'maravillosa historia' [marvellous history] is significantly narrated by Forest to his niece, penetrates the *real* dimension in the novel by appearing *really* on the beach with the young child in a process which undermines 'las junturas de lo real y lo soñado, el cosido del tiempo y del espacio'⁹⁹ [the seams of the real and the dreamed, the patterns of time and space].

Juan Marsé repeatedly highlights how the *imagined* sphere penetrates into the *real* one through the appearance of physical, tangible, paradoxically undeniable objects 'una caja de pañuelos [...] y en su interior el anochecido volumen de poemas, la navaja y el espejito; objetos que habían envejecido visiblemente juntos...'¹⁰⁰ [a box of tissues [...] and inside it, the benighted volume of poems, the knife and mirror; objects that had clearly aged together].

Significantly, Wittgenstein similarly insists on the mediating function of the notion of *object* and on the capacity of *objects* of being situated on the borderline, on giving tangibility to the turning point, the frontier between the two ontological dimensions we have evoked: 'It follows from this [...] that all possible or conceivable worlds must consist of precisely the same objects that this actual world of ours consists of'.¹⁰¹

The process reaches a culminating point as the characters appear to become irrevocably detached from the dimension of the *real*, as they come to doubt the existence of *life* itself beyond the sphere of what they can perceive, the *internal* sphere in which they appear to be irrevocably enclosed: 'Pero sí que estoy confusa. ¿Será verdad que existe otra vida exterior con la que ne yo ni Elemyr tenemos ya contacto y en la que cuentan todavía las cicatrices y los impactos?'¹⁰² [Indeed, I am confused. Is it really true that there is an outer life with whom neither I nor Elemyr have contact and where, nevetherless, scars and hits still count?]. Similarly, as early as in his 1947 novel, Miguel Delibes displays his characters' incapacity of distinguishing between suggestions, imaginations, illusions and reality as they wonder

> ... si lo que veían diariamente nuestros ojos no sería más que una sugestión creada en torno de algo inesistente; si la vitalidad de los demás sentidos no sería igualmente una mera y simple ilusión; si el mundo, en fin, carecería un carácter objetivo, real, verdadero, para pasar a ser algo ficticio, iluminado solamente por el carácter que individualmente cada humano queríamos attribuirle.¹⁰³

> [... if what our eyes saw every day was no more than a suggestion built around something which did not exist; if the vitality of the senses were nothing more than a pure and simple illusion; if the world, in short, had no real, objective nature and had become a fiction, illuminated only by the character that every human individual wanted to give it.]

Narration as lying

Delibes's concern with perception and vision is particularly significant in that it appears to be a constant in the narratives of the period. The lexical field of vision seems, in particular, to match a strong thematic emphasis on narration as a process of re-construction/re-creation of events. One example is given in the following passage, when Señorita Mirentxu's hypotheses add themselves to one another to form an increasingly complex narration of events which may or may not have occurred:

No puedo saber cúando vi yo este rostro. No sé si lo soñé, de niña. O si lo vi, tal vez, una tarde, en el parque, cuando llegó el hombre del pequeño 'guignol', con su campanella y su voz cascada. No sé si lo vi, un atardecer, al pasear junto a la ría, cuando aquella tribu de gitanos acampó con sus carros bajo el puente. No sé si lo vi en el mascarón de un velero, o si lo soñé, o si no lo vi nunca y era lo que temía ver surgir de los rincones obscuros.[104]

[I cannot know when I saw this face. I do not know if I dreamt about it as a child. Or if, perhaps, I saw him one afternoon in the park, when the puppet-master, with his bell and his cracked voice, came. I do not know if I saw him at sunset one day, when strolling along the river, when that tribe of Gypsies camped with their wagons under the bridge. I do not know if I saw him in the figurehead of a sailboat, or if I dreamt about him, or if I never saw him and he was what I was afraid of seeing emerging from dark corners.]

The *real*, the *viewed/perceived* and the *narrated* appear to be linked through an explicit relation, a relation which moreover seems to be marked by a continuity between early works and later narrations.

Indeed, let us consider once more Roland Barthes's use of *realist operators* which we have previously mentioned. We have discussed the degree to which the articulation of the spatial dimension relies on the construction of a geographical sphere in which concepts of proximity and relative distance aim to provoke in the audience a sense of empathy with the physical position of the characters in the novel. One notices, however, that such a location of objects within the scenes entails a carefully constructed frame in which the question of the position of the viewer/s and the use of the lexical field of vision or observation are predominant: 'mirando', 'vi a Sabas', etc.

The focus appears to be not so much on the landscape but on the act of vision, of perception, of presentation of the scene. With the unfolding action, the *realist* opening of *El Cacique* [The Chief], with Marcelino's apparently detached observation of the surrounding landscape, is almost immediately challenged at the thematic level, as Doctor Gabriel's schemes aimed at changing the appearance of the dead man's bedroom — in an attempt to actually transform the potential viewers' understanding of the events which took place at the deathbed — are highlighted. The mediating presence of the viewer and his/her potential intervention on the link between spatial organisation and temporal re-construction (re-fashioning) of events is thus underlined in a process which actually entails the dramatisation of the notion of *reality,* understood as something expressed and perceived through the filter of subjective description:

He pedido a la ciudad algunos específicos nuevos que no tienen en la botica y un aparato de inyección de suero artificial. Lo llevaré todo a la Casa y destaparé los frascos como se le hubiesen administrado los medicamentos. Y el aparato también quedará allí. Toda la farmacia la he retirado al tocador que está junto a la alcova, y he dado orden de que la conserven tal como la he dejado por si se le ocurriera presentarse al Barbuto.[105]

[I have asked in the city for some new medicines that they do not have in the pharmacy, together with a device for the injection of artificial serum. I'll take it all up to the House and will uncork the bottles as if the drugs had been given. And the device will also remain there. I have taken all the drugs away from the vanity table, near the bedroom, and I have given orders that the medicines be conserved exactly the way I left them, in case the Barbuto happened to come.]

As a result, what is *true* and what is *false* often entirely depends on the very personal vision of each character in a context in which conversation and dialogic exchange are shown as being ironically thwarted and doomed to failure:

> Tu obra parece tener dos vertientes muy diferenciadas. De un lado, la crónica de la posguerra. Es la que te dió prestigio y dinero pero a mí no me gusta, está llena de lomas triunfalistas, da basura ideológica y de embustes [...] En cambio, tus libros de relatos y tu novelas [...] me encantan. Es extraño: cuando pretendes ser testimonial no resultas verosímil, no te creo, y cuando inventas descaradamente, digamos cuando mientes sin red, consigues reflejar la verdad.[106]

> [Your work seems to have two very different aspects. On the one hand, the chronicle of the war. It's the one that gave you prestige and money but I do not like it. It is full of triumphant tones, ideological garbage and lies [...] On the other hand, I love your stories and your novels [...]. It's strange: when you pretend to be a witness you do not appear to be credible, I do not believe you. When you invent shamelessly, let us say, when you lie without a net, you succeed in reflecting the truth.]

At the stylistic level, such a thematic focus is matched by a sophisticated manipulation of focalisation and complex handling of the characters' point of view. An interesting example of a fragment oscillating between those two tendencies of the fictional process is provided by Juan Marsé's description of Forest's past through the use of the lexical field of vision. The narration of a past characteristic becomes the *visual* sketching of a stereotyped cultural model — the narrated '*invenciones*' [inventions] — accusingly unveiled by his niece: 'Veo un joven introvertido y algo fúnebre, con un volumen de Garcilaso enternamente pegado al sobaco, una camisa blanca abierta a lo Byron y una colera añeja, romántica'[107] [I see a young man, introverted and somewhat funereal, with a volume of Garcilaso eternally attached to the armpit, an open white shirt in the Byronic style and a Romantic, old-style mood]. Such a visual emphasis is similarly displayed in *Pequeño Teatro* [Little Theatre] as the characters are repeatedly shown as playing the role of observers and are represented as being studied[108] or spied upon: 'Y a Kepa Devar, a quien veía pasear en el atardecer, solitario, pensativo, imponente, se convirtió para Ilé Eroriak en un ser fantástico, en el más grande de los hombres'[109] [And Kepa Devar, whom he saw walking at sunset, lonely, thoughtful, imposing, became for Ile Eroriak a fantastic being, the greatest of men].

If the notion of truth in novels which display an internally focalised, autodiegetic, overt narrator such as *La Gangrena* [Gangrene] or *La Sombra del Ciprés es Alargada* [The Shadow of the Cypress is Extended] is undermined through the thematic referring to the act of lying, novels such as *El Cacique* [The Chief] or *La Noria* [The Ferris Wheel] translate such a tension at the stylistic level by projecting a seemingly endless series of juxtaposed fragmented visual acts. El *Cacique* is particularly evocative of such a procedure in that, as opposed to *La Noria*, a single event — the death of Isabel's father — ostensibly appears to be the focus of such a fragmented game of characters' visions and opinions. Thus each chapter is constructed on the act of focalisation of an isolated character or group of characters which provide a personal perception of the events, a vision which indeed often significantly contrasts with both those which precede it and those which follow it. If the novel opens with a slow closing-in on the village which is first perceived from the outside through Marcelino's view, a view which stresses a spatial distance, and Machiste's view in chapter three,[110] a view which stresses a social and cultural distance instead, it then proceeds to display all the contrasting perceptions of the central narrated event through the characters inhabiting the village and its surroundings.[111] The contradictory nature of the portrait which finally emerges from the narrative expresses the impossibility of reaching a coherent and univocal description. Thus, by slow, superimposed, brush strokes, the portrait that finally arises comprises all its contradictions, as a cubist composition in which all angles and views of the same seemingly tangible object are impossibly and simultaneously expressed on the same visual plane. The dead protagonist is therefore considered as 'un putero, y lo ha continuado siendo hasta el último estertor'[112] [a whoremonger, and he remained one until his last breath] while also being simultaneously described as 'el muy ilustre y preclaro vecino'[113] [the most illustrious neighbour].

A similar process is at work in *La Muchacha de las Bragas de Oro* [Golden Girl], as can be illustrated by a short analysis of the first four chapters of the novel. The first chapter oscillates between a third person, externally focalised, hetero-diegetic narrator and an internally focalised, third person, homo-diegetic narrator. The second chapter offers an alternating movement between an auto-diegetic narration, as expressed in the fragments based on the letters, a third person externally focalised narration, corresponding to authorial narration, and the niece's focalisation, which is expressed through an internally focused perspective.[114] Forest's internally focalised narrative is once more contrasted, in the third chapter, with the model of authorial narration, while the fourth chapter displays a shift to free direct style and a sustained focus on auto-diegetic narration.

In *La Noria* [The Ferris Wheel], both techniques, the thematic alternation of different points of view and the stylistic oscillation between an omniscient narrator and internally focalised perspectives, are united as the author stages the description of a day in Barcelona through thirty-six different characters, whose tenuous links with one another hardly go beyond the thread of casual juxtaposition. Thus, as the first and second chapters are connected by the protagonist of the first chapter taking the taxi driven by the protagonist of the second,[115] the transition is then made to the driver's daughter in the third[116] and to the customer of the shop where the girl works in the fourth. The style is characterised by a subtle oscillation in the process of focalisation as the externally focalised narrator leaves way to free direct[117] or indirect style and internal focalisation:

> Aunque este taxista se queja y se pasa el día refuñando, la vida no le va del todo mal. Claro que ha de trabajar mucho, aguantar impertinencias y hacer la vista

gorda muchas veces, pero se saca un buen jornal. La María es, además, muy trabajadora y sabe cómo se compra, y en estos tiempos la buena administración en una casa equivale a un sueldo elevado. La hija está empleada en una librería.[118]

[Although this driver complains and spends the day whining, life is not going too badly. Of course, he has to work hard, endure insolence and turn a blind eye many a time, but he earns a good wage. Maria is moreover very hardworking and knows how to buy at a good price, and these days having good house-keeping is like earning a high salary. The daughter is employed in a library.]

As observers and narrators and, often, observers/narrators proliferate throughout the pages of the winning novels, one notices how *truth* as a concept is unveiled as being artificially constructed, often by a minority of people who fashion *truth* and *falsehood* without striving for an open dialogue and acting, in fact, in secret and for their own interests. An instance of such a trend is expressed in Luis Romero's *El Cacique* [The Chief], in the illustration of the preparation of the funerals[119] — as the commemorative speech is written — or during the description of the police investigation: 'Pretextaremos que se ha extraviado, y se redactará de nuevo de acuerdo con lo que más convenga. Y esta declaración también sera preferable que desaparezca'[120] [we will pretend that it was lost, and it will be redrafted according to what suits best. And it would also be preferable for this statement to disappear].

In his seemingly endless capacity of 'contar un cuento'[121] [telling a tale], Marco comes to personify and embody the characteristics of all the narrators which appear in the novels under examination. Magnifying the story-telling capacity to its most extreme potential, Marco spins an endless tale of past drama[122] and future adventures, of half-lies and distorted truths, which ensnares the small village while also causing the eventual destruction of its inhabitants. Marco's figure is the ultimate expression of characteristics which appear actually to be present in the majority of the novels examined: the instability of the narrative act, the unreliability of the narrating figure and of the narrated events. Indeed, weaving his complex web of recurring lies, Marco juxtaposes contradictory and contrasting versions of his own life — '[...] de todos mis males tiene la culpa mi madre. Sí, yo naufragué en su amor, yo me anulé en su amor. Sí, mi madre fue despótica en su amor hacia mí, fue egoísta, fue Tirana'[123] [I blame my mother for all my problems. Yes, her love drowned me, I was annihilated in her love. Yes, my mother was overbearing, was selfish, was a tyrant] — while simultaneously managing to convince the surrounding characters to perceive their own past and their own present under the distorted length of his own narration.

Marco's voice is but the magnified echo of the voices of all other narrators which haunt the pages of the winning Spanish novels of the Francoist era and which display a similar capacity for lying and presenting themselves as both victims of distorted narrations and masterly authors of deceitful narrative constructions.

Thus, in *La Gangrena* [Gangrene], the narrator-protagonist discovers the figure of his deceased father uniquely through the stories of Uncle Rodolfo — 'Fueron los relatos del tío Rodolfo los que consiguieron darme una imagen viva de mi padre: mucho más viva que la conseguía mi madre cuando se lanzaba a hablarme de su marido'[124] [the stories told by my Uncle Rodolfo gave me a picture of my father that was much more lively than the one provided by my mother, when she ventured to talk about her husband] — only to discover later that the uncle-narrator is nothing other than his mother's secret lover and has lied to him throughout his childhood. In turn, the protagonist-narrator finally plays a similar intra-diegetic narrative function as he deceives Rodolfo's own family while the Tío is dying.

Similarly, Ana María Matute's characters are presented as being both affabulators and victims of narratorial distortions, as in the case of Kepa's listening to the exotic tales told by the mysterious sailor — a figure significantly echoing the Captain who is supposed to carry Marco away at the end of the novel.

Repeatedly, the lexical field of lying thematically undermines the stability of both narrator and narrated events. To the open recognition of the lack of veridicity of expressed events — 'Pero no hablo de cómo soy ni cómo fui, sino de cómo hubiese querido ser'[125] [however I'm not talking about how I am or was, but how I would have wanted to be] — one can add the widespread anxiety manifested by the protagonists with regards to the status of the *récit* and its relation with *truth*. Carlota's questioning of her lying father '¿Cómo saber quién miente y quién es sincero ?'[126] [How to tell who is lying and who is sincere?] in *La Gangrena* [Gangrene] could also be applied to Illé's perplexed perception of Marco's ever-changing narrations in *Pequeño Teatro* [Little Theatre]:

> Vaya, no quiero mentirte a ti ¿sabes?... Soy muy pueril. No es verdad eso que acabo de decirte. Mis desdichas no tienen ni remotamente nada que ver con mi madre, a quien ni siquiera conocí. Nada tiene que ver eso con mi verdadero dolor. ¿Por qué habré hablado de una madre? Nada, nada creas.[127]

> [I do not wish to lie to you, you know... I am very childish. What I just told you... it's not true. My misfortunes have nothing to do with my mother, whom I never even met. This has nothing to do with my real pain. Why have I spoken of a mother? Believe nothing, nothing],

while similarly resonating in the childish lies of *La Sombra del Ciprés es Alargada*[128] [The Shadow of the Cypress is Extended].

In this context, one notices how Richard Rorty's assessment of the relationship between *truth* and *language* offers an illuminating perspective on the thematic and stylistic concerns of the novels evoked. Indeed, one notices how, far from spiralling out of control in pure self-reflexive meta-fictions, the Spanish novels under consideration, with perhaps the sole noticeable exception of *La Muchacha de las Bragas de Oro* [Golden Girl] (with its open confusion of ontological levels), remain in a space in which the relationship between language and the real is powerfully dramatised rather than deliberately undermined. In this context, the studied novels appear to embody Rorty's observation that

> we need to make a distinction between the claim that the world is out there and the claim that the truth is out there. To say that the world is out there, that it is not our creation, is to say, with common sense, that most things in space and time are the effects of causes which do not include human mental states. To say that the truth is not out there is simply to say that where there are no sentences there is no truth, that sentences are elements of human languages, and that

human languages are human creations. Truth cannot be out there, cannot exist independently of the human mind — because sentences cannot so exist, or be out there. The world is out there, but descriptions of the world are not. Only descriptions of the world can be true or false. The world on its own — unaided by the describing activities of human beings — cannot.[129]

The recognition is one of the illusory nature of the supposedly stable relation between language and truth. The predominance of language over *facts* often illustrates such a position in the analysed novels. Anticipating not simply the reaction of the intra-diegetic narratee — his niece — but also that of the external audience of the novel, similarly aware of the contradiction and inner contrasts of his ongoing tale, Juan Marsé's protagonist is made to exclaim: 'Por una vez, sobrina, me anticipo a tus irritantes paréntesis. No estoy alardeando de una memoria total, ni siquiera de alguna facultad premonitoria: esta reiterada furgoneta fantasma no es real [...] sino inventada'[130] [For once, niece, I would like to anticipate your irritating parentheses. I'm not boasting about an all-encompassing memory capacity or about some premonitory capacity: this reappearing ghostly van is not real [...] but invented].

Social division and isolation: lack of communication

As the 'relative' dimension of the 'real' is enhanced, one notices how the reader is increasingly brought to face the absence of what Rorty establishes at the basis of his non-representational view of language: namely, common agreement and understanding, which form the basis for social communication.

If, according to Rorty, common agreement can be made to compensate for the lack of any representational relation between reality and language, one notices how, on the contrary, the dramatisation of the construction of 'truth' in the novels under examination is characterised by the undermining of the possibility of such a stabilising frame.

Indeed, in the context of the winning Spanish novels, one notices how, not only are the limits of reality presented to correspond to the limits of language,[131] but additionally, the Wittgensteinean belief that the 'limits of language', namely the specific linguistic utterance born out of the specific vision of the world proper of each character, are 'the limits of [one's] world'[132] is dramatised and accentuated in order to highlight the degree to which neither linguistic constructs nor perceptions of the external dimension are actually shared by the characters in the novels.

We have already highlighted the degree to which these novels display a shift between focus on *narration* (temporally characterised) and *vision/representation* (spatially characterised). The narrative — thus temporal — act finds its counterpart in a stylistically visual — primarily spatial — act which emphasises the presence of an observer within the narrative flow. In turn, the visual processes of such an observer, characterised by their intrinsically connected framing processes, are typified by the singularity and the incommunicability they possess. In this context, individual views appear to be incompatible with one another and the dialogic exchange becomes a monologic stream which highlights the loneliness of the depicted characters.

In the case of *Nada*, one notices how the shift to the *dramatic* mode we have evoked in the context of the generic mixing of different cultural media is complicated by the insertion of an inner instability of the dialogic mode illustrating a growing disconnection between the perceptions and the understanding of the different characters.

Thus, not only are the points of view, exposed and expressed in the sequence, often completely opposed to one another, but they become so incompatible as to reduce the theatrical dialogue to a dramatic series of monologues, echoed at the thematic level by the wholly contrasting representations of *reality* which are displayed:

> GLORIA — Román había cambiado antes. En el momento mismo que entramos en Barcelona en aquel coche oficial. ¿Tú sabes que Román tenía un cargo importante con los rojos? Pero era un espía, una persona [...] que vendia a los que le favorecieron. Sea por lo que sea, el espionaje es de cobardes...
>
> ABUELA — ¿Cobardes? Niña, en mi casa no hay cobardes... Román es bueno y valiente y exponía su vida por mí, porque yo no quería que estuviera con aquella gente. Cuando era pequeño...
>
> GLORIA — Te voy a contar una historia, mi historia, Andrea, para que veas que es como una novela de verdad...[133]
>
> [GLORIA — Roman had changed before. When we arrived in Barcelona in that official car. Did you know that Roman had an important position with the Reds? But he was a spy, a person [...] who sold those who helped him. Be that as it may, spying is for cowards...
>
> GRANDMA — Cowards? Girl, in my house there are no cowards... Roman is good and brave and he put his life on the line for me, because I did not want him to be with these people. When he was young...
>
> GLORIA — I'll tell you a story, my story, Andrea, so that you may see how it really seems to be like a novel...]

Since only 'one's own self and what one experiences exist',[134] characters are often shown not only to observe one another but also to spy, to watch one another obsessively in a process in which voyeurism[135] comes to embody the absolute lack of contact and reciprocity in the relations which are established in the novels.

An instance of such a voyeuristic tendency is strongly expressed in a recurrent emphasis on stolen glances, secret observers in *La Sombra del Ciprés es Alargada* [The Shadow of the Cypress is Extended], in *Nada* and, with a strong sexual emphasis, in *La Muchacha de las Bragas de Oro* [Golden Girl]: 'Forest pudo distinguir, mediante un leve desplazamiento del torso que dejó pasar la luz de la ventana, la furtiva mano ahora en su pecho y el pezón rebrincando entre los dedos. Pero ella ni caso'[136] [Thanks to a slight movement of the torso, which let in the window light, Forest could see the furtive hand now on her breast and the puckered nipple between his fingers. She, however, took absolutely no notice].

Alternatively, contrasting versions lead to embittered rows — symbolically embodying the impossible coherence and social division plaguing the narrative worlds depicted — such as those provided by the villagers' description of Marco in *Pequeño Teatro*: '[...] y dicen que era un gitano. Y otros dicen que era un contrabandista, como el portugués. Y otros que era un estafador perseguido'[137] [... and they say that he was a gypsy. And others say he was a smuggler, like the Portuguese. And others, that he was a pursued con-artist].

Significantly, one notices a reiterated dramatisation of the impossibility of obtaining an agreement, a common voice, a coherent picture as characters are displayed as being enclosed within their own inner world of preoccupations and fears.

Such an effect is similarly evoked in Ramiro Pinilla's *Las Ciegas Hormigas* [The Blind Ants] where the juxtaposition of different characters' perceptions, emphasised by the juxtaposition of paragraphs and textual segments announced and introduced by each character's name, is dramatised by the growing disconnection occurring at the thematic level between one character's thoughts and the next character's preoccupations. Thus if, in the early parts of the novel, the shift from Ismael to Nerea simply allows the reader to gain an understanding of the contrasting thoughts of the persons involved in the story,[138] it is precisely the dramatisation of the contrasting nature of such thoughts which takes place in the middle and, increasingly, in the later part of the novel:

> Nerea.
> Tengo que dar con un escondrijo para los tres gatitos, y con una cesta, o algo parecido, para que estén recojidos, sin poder salir, y así no me los maten.
> Berta.
> Pedro llega a casa y me dice que era la verdad que el barco traía carbón, y que va a ir con Sabas a las peñas, esta misma noche, a coger lo que se pueda.[139]

> [Nerea.
> I have to provide a hiding place for the three kittens, with a basket or something similar, so that they may stay together, unable to leave, and so that they do not kill them.
> Bertha.
> Peter comes home and tells me that it was true that the ship brought coal, and that he will go with Sabas to the rocks, tonight, to take what he can find.]

Thus the narration is fragmented into a series of isolated monologues rather than a unique thread of interconnected dialogue, an effect similarly obtained in Marcos Aguinis's *La Cruz Invertida* [The Inverted Cross] where the dense pattern of juxtaposed points of view reaches its culmination in the cancellation of the characters' names and in the replacement of their distinctive identities with the letters of the alphabet during the episode in which the characters comment upon Torres's discourse on Church issues:

> C
> ¿Qué te pareció? Bello ha quedado mal. Fastidió con tantas preguntas y explicaciones. Si se hubiera limitado a decir unas pocas palabras, quizás habría pasado. Pero se despachó una perorata interminabile sin añadir nada nuevo [...]
> B
> Analizó tendenziosamente la historia latinoamericana. Se apartó del tradicional respeto que debemos a nuestros próceres y no hizo justicia a la obra misionera de España.[140]

[C

What did you think about it? Bello has performed badly. He was annoying with so many questions and explanations. If he had only said a few words, he might have succeeded. But he produced an interminabile rant without adding anything new [...].

B

He analysed Latin American history in a biaised manner. He ignored the traditional respect we owe to our heroes and did not do any justice to the missionary work of Spain.]

Ultimately, one notices how the projection of a divided community emerging from the winning narratives is at odds with the identity-forming and uniforming function of the social institution which establishes the cultural status of those self-same narratives. If the literary prize as an institution can be understood to embody the Francoist desire to proceed to the shaping and formation of a new and non-divided Spanish identity through the endorsement of a specific cultural frame and through the use of the cultural product as identity-shaping tool on the cognitive landscape, the cultural products emerging from such a social institution openly contrast with the function which the institution itself can arguably be understood to fulfil.

Notes to Chapter 3

1. Bloch (1988), p. 43.
2. Derek Edwards (1991), p. 518.
3. Ibid., p. 519.
4. Ibid., p. 519.
5. Ibid., p. 523.
6. José María Martínez Cachero, *La novela española entre 1936 y el fin de siglo* [The Spanish Novel between 1936 and the End of the Century] (Madrid: Editorial Castalia, 1997), p. 54.
7. Ibid., p. 94.
8. Ibid., p. 68.
9. Ibid., p. 69.
10. Ibid., p. 96.
11. Translated in the United States in 1963 by Elaine Kerrigan as *The School of the Sun* and in the United Kingdom, also in 1963, by James Mason as *Awakening*.
12. 'Premio Planeta', *Wikipedia*, <http://en.wikipedia.org/wiki/Premio_planeta> [accessed 3 July 2017] (Introduction). The most famous episode in that respect is possibly the refusal of the prize by Miguel Delibes in 1994. As the 1994 *Planeta* was granted to Camilo José Cela for *La Cruz de San Andrés* [St. Andrew's Cross], Delibes accused the *Planeta* organisation of having offered Cela the prize in the first instance. It was refused by Ernesto Sábato and the prize also met with some controversy in Latin America where, in 2005, an 'Argentinian court fined *Planeta* 10,000 pesos after finding that there had been fraud in awarding the Argentinian version of the prize to Ricardo Piglia in 1997'.
13. Martínez Cachero (1997), p. 103.
14. Ibid., p. 73.
15. See Hevia <http://www.nodulo.org/ec/2005/n042p01.htm> [accessed 3 July 2017] (paragraph 16).
16. Gustavo Bueno, *El mito de la cultura: Ensayo de una filosofía materialista de la cultura* [The Myth of Culture: Essay on a Materialist Philosophy of Culture] (Barcelona: Editorial Prensa Ibérica, 1996).

17. Hevia (paragraph 1).
18. Luis de Llera, *La modernización cultural de España 1898–1975* [The Cultural Modernisation of Spain 1898–1975] (Madrid: Editorial Actas, 2000), p. 157.
19. Edwards] (1991), pp. 515–42.
20. Talon-Hugon (2004), p. 39.
21. Ibid., p.39 : 'Entre les notions neuves de beaux-arts et de public apparaît donc, aussi, au XVIIIe siècle, la figure du critique qui, lui, pratique l'art de juger.' [In the eighteenth century, between the new notions of fine arts and the public, there appears the figure of the critic, whose function is that of judging.]
22. Ibid., p. 61.
23. Ibid., p. 39.
24. Martínez Cachero (1997), p. 97.
25. Ibid., p. 100.
26. Ibid., p. 73.
27. Geneviève Champeau, *Les Enjeux du réalisme dans le roman sous le Franquisme* [The Issue of Realism in Novels in the Francoist Period] (Madrid: Casa de Velásquez, 1993), p. 379.
28. Ibid., p. 11.
29. Martínez Cachero (1997), p. 80.
30. Ibid., p. 79.
31. Luis Romero, *El cacique* [The Chief], [1963], 24th edn (Barcelona: Planeta, 1980), p. 41.
32. Martin Montgomery et al., *Ways of Reading* (London: Routledge, 1992), p. 214.
33. Romero (1980), p. 6.
34. Ibid., p. 6.
35. Ibid., p. 6.
36. Montgomery (1992), p. 214.
37. Romero (1963), p. 108.
38. Jorge Semprún, *Autobiografía de Federico Sánchez* [Federico Sánchez's Autobiography], 8th edn (Barcelona: Planeta, 1978), p. 9.
39. Ibid., p. 9.
40. Eduardo Caballero Calderón, *El Buen Salvaje* [The Noble Savage], [1965], 7th edn (Barcelona: Ediciones Destino, 1967), p. 20.
41. Montgomery (1992), p. 212.
42. Gonzalo Sobejano, in *The Cambridge Companion to the Spanish Novel*, ed. by Harriet Turner and Adelaida López de Martínez (Cambridge: Cambridge University Press, 2003), p. 174.
43. Semprún (1977), p. 10.
44. David K. Herzberger, in *Intertextual Pursuits*, ed. by Jeanne P. Brownlow and John W. Kronik (Lewisburg: Bucknell University Press, 1998), p. 127.
45. Semprún (1978), p. 9.
46. Romero (1980), p. 32.
47. Barry Jordan, 'Sartre, Engagement and the Spanish Realist Novel of the 1950s', *Journal of European Studies*, 20 (1990), 299–323 (p. 301).
48. Martínez Cachero (1997), p. 181.
49. Ibid., p. 185.
50. Ibid., p. 193.
51. Randolph D. Pope, in *The Cambridge Companion to Modern Spanish Culture*, ed. by David T. Gies (Cambridge: Cambridge University Press, 1990), p. 140.
52. Ramiro Pinilla, *Las Ciegas Hormigas* [The Blind Ants], [1960], 2nd edn (Barcelona: Ediciones Destino, 1961), p. 7.
53. Martínez Cachero (1997), p. 191.
54. Pinilla (1961), p. 93: 'La vaca. Me pregunté: ¿qué podía ser más fuerte : mi voluntad de resistir o las sucesivas negativas de Benito a venderla ? Pues él, Sabas, seguía insistiendo tercamente.' [The cow. I wondered, what could be stronger: my will to resist or Benito's reiterated refusal to sell? At any rate, Sabas, stubbornly, kept insisting.]
55. Ibid., p. 97.

56. Ibid., p. 123.
57. Gonzalo Sobejano in Turner & López de Martínez, eds (2003), p. 174.
58. Ibid., p. 173.
59. Ibid., p. 173.
60. Ibid., p. 182.
61. Bradley Epps, in Turner and López de Martínez, eds (2003), p. 193.
62. Ibid., p. 193.
63. Semprún (1978), p. 94.
64. Caballero Calderón (1965), p. 28.
65. Ibid., p. 100.
66. Carmen Laforet, *Nada* [1945], 22nd edn (Barcelona: Ediciones Destino, 1973), p. 46.
67. Ramón J. Sender, *En la vida de Ignacio Morel* [In Ignacio Morel's Life] (Barcelona: Planeta, 1969), p. 73.
68. Juan Marsé, *La muchacha de las bragas de oro* [Golden Girl] (Barcelona: Planeta, 1978), p. 123.
69. Caballero Calderón (1965), p. 13.
70. Semprún (1978), p. 50.
71. Rafael Sánchez Ferlosio, *El jarama* [The River], [1953], 9th edn (Barcelona: Ediciones Destino, 1969), p. 6.
72. Caballero Calderón (1965), p. 18.
73. Miguel Delibes, *La sombra del ciprés es alargada* [The Shadow of the Cypress is Extended], [1947], 8th edn (Ediciones Destino: Barcelona, 1969), p. 42.
74. Ibid., p.13.
75. Ibid., p.52.
76. Ana María Matute, *Pequeño Teatro* [Little Theatre] (Barcelona: Ediciones Destino, 1971), p. 35.
77. Marsé (1978), p. 18.
78. Delibes (1969), p. 53.
79. Marsé (1978), p. 77.
80. Sánchez Ferlosio (1969), p. 6.
81. Delibes (1969), p. 263.
82. Champeau (1993), p. 370.
83. Ibid., p. 371.
84. Ibid., p. 380.
85. Ibid., p. 11.
86. Semprún (1978), p. 29.
87. Ibid., p. 88.
88. Matute (1970), p. 36.
89. José María Gironella, *Un hombre* [A Man], [1946], 4th edn (Barcelona: Ediciones Destino, 1961), p. 29.
90. Delibes (1969), p. 154.
91. Romero (1980), p. 56.
92. Ibid., p. 105.
93. Matute (1970), p. 41.
94. Marsé (1978), p. 8.
95. Gironella (1961), p. 23.
96. Delibes (1969), p. 68.
97. Merleau-Ponty (2005), p. xi.
98. In George Pitcher, *The Philosophy of Wittgenstein* (Englewood Cliffs, NJ: Prentice Hall, 1964), pp. 49–50.
99. Ibid., p. 223.
100. Marsé (1978), p. 111.
101. Pitcher (1964), pp. 49–50.
102. Marsé (1978), p. 23.
103. Delibes (1969), p. 163.
104. Matute (1970), p. 106.

105. Romero (1980), p. 15.
106. Marsé (1978), p. 221.
107. Ibid., p. 54.
108. Matute (1970), p. 59.
109. Ibid., p. 31.
110. Romero (1980), p. 18.
111. Structure of *El Cacique*: Ch. 1: Marcelino, Ch. 2 Don Gabriel, Ch. 3 Machiste, Ch. 4: Zacarías, Ch. 5 Voluntario, Ch. 6 El Tío Vivo, Ch. 7 Daniel, Ch. 8 El maestro, Ch. 9 Don Pablito, Ch. 10 El Tío Raposo, Ch. 11 Don Fernando y Don Eloy, Ch. 12 Isabel, Ch. 13 Saturio y Señor Aquilino, Ch. 14 Telesforo, Ch. 15 Hombre y Mujer, Ch. 16 Oficial Lopez y Don Paciano, Ch. 17 Ceferino y Simeón, Ch. 18 Balbino, Ch. 19 Rosita and her Lover, Ch. 20 Don Onore.
112. Ibid., p. 52.
113. Ibid., p. 50.
114. Ibid., p. 17.
115. Romero (1980), p. 16.
116. Ibid., p. 23.
117. Ibid., p. 11.
118. Ibid., p. 19.
119. Ibid., p. 49.
120. Ibid., p. 98.
121. Matute (1970), p. 85.
122. Ibid., p. 87.
123. Ibid., p. 72.
124. Mercedes Salisachs, *La Gangrena* [Gangrene], [1975], 5th edn (Barcelona: Editorial Planeta, 1969), p. 8.
125. Marsé (1978), p. 14.
126. Salisachs (1976), p. 502.
127. Matute (1970), p. 72.
128. Delibes (1969), p. 52.
129. Richard Rorty, *Contingency, Irony and Solidarity* (Cambridge: Cambridge University Press, 1989), p. 5.
130. Marsé (1978), p. 150.
131. Pitcher (1964), p. 141.
132. Ibid., p. 145.
133. Romero (1980), p. 48.
134. Pitcher (1964), p. 145.
135. Marsé (1978), p. 29.
136. Ibid., p. 59.
137. Matute (1970), p. 256.
138. Pinilla (1961), p. 10.
139. Ibid., p. 24.
140. Marcos Aguinis, *La Cruz Invertida* [The Inverted Cross], [1970] (Barcelona: Planeta, 1980), p. 12.

CONCLUSION

When considering the reading process, Peter Stockwell underlines the importance of remaining faithful to its 'essentially dynamic nature',[1] highlighting how the constitution of a written theoretical and critical approach to a literary phenomenon often entails a process of 'solidification' in which the grasp of its essentially dynamic nature is lost. This observation can be extended beyond the single act of reading to the consideration of the whole process of literary creation, diffusion and reception. Indeed, critical approaches often forego to integrate an awareness of the degree to which the temporal dimension — with its evolving, changing, dynamic nature — can affect a given critical position. This does not simply refer to the fact that an older critical approach can be challenged by a more recent one, but it refers to the degree to which time can and should be successfully integrated *within* any given critical approach, as a determining and significant factor. In other words, not only should time be considered as part of any process of cognition under examination but it should also be self-consciously apprehended and accounted for within the framework of the critical act itself.

The theoretical framework here developed for the study of literary competitions has been conceived to attempt such an integration. It is my contention that though historical and political events, subjective preferences and needs and aesthetic features are certainly key factors influencing the functioning of literary prizes and their lasting success, an apprehension of the combined influence of the multiple factors involved — in a *simultaneous* and *temporally dynamic* perspective — provides new possibilities for the interpretation and understanding the phenomenon.

Specifically, the theoretical scheme sketched at the opening of the current study has been gradually amended in order to express such a view and can arguably be now represented as shown in Figure C.1.

Moving away from an understanding of literary competitions as 'solidified' objects to a view of the phenomenon as a process immersed within and determined by time points to a shift in critical perception. Time is not simply seen as belonging to *inner* dimension of the literary competition and its winning texts — one thinks, for instance, of historical novels or of narrations in which the temporal element is central for the plot or the style of the work — but it is seen as that which encompasses the competitions themselves. The time in which the competitions were created, the time in which they operate, the temporal tension between the present and the past, the future orientation given by yearly repetition. Temporal dimensions become a complex layer of meaning which cannot be ignored if the phenomenon is to be understood in its complexity.

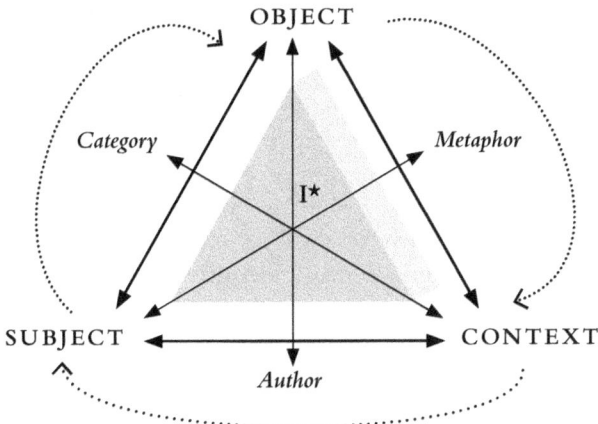

Fig. C.1. Theoretical Scheme — Dynamism (* Literary Prize)

Time can hardly be considered without a conceiving mind. How does the interaction between subject, object and context operate? How is each and every element in the equation sketched above affected by such an interaction? My contention is that, as argued in the preceding chapters, a key aspect of such an interaction rests on processes of identity constitution and negotiation, emerging from the cognition of time and space within and without the literary world.

Can cognitive processes actually prescind from identity construction drives? This question goes beyond the scope of the present study. What certainly emerges from the case of literary competitions is a link between cultural and social identity and processes of understanding and assessment of literary creation.

A key function is played, in this context, by the notions of circularity and reciprocity. We have described, in the course of the study, both the degree to which literary competitions appear to emerge in specific socio-historical contexts as well as the degree to which they appear to survive and, indeed, thrive in very different social, cultural and historical realities. Within such an evolution, the reciprocal, circular, nature of identity construction appears to play a key role and points to the remarkably complex relationship of cause and effect in identity dynamics. Products and producers within the process of identity formation appear to be linked and are seen as reciprocally influencing each other in an organic and evolutive pattern. Thus, considering processes of identity formation in terms of origin and end would appear as a reduction to a linear — one directional — process of what is in fact a multi-dimensional and reciprocal dynamic. This, in turn, calls into question the degree to which the origin (historical, cultural, social) of a phenomenon can be traced without falling into the *solidification* trend denounced by Stockwell. This is all the more true for phenomena for which no precise founding date can be traced. Even for literary competitions, where biographical and institutional information allow for a rather precise framing of the phenomenon origins, it can indeed be argued that the simultaneous emergence of related institutions transcends the single, anecdotal, episode of foundation and points to diffuse processes rather than to isolated occurrences.

How can one take into account such a dynamism while also producing a coherent and, to a degree, stable and truthful representation of the phenomenon? As argued in the first part of the study — while considering the potential nationalist interpretation of French competitions — solidification might entail distortions. This issue can also be directly related to the phenomenon of competitions itself. As considered in the study, the attempt at stabilising collective identity through the selection of a winning literary work is inherently submitted to displacement and self-undermining. The yearly renewal of selection, and definition of winners, points to the fundamental fragility of any identity temporarily achieved.

It is indeed in such a dimension of fragility that Bloch's utopian view finds its embodiment. Crucially, the case of literary competitions appears to conflate the two sides of what Fredric Jameson considers as Bloch's hermeneutic contradiction. On the one hand, the critic identifies 'deliberate and fully self-conscious utopian programmes as such'.[2] On the other hand, he points to the Blochean view of the 'utopian impulse governing everything future-oriented in life and culture'.[3] Literary competitions, as shown in the case of the Goncourt, may display a deliberateness, an intention of utopian construction in their desire to overcome dissolution and change. On the other hand, their embracing of the utopian 'impulse' unveils their capacity to actually thrive in a context of transformation, embracing ever-changing identities and dynamics. Thus, as noted by Jameson, Bloch's utopian impulse goes beyond the category of 'totality' which characterises the traditional view of the utopian programme, allowing the literary competitions here under examination to transcend the limits potentially posited by their own utopian, in the somewhat more traditional sense of the term, ideological drive.

A critical awareness of the dynamics at work in processes of competition, selection, artistic creation and affirmation of identity can highlight further areas of study.

An interesting approach to writing in academia is suggested by Eli Thorkelson in his paper on academic writing and the construction of critical authorship *The Case of the Bad Writing Contest: Literary Theory as Commodity and Literary Theorists as Brands*[4] when he investigates the case of a contest organised in the late 1990s by the Journal *Philosophy and Literature* in order to consider issues related to academic writing, the selection of academic texts and articles and the construction of academic authorial identities. How can authorship be defined for writers of theory and criticism? Are they less *authorial* than creative writers? What role is played by competitive dynamics and selection criteria in academia?

Exploring further the link between construction of identity and competition processes also interestingly points to the use of literary challenges in educational contexts. What is the link between writing competitions organized, for instance, in university contexts and the pedagogic dimension? How are student identity dynamics affected, influenced or determined by creative contests?

The consideration of literary competitions also raises the question of non-literary contests. Are competitions based on visual arts or theatrical performances similarly characterised by the elements identified in this study?

Such questions naturally go beyond the scope of the present study but it is my contention that the consideration of the interaction between processes of creation, of selection and of definition and affirmation of the self can offer some interesting openings for further research.⁵

Notes to the Conclusion

1. Stockwell (2002), p. 168.
2. Fredric Jameson, *Archaeologies of the Future: The Desire Called Utopia and Other Science Fiction* (London: Verso, 2005), pp. 1–9.
3. Ibid., pp. 1–9.
4. Eli Thorkelson, *The Case of the Bad Writing Contest: Literary Theory as Commodity and Literary Theorists as Brands*, <http://decasia.org/papers.html> [accessed 3 July 2017].
5. *Isocrates*, trans. by T. L. Papillon (Austin, Texas: University of Texas Press), Panegyricus 1–4, in Tarik Wareh, *The Theory and Practice of Life: Isocrates and the Philosophers*. Hellenic Studies Series 54 (Washington, DC: Center for Hellenic Studies, 2013). Available at <http://nrs.harvard.edu/urn-3:hul.ebook:CHS_WarehT.The_Theory_and_Practice_of_Life.2012> [accessed 3 July 2017]:

   'I have often marveled that those who established panegyric festivals and set up athletic contests considered athletic success [tas tōn sōmatōn eutukhias] worthy of such great prizes, but established no such prize for those who work hard as private citizens for the public good and prepare their own lives [tas hautōn psukhas] so that they can benefit others. They should have given more thought to the latter, for even if the athletes acquired twice their current strength, there would be no greater benefit for the people, while if one person has good ideas, all who wish to share in those ideas would benefit. Nonetheless, I have not lost heart about these things or chosen to give up. Rather, I think that there is sufficient reward for me in the glory this discourse will bring, and so I have come to give advice about the war against the barbarians and the need for unity among ourselves. I know that many who claim to be sophists have attempted this task, but I expect to speak so much better that people will think nothing has ever even been spoken on these matters before, and I consider those discourses most beautiful that treat the greatest subjects, best demonstrate the speaker's talent, and most help those who hear them. This is just such a discourse.'

BIBLIOGRAPHY

Primary Sources

Narrative and Poetry

AGUINIS, MARCOS, *La cruz invertida* [1970] (Barcelona: Planeta, 1980)
AUDOUX, MARGUERITE, *Marie-Claire* [1910] (Paris: Arthème Fayard & Cie [193- (?)])
BARRÈS, MAURICE, *Un homme libre* (see 'on-line resources')
BELFOND, PIERRE, *La Délibération* (Paris: Lansman, 2002)
BOURGET, PAUL, *L'Etape* (Paris: Plon-Nourrit, [1902 (?)])
CABALLERO CALDERÓN, EDUARDO, *El buen salvaje*, [1965], 7th edn (Barcelona: Ediciones Destino, 1967)
CARDARELLI, VINCENZO, *Opere*, rev. by Clelia Martignoni (Milano: Arnoldo Mondatori Editore, 1981)
DELIBES, MIGUEL, *La sombra del ciprés es alargada*, [1947], 8th edn (Ediciones Destino: Barcelona, 1969)
ESTAUNIÉ, EDOUARD, *La Vie secrète*, [1908], 33rd edn (Paris: Librairie Académique Perrin, 1935)
FARRÈRE, CLAUDE, *Les Civilisés*, [1905] (Paris: Ernest Flammarion, 1921)
GADDA, CARLO EMILIO, *Il castello di Udine* [1934], intro. by Guido Lucchini (Milano: Garzanti, 1989)
GIRONELLA, JOSÉ MARÍA, *Un hombre*, [1946], 4th edn (Barcelona: Ediciones Destino, 1961)
JALOUX, EDMOND, *Le Reste est silence* (Paris: Editions Lapina, 1924)
LAFORET, CARMEN, *Nada* [1945], 22nd edn (Barcelona: Ediciones Destino, 1973)
MARSÉ, JUAN, *La muchacha de las bragas de oro* (Barcelona : Planeta, 1978)
MATUTE, ANA MARÍA, *Pequeño teatro*, [1954], 6th edn (Barcelona: Planeta, 1970)
MIOMANDRE, FRANCIS DE, *Ecrit sur de l'eau*, [1908] (Paris: Emile-Paul Frères, 1919)
PEA, ENRICO, *L'arca di Noè: racconti, memorie, elzeviri, 1945–1953*, rev. by Enrico Lorenzetti (Viareggio, Lucca: Mario Baroni Editore, 1997)
PERGAUD, LOUIS, *De Goupil à Margot: histoires de bêtes* [1910], 13th edn (Paris: Mercure de France, 1914)
PINILLA, RAMIRO, *Las ciegas hormigas* [1960], 2nd edn (Barcelona: Ediciones Destino, 1961)
ROMERO, LUIS, *El cacique* [1963], 24th edn (Barcelona: Planeta, 1980)
SALISACHS, MERCEDES, *La gangrena* [1975], 5th edn (Barcelona: Editorial Planeta, 1976)
SÁNCHEZ FERLOSIO, RAFAEL, *El jarama* [1953], 9th edn (Barcelona: Ediciones Destino, 1969)
SAVIGNON, ANDRÉ, *Filles de la pluie: scènes de la vie ouessantine* (Paris: Bernard Grasset Editeur, 1912)
SEMPRÚN, JORGE, *Autobiografía de Federico Sánchez* [1977], 8th edn (Barcelona: Planeta, 1978)
SENDER, RAMÓN JOSÉ, *En la vida de Ignacio Morel* (Barcelona: Planeta, 1969)
TUMIATI, CORRADO, *Tetti rossi: ricordi di manicomio* [1931] (Venezia: Marsilio Editore, 1987)

Philosophy

ARISTOTLE, *Poetics*, trans. with notes by Richard Janko (Indianapolis: Hackett Publishing Company, 1987)
BENJAMIN, WALTER, *The Arcades Project* [1982], ed. by Roy Tiedemann, trans. by Howard Eiland and Kevin McLaughlin (Cambridge, MA: Harvard University Press, 1999)
BERGSON, HENRI, *Essai sur les données immédiates de la conscience* [1888], 144th edn (Paris: Presses Universitaires de France, 1970)
—— *Le Rire*, [1900], 23rd edn (Paris: Editions Alcan, 1924)
—— 'L'Evolution créatrice', [1907], in *Oeuvres* (Paris: Presses universitaires de France, 1959)
BLANCHOT, MAURICE, *The Space of Literature*, [1955], trans. by Ann Smock (Lincoln: University of Nebraska Press, 1982)
BLOCH, ERNST, *A Philosophy of the Future*, trans. by John Camming (New York: Herder and Herder, 1970)
—— *The Utopian Function of Art and Literature* [1974/1975], trans. by Jack Zipes & Frank Mecklenburg (Cambridge, MA: MIT Press, 1988)
BOURDIEU, PIERRE, *Les Règles de l'art. Genèse et structure du champ littéraire* (Paris: Le Seuil, 1992)
EPICURUS, 'Letter to Herodotus' (see 'on-line resources')
KANT, IMMANUEL, *The Critique of Judgment* [1790], trans. by James Creed Meredith (Oxford: The Clarendon Press, 1982 [rpt.])
LACAN, JACQUES, 'Le Stade du miroir' [1936/1949], in *Écrits* (Paris: Editions du Seuil, 1999 [rpt.])
MAUSS, MARCEL and DURKHEIM, EMILE 'De quelques formes primitives de classification' (see 'on-line resources')
MERLEAU-PONTY, MAURICE, *Phenomenology of Perception* [1945], trans. by Colin Smith (London: Routledge, 2005)
PEIRCE, CHARLES SANDERS, *Collected Writings* (8 vols), ed. by Charles Hartshorne, Paul Weiss, and Arthur W. Burks (Cambridge, MA: Harvard University Press, 1931–1958)
PLATO, *The Republic*, trans. by Georges M. A. Grube and rev. by C. D. C. Reeve (Indianapolis: Hackett Publishing Company, 1992)
—— *Complete Works*, ed. by John M. Cooper and D. S. Hutchinson (Indianapolis: Hackett Publishing Company, 1997)
RORTY, RICHARD, *Contingency, Irony and Solidarity* (Cambridge: Cambridge University Press, 1989)
SARTRE, JEAN-PAUL, *Qu'est-ce que la Littérature?* (Paris: Gallimard, 1948)

Secondary Sources

ALLEMAND, ROGER MICHEL, *L'Utopie* (Paris: Ellipses, 2005)
ANDERSON, BENEDICT, *Imagined Communities* (London: Verso, 1991)
ANGENOT, MAURICE, *1889: Un état du discours social* (Longueuil: Le Préambule, 1989)
ANGIOLETTI, GIOVAN BATTISTA and ORIO VERGANI, *Il primo Bagutta* (Milano: Ceschina, 1955)
ARKINSTALL, CHRISTINE, ed., *Literature and Quest* (Amsterdam & Atlanta: Rodopi, 1993)
ARON, PAUL, DENIS SAINT-JACQUES, and ALAIN VIALA, eds, *Le Dictionnaire du littéraire* (Paris: PUF, 2002)
ARONSON, ELLIOT, TIMOTHY WILSON, and ROBIN AKERT, *Social Psychology* (New York: Pearson Prentice Hall, 2007)

ARSLAN, ANTONIA and PATRIZIA ZAMBON, *Enrico Pea* (Firenze: La Nuova Italia, 1983)
ASHLEY, KATHERINE, ed., *Prix Goncourt, 1903–2003: essais critiques* (Oxford: Peter Lang AG, 2003)
ASSOCIAZIONE ITALIANA EDITORI — Fondazione Maria e Goffredo Bellonci, eds, *A Catalogue of Literary Awards* (Roma: Istitituto Poligrafico e Zecca dello Stato, 1990)
BALDASSARRI, RITA, *Lorenzo Viani* (Firenze: La Nuova Italia, 1982)
BARAŃSKI, ZYGMUNT G. and REBECCA J. WEST, eds, *The Cambridge Companion to Modern Italian Culture* (Cambridge: Cambridge University Press, 2001)
BÁRBERI SQUAROTTI, GIORGIO, *L'Orologio d'Italia — Carlo Levi ed altri racconti* (Limena: Libroitaliano World, 2001)
BARKER, CHRIS, *Cultural Studies: Theory and Practice* (London: Sage Publications, 2003)
BEAUPRÉ, NICOLAS, *Écrire en guerre, écrire la guerre. France-Allemagne 1914–1920* (Paris: CNRS Editions, 2006)
BELL, CLIVE, *Art* (Oxford: Oxford University Press, 1987)
BELLONCI, MARIA, *Il Premio Strega* (Milano: Mondadori, 2003)
BILLY, ANDRÉ, *Les Frères Goncourt* (Paris: Flammarion, 1954)
BONSAVER, GUIDO and ROBERT GORDON, eds, *Culture, Censorship and the State in Twentieth-Century Italy* (Oxford: Legenda, 2005)
BONSAVER, GUIDO, *Literature and Censorship in Fascist Italy* (Toronto: Toronto University Press, 2007)
BOURA, OLIVIER, *Un siècle de Goncourt* (Paris: Arléa, 2003)
BOWIE, ANDREW, ed., *Manfred Frank. The Subject and the Text: Essays on Literary Theory and Philosophy* (Cambridge: Cambridge University Press, 1997)
BROWNLOW, JEANNE P. and JOHN W. KRONIK, eds, *Intertextual Pursuits* (Lewisburg: Bucknell University Press, 1998)
BUENO, GUSTAVO, *El mito de la cultura: ensayo de una filosofía materialista de la cultura* (Barcelona: Editorial Prensa Ibérica, 1996)
BURDETT, CHARLES, *Vincenzo Cardarelli and his Contemporaries* (Oxford: Clarendon Press, 1999)
BURKE, P. J. and JAN E. STETS, *Identity Theory* (Oxford: Oxford University Press, 2009)
CANNELLIS, PATRICIA, ed., *Aristeion* (Brussels: The Commission of the European Communities, 1995)
CAPOZZA, DORA and RUPERT BROWN, eds, *Social Identity Processes* (London: Sage Publications Limited, 2000)
CASSATA, FRANCESCO and MASSIMO MORAGLIO, eds, *Manicomio, società e politica* (Pisa: BFS Edizioni, 2005)
CASSATA, FRANCESCO, *Molti, sani e forti. L'eugenetica in Italia* (Torino: Bollati Boringhieri, 2006)
CHAMPEAU, GENEVIÈVE, *Les Enjeux du réalisme dans le roman sous le franquisme* (Madrid: Casa de Velásquez, 1993)
CHAMPEAU, STÉPHANIE, *La Notion d'artiste chez les Goncourt* (Paris: Honoré Champion Editeur, 2000)
CHEMELLO, ADRIANA, ed., *Filippo Sacchi e Silvio Negro scrittori-giornalisti vicentini del Novecento* (Venezia: Marsilio Editore, 2001)
CLARK, TIMOTHY, *Martin Heidegger* (London: Routledge, 2002)
COHEN, ANTHONY, *The Symbolic Construction of Community* (London: Tavistock, 1985)
COLLECTIF, ed. *Les prix littéraires. Programmes, valeurs, dates, jurys, historique* (Paris: Jouve & Cie Editeurs, 1934)
COLLINGWOOD, ROBIN G., *Principles of Art* (Oxford: Oxford University Press 1938)
DE SETA, CESARE, ed., *Storia d'Italia*, Annali 8 (Torino: Giulio Einaudi Editore, 1985)

DEL BUONO, ORESTE, *Achille Campanile: Opere. Romanzi e Racconti 1924–1933* (Milano: Classici Bompiani, 1989)
DEWEY, JOHN, *Art as Experience* (New York: Capricorn, 1958)
DOGLIANI, PATRIZIA, *Il fascismo degli italiani* (Novara : De Agostini S.p.A., 2014)
DUCHET, CLAUDE, *Sociocritique* (Paris: Nathan, 1979)
DYER, GEOFF, ed., *Selected Essays of John Berger* (New York: Pantheon Books, 2001)
ENGLISH, JAMES F., *The Economy of Prestige: Prizes, Awards and the Circulation of Cultural Value* (Cambridge, MA: Harvard University Press, 2005)
ESPOSITO, ROSSANA, *Invito alla lettura di Giovanni Comisso* (Milano: Mursia, 1990)
FARRELL KRELL, DAVID, *Basic Writings: Martin Heidegger* (London: Routledge, 1993)
FERRERO, ERNESTO, ed., *Maria Bellonci: Opere* (Milano: Arnoldo Mondatori Editore, 1994)
FORBES, JILL and MICHAEL KELLY, *French Cultural Studies: An Introduction* (Oxford: Oxford University Press, 1995)
GALLOIS, ANDRÉ, *Occasions of Identity* (Oxford: Oxford University Press, 1998)
GAUT, BERYS and DOMINIC MCIVER LOPES, eds, *The Routledge Companion to Aesthetics* (London and New York: Routledge, 2005)
GAVINS, JOHANNA and GERARD STEEN, eds, *Cognitive Poetics in Practice* (London: Routledge, 2003)
GIES, DAVID T., ed. *The Cambridge Companion to Modern Spanish Culture* (Cambridge: Cambridge University Press, 1990)
GOODMAN, NELSON, *Languages of Art* (Indianapolis: Hackett Publishing Company, 1976)
GRISONI, DOMINIQUE-ANTOINE, ed., *Goncourt: cent ans de littérature* (Paris: Noésis, 2003)
GUAGNINI, ELVIO, *Viaggi d'inchiostro* (Pasian di Prato: Campanotto Editore, 2000)
HALLIWELL, STEPHEN, *The Aesthetics of Mimesis: Ancient Texts and Modern Problems* (Princeton: Princeton University Press, 2002)
HEINICH, NATALIE, *L'Epreuve de la grandeur: prix littéraires et reconnaissance* (Paris: La Découverte, 1999)
INGOLD, TIM, ed., *Companion Enciclopedia of Anthropology* (London: Routledge, 2002)
ISTITUTO POLIGRAFICO, ed. *A Catalogue of Literary Awards* (Roma: Istituto Poligrafico e Zecca dello Stato, 1990)
JAMESON, FREDERIC, *The Political Unconscious: Narrative as a Socially Symbolic Act* (Methuen: Cornell University Press, 1981)
—— *Archaeologies of the Future: The Desire Called Utopia and Other Science Fiction* (London and New York: Verso, 2005)
KENNEDY, GEORGE A., ed., 'Classical Criticism' (vol. 1), *The Cambridge History of Literary Criticism* (Cambridge: Cambridge University Press, 1989)
KONOPNICKI, GUY, *Prix littéraires: la grande magouille* (Paris: Jean-Claude Gawsewitch Editeur, 2004)
KUSPISZ, KAZIMIERZ et al., eds, *Le Portrait littéraire* (Lyon: Presses Universitaires de Lyon, 1989)
LABES, BERTRAND, *Guide Mont-Blanc des prix et concours littéraires* (Paris: Le Cherche-midi Editeur, 1992)
—— *Guide Cartier des prix et concours littéraires* (Paris: Le Cherche-midi Editeur, 1999)
—— *Guide Lire des prix et concours littéraires* (Paris: L'Express Editions, 2004)
LAKOFF, GEORGE and MARK JOHNSON, *Metaphors We Live By* (Chicago: Chicago University Press, 1980)
LEACH, EDMUND, *Culture and Communication: The Logic by which Symbols are Connected* (Cambridge: Cambridge University Press, 1976)
LE BRIS, MICHEL and JEAN ROUAUD, eds, *Pour une littérature-monde* (Paris: Gallimard, 2007)

LEJEUNE, PHILIPPE, *On Autobiography* (Minneapolis: University of Minnesota Press, 1989)
LLERA, LUIS DE, *La modernización cultural de España 1898–1975* (Madrid: Editorial Actas, 2000)
MAINGUENEAU, DOMINIQUE, *Le Discours littéraire* (Paris: Armand Colin, 2004)
MANCHESTER, MARTIN, *The Philosophical Foundations of Humboldt's linguistic doctrines* (Amsterdam: John Benjamins, 1985)
MARTÍNEZ CACHERO, JOSÉ MARÍA, *La novela española entre 1936 y el fin de siglo* (Madrid: Editorial Castalia, 1997)
MONTGOMERY, MARTIN, et al., *Ways of Reading* (London: Routledge, 1992)
MÜNSTER, ARNO, *Figures de l'utopie dans la pensée d'Ernst Bloch* (Paris: Aubier, 1985)
PARENTI, MARINO, *Bagutta* (Milano: Casa Editrice Ceschina, 1928)
PARKHURST CLARK, PRISCILLA, *Literary France: The Making of a Culture* (Berkeley: University of California Press, 1987)
PELOSO, PAOLO FRANCESCO, *La guerra dentro. La psichiatria italiana tra fascismo e resistenza (1922–1945)* (Verona: Ombre Corte, 2008)
PERFETTI, FRANCESCO, *Il nazionalismo italiano dalle origini alla fusione col Fascismo* (Bologna: Cappelli Editore, 1977)
PERLOFF, MARJORIE, *The Futurist Moment* (Chicago and London: The University of Chicago Press, 1986)
PETROCCHI, MARIA FRANCESCA, *Esperienze e scritture di viaggio* (Viterbo: Settecittà, 2003)
PILKINGTON, ANTHONY EDOUARD, *Bergson and his Influence: A Reassessment* (Cambridge: Cambridge University Press, 1976)
PITCHER, GEORGE, *The Philosophy of Wittgenstein* (Englewood Cliffs, NJ: Prentice Hall, 1964)
PRAETORIOUS, NINI, *Principles of Cognition, Language and Action* (Dordrecht, Netherlands: Kluwer Academic Publishers, 2000)
ROBERTSON, GEORGE ET AL., eds, *Travellers' Tales* (London: Routledge, 1998)
SACKS, SHELDON, ed., *On Metaphor* (Chicago: The University of Chicago Press, 1978)
SOCIÉTÉ DES ECRIVAINS, eds, *Guide des prix littéraires 2006* (Paris: Société des Ecrivains, 2006)
STOCKWELL, PETER, *Cognitive Poetics: An Introduction* (London: Routledge, 2002)
TALBOT, GEORGE, *Censorship in Fascist Italy, 1922–43* (London: Palgrave Macmillan, 2007)
TALON-HUGON, CAROLE, *L'Esthétique* (Paris: Presses Universitaires de France, 2004)
TANI, CINZIA, *Premiopoli* (Milano: Arnoldo Mondadori Editore, 1987)
TODD, RICHARD, *Consuming Fictions: The Booker Prize and Fiction in England Today* (London: Bloomsbury, 1996)
TURNER, HARRIET and ADELAIDA LÓPEZ DE MARTÍNEZ, eds, *The Cambridge Companion to the Spanish Novel* (Cambridge: Cambridge University Press, 2003)
TURNER, VICTOR W. and EDOUARD M. BRUNER, eds, *The Anthropology of Experience* (Urbana: University of Illinois Press, 1986)
UBALDO, NICOLA, *Antologia illustrata di filosofia* (Firenze: Demetra, 2002)
VAN DELFT, LOUIS, *Littérature et anthropologie* (Paris: Presses Universitaires de France, 1993)
VERGANI, GUIDO, ed., *Milano degli scrittori. Bagutta 50 premi letterari 1927–1986* (Milano: Campari, 1986)
VERGANI, GUIDO, *Bagutta e baguttiani* (Milano: Lucini, 2005)
VERGANI, ORIO, *Alfabeto del XX secolo* (Milano: Baldini & Castoldi, 2000)
VIVANTI, CORRADO, ed., *Storia d'Italia*. Annali 4 (Torino: Giulio Einaudi Editore, 1981)
VOLLI, GEMMA, *Le escluse* (Empoli: Ibiskos Editrice Risolo, 2006)
WAREH, TARIK, *The Theory and Practice of Life: Isocrates and the Philosophers*, Hellenic Studies Series, 54 (Washington, DC: Center for Hellenic Studies, HUP, 2013)
WUNENBURGER, JEAN-JACQUES, *Questions d'éthique* (Paris: PUF, 1993)

Articles and Journals

BOURDIEU, PIERRE, 'Le Marché des biens symboliques', *L'Année sociologique*, 22 (1971)
EDWARDS, DEREK, 'Categories Are for Talking', *Theory and Psychology*, 1.4 (Sage, 1991)
ENGSTROM, STEPHEN, 'Understanding and Sensibility', *Inquiry*, 49 (2006), 2–25
EVEN-ZOHAR, ITAMAR, 'The Making of Culture Repertoire and the Role of Transfer', *Target*, 9.2 (1997)
JORDAN, BARRY, 'Sartre, Engagement and the Spanish Realist Novel of the 1950s', *Journal of European Studies*, 20 (1990)
LEYMARIE, MICHEL, 'Peurs françaises et désirs d'empire', *French Cultural Studies*, 17.2 (2006)
Official Journal of the European Communities, C 035 (15 February 1990)
PROSHANSKY, HAROLD M., ABBE K. FABIAN, and ROBERT KAMINOFF, 'Place-identity: Physical world socialization of the self', *Journal of Environmental Psychology*, 3.1 (1983)

On-Line Resources

BARRÈS, MAURICE *Un homme libre* [1889] (Paris: Perrin, 19[?]), electronic edition in 'Barrès, Maurice', *Gallica* <http://gallica.bnf.fr/ark:/12148/bpt6k87498z.item>
CABRERA SANTANA, ANTONIA MARÍA, 'El Premio Eugenio Nadal y Carmen Laforet', *Vector Plus*, 18 (July-December 2001) <http://www.fulp.ulpgc.es/publicaciones/vectorplus/articulos/vp18_04_articulo01.pdf>
'Categorization', *Wikipedia* <http://en.wikipedia.org/wiki/Categorisation>
DI STEFANO, PAOLO, 'Il Premio Letterario? Era Strega e diventa fata', *Giangiacomo Feltrinelli Editore* <http://www.feltrinelli.it/FattiLibriInterna?id_fatto=5106 >
DODILLE, NORBERT, 'Les théories du roman colonial', *Introduction aux discours coloniaux*, <http://unt.univ-reunion.fr/fileadmin/Fichiers/UNT/UOH/idc/co/Cours102.html>
EPICURUS, 'Letter to Herodotus', <http://www.epicurus.net/en/herodotus.html>
FISHER, TIBOR, 'Worthy but Forgettable', *The Guardian* (11 October 2005) <http://books.guardian.co.uk/bookerprize2005/story/0,,1589468,00.html>
FORNACIARI, PAOLO 'Lorenzo Viani e la grande guerra', *Comune di Viareggio*, <http://www.comune.viareggio.lu.it/index.php?option=com_content&view=article&id=911&Itemid=12>
GATTA, MASSIMO, 'Letteratura ai tavoli del Bagutta. Ritrovo di galantuomini', *MenSA* <http://www.mensamagazine.it/articolo.asp?id=740>
GONZÁLEZ HEVIA, LEONCIO, 'La Idea de Cultura durante la España franquista', *El Catoblepas*, 42 (August 2005) <http://www.nodulo.org/ec/2005/n042p01.htm>
JANIAK, ANDREW 'Kant's Views on Space and Time', *Stanford Encyclopedia of Philosophy* <http://plato.stanford.edu/entries/kant-spacetime/#IntPhiQueAboSpaTim>
'Jean Paul Dubois : Prix Femina', *Le Nouvel Observateur* (Littérature) <http://archquo.nouvelobs.com/cgi/articles?ad=culture/20041103.OBS0648.html&host=http://permanent.nouvelobs.com/>
'Le Polemiche', *Premio Letterario Viareggio Répaci* <http://premioletterarioviareggiorepaci.it/polemiche.htm>
LORENCI, MIGUEL, 'Álvaro Pombo logra el Premio Planeta 2006 con una crónica familiar', *Gibralfaro* (Hemeroteca, n.44, October 2006) <http://www.gibralfaro.net/hemeroteca/pag_1311.htm>
MAUSS, MARCEL and DURKHEIM, EMILE 'De quelques formes primitives de classification', *www.philagora.net* (Philosophie de Philagora, Epistémologie) <http://www.philagora.net/capes-agreg/mauss-durkheim4.htm>

'Mussolini contro Bacchelli: niente premio, non è fascista', *Il Corriere della Sera*, <http://archiviostorico.corriere.it/1995/dicembre/19/Mussolini_contro_Bacchelli_Niente_premio_co_0_95121913688.shtml>

PAGE, MARTIN, 'Sous la surface', *Evene.fr Toute la Culture* (Livres, September 2005) <http://www.evene.fr/livres/actualite/interview-de-martin-page-180.php>

'Premi Letterari: Un'inflazione ed una febbre che non accenna ad acquietarsi', *Le reti di Dedalus* (La Newsletter del Sindacato Nazionale Scrittori n.1, febbraio 2005) <http://www.sindacatoscrittori.net/comunicazione/news/premiletterari.htm>

Premio Letterario Viareggio Repaci <www.premioletterarioviareggiorepaci.it/>

'Premio Planeta', *Wikipedia* <http://en.wikipedia.org/wiki/Premio_planeta>

'Premio Viareggio', *Wikipedia* <http://it.wikipedia.org/wiki/Premio_Viareggio>

'Presentation', *Prix Renaudot* <http://www.renaudot.com/>

SHORE, CHRIS, 'European Union and the Politics of Culture', *The Bruges Group* <http://www.brugesgroup.com/mediacentre/index.live?article=13>

STOCKWELL, PETER, 'Cognitive Poetics and Literary Theory', *<http://www.academia.edu/718974/Cognitive_poetics_and_literary_theory>*

THE ECONOMIST, 'Reflections of a Man Booker Prize Judge', *Economist.com* (21 October 2004) <http://www.economist.com/books/displayStory.cfm?story_id=3308497>

THORKELSON, ELI, *The Case of the Bad Writing Contest: Literary Theory as Commodity and Literary Theorists as Brands*, <http://decasia.org/papers.html>

WORMS, FRÉDÉRIC, 'Henri Bergson' , *PUF*, http://www.puf.com/Espace_Bergson/Henri_Bergson>

APPENDIX

In bold: novels discussed in this book

Goncourt

The following list does not include works having obtained the 'Prix Goncourt des Lycéens' established in 1987.

1903	**John Antoine Nau**	**Force ennemie**
1904	Léon Frapié	La Maternelle
1905	**Claude Farrère**	**Les Civilisés**
1906	J. and J. Tharaud	Dingley, l'illustre écrivain
1907	Emile Moselly	Le Rouet d'ivoire
1908	**F. de Miomandre**	**Ecrit sur l'eau**
1909	Marius-Ary Leblond	En France
1910	**Louis Pergaud**	**De Goupil à Margot**
1911	A. de Chateaubriant	Monsieur de Lourdines
1912	**André Savignon**	**Les Filles de la pluie**
1913	Marc Elder	Le Peuple de la mer
1914	*not awarded*	
1915	René Benjamin	Gaspard
1916	Henri Barbusse	Le Feu
	Adrien Bertrand	L'Appel du sol
1917	Henri Malherbe	La Flamme au poing
1918	Georges Duhamel	Civilisation
1919	Marcel Proust	A l'ombre des jeunes filles en fleur
1920	Ernest Perochon	Nene
1921	René Maran	Batouala
1922	Henry Béraud	Le martyre de l'obèse
1923	Lucien Fabre Fabre	Rabevel
1924	Thierry Sandre	Le Chèvrefeuille
1925	Maurice Genevoix	Raboliot
1926	Henry Deberly	Le Supplice de Phèdre
1927	Maurice Bedel	Jérôme 60° latitude nord
1928	Maurice C. Weyer	Un homme se penche ...
1929	Marcel Arland	L'Ordre
1930	Henri Fauconnier	Malaisie
1931	Jean Fayard	Mal d'amour
1932	Guy Mazeline	Les Loups
1933	André Malraux	La Condition humaine

1934	Roger Vercel	Capitaine Conan
1935	Joseph Peyré	Sang et lumières
1936	M. Van Der Meersch	L'Empreinte de Dieu
1937	Charles Plisnier	Faux passeports
1938	Henri Troyat	L'Araigne
1939	Philippe Hériat	Les Enfants gâtés
1940	Francis Ambrière	Les Grandes vacances
1941	Henri Pourrat	Le Vent de Mars
1942	Bernard Marc	Pareil à des enfants
1943	Marius Grout	Passage de l'homme
1944	Elsa Triolet	Le premier accroc coûte 200 francs
1945	Jean-Louis Bory	Mon village à l'heure allemande
1946	Jean-Jacques Gautier	Histoire d'un fait divers
1947	Jean-Louis Curtis	Les Forêts de la nuit
1948	Maurice Druon	Les grandes familles
1949	Robert Merle	Week-end à Zuydcoote
1950	Paul Colin	Les jeux sauvages
1951	Julien Gracq	Le Rivage des Syrtes (*refused*)
1952	Béatrice Beck	Léon Morin, prêtre
1953	Pierre Gascar	Les bêtes et le temps
1954	Simone de Beauvoir	Les Mandarins
1955	Roger Ikor	Les eaux mêlées
1956	Romain Gary (*Emile Ajar*)	Les racines du ciel
1957	Roger Vailland	La Loi
1958	Francis Walder	Saint Germain ou la négociation
1959	André Schwartz-Bart	Le dernier des justes
1960	Vintila Horia	Dieu est né en exil
1961	Jean Cau	La pitié de Dieu
1962	Anna Langfus	Les bagages de sable
1963	Armand Lanoux	Quand la mer se retire
1964	Georges Conchon	L'Etat sauvage
1965	Jacques Borel	L'Adoration
1966	E. Charles-Roux	Oublier Palerme
1967	A. P. de Mandiargues	La Marge
1968	Bernard Clavel	Les fruits de l'hiver
1969	Félicien Marceau	Creezy
1970	Michel Tournier	Le Roi des Aulnes
1971	Jacques Laurent	Les Bêtises
1972	Jean Carrière	L'Epervier de Maheux
1973	Jacques Chessex	L'Ogre
1974	Pascal Lainé	La Dentellière
1975	Emile Ajar (*Romain Gary*)	La Vie devant soi
1976	Patrick Grainville	Les Flamboyants
1977	Didier Decoin	John l'enfer

1978	Patrick Modiano	Rue des boutiques obscures
1979	Antonine Maillet	Pélagie-la-charrette
1980	Yves Navarre	Le Jardin d'acclimatation
1981	Lucien Bodard	Anne Marie
1982	D. Fernandez	Dans la main de l'Ange
1983	Frédérick Tristan	Les égarés
1984	Marguerite Duras	L'Amant
1985	Yann Queffelec	Les Noces barbares
1986	Michel Host	Valet de nuit
1987	Tahar ben Jelloun	La Nuit sacrée
1988	Erik Orsenna	L'Exposition coloniale
1989	Jean Vautrin	Un grand pas vers le Bon Dieu
1990	Jean Rouaud	Les Champs d'honneur
1991	Pierre Combescot	Les Filles du Calvaire
1992	Patrick Chamoiseau	Texaco
1993	Amin Maalouf	Le Rocher de Tanios
1994	D. Van Cauwelaert	Un Aller simple
1995	Andreï Makine	Le Testament français
1996	Pascale Roze	Le Chasseur Zéro
1997	Patrick Rambaud	La Bataille
1998	Paule Constant	Confidence pour confidence
1999	Jean Echenoz	Je m'en vais
2000	Jean-Jacques Schuhl	Ingrid Caven
2001	J. C. Rufin	Rouge Brésil
2002	Pascal Quignard	Les Ombres errantes
2003	J. P. Amette	La Maîtresse de Brecht
2004	Laurent Gaudé	Le soleil des Scorta
2005	François Weyergans	Trois jours chez ma mère
2006	Jonathan Littel	Les Bienveillantes
2007	Gilles Leroy	Alabama Song
2008	Atiq Rahimi	Syngué sabour. Pierre de patience.
2009	Marie NDiaye	Trois femmes puissantes
2010	Michel Houellebecq	La Carte et le territoire
2011	Alexis Jenni	L'Art français de la guerre
2012	Jérôme Ferrari	Le sermon sur la chute de Rome
2013	Pierre Lemaitre	Au revoir là-haut
2014	Lydie Salvayre	Pas pleurer
2015	Mathias Énard	Boussole

Femina

In the 'Prix Femina', there are today three distinct categories: 'Prix Femina', 'Prix Femina Essai', 'Prix Femina Étranger'. Only the first category is here listed.

1904	Myriam Harry	La Conquête de Jérusalem
1905	**Romain Rolland**	**Jean-Christophe**
1906	André Corthis	Gemmes et moires
1907	Colette Yver	Princesses de science
1908	**Edouard Estaunié**	**La Vie secrète**
1909	**Edmond Jaloux**	**Le reste est silence**
1910	**Marguerite Audoux**	**Marie-Claire**
1911	Louis de Robert	Le Roman du malade
1912	Jacques Morel	Feuilles mortes
1913	Camille Marbo	La Statue voilée
1914–1916: *not awarded*		
1917	René Milan	L'Odyssée d'un transport torpillé
1918	Henri Bachelin	Le Serviteur
1919	Roland Dorgelès	Les Croix de bois
1920	Edmond Gojon	Le Jardin des dieux
1921	Raymond Escholier	Cantegril
1922	Jacques de Lacretelle	Silbermann
1923	Jeanne Galzy	Les Allongés
1924	Charles Derennes	Le Bestiaire sentimental
1925	Joseph Delteil	Jeanne d'Arc
1926	Charles Silvestre	Prodige du coeur
1927	Marie Le Franc	Grand-Louis l'innocent
1928	Dominique Dunois	Georgette Garou
1929	Georges Bernanos	La Joie
1930	Marc Chadourne	Cécile de la Folie
1931	A. de Saint-Exupéry	Vol de nuit
1932	Ramon Fernandez	Le Pari
1933	G. Fauconnier	Claude
1934	Robert Francis	Le Bateau-refuge
1935	Claude Silve	Bénédiction
1936	Louise Hervieu	Sangs
1937	Raymonde Vincent	Campagne
1938	Félix de Chazournes	Caroline ou le Départ pour les îles
1939	Paul Vialar	La Rose de la mer
1940–1903: *not awarded*		
1944	*awarded to the Editions de Minuit*	
1945	Anne-Marie Monnet	Le Chemin du soleil
1946	Michel Robida	Le Temps de la longue patience
1947	Gabrielle Roy	Bonheur d'occasion
1948	Emmanuel Roblès	Les Hauteurs de la ville
1949	Maria Le Hardouin	La Dame de coeur

1950	Serge Groussard	La Femme sans passé
1951	Anne de Tourville	Jobadao
1952	Dominique Rolin	Le Souffle
1953	Zoé Oldenbourg	La Pierre angulaire
1954	Gabriel Veraldi	La Machine humaine
1955	André Dhôtel	Le pays où l'on n'arrive jamais
1956	F. R. Bastide	Les Adieux
1957	Christian Mégret	Le Carrefour des solitudes
1958	F. Mallet-Joris	L'Empire céleste
1959	Bernard Privat	Au pied du mur
1960	Louise Bellocq	La Porte retombée
1961	Henri Thomas	Le Promontoire
1962	Yves Berger	Le Sud
1963	Roger Vrigny	La Nuit de Mougins
1964	Jean Blanzat	Le Faussaire
1965	Robert Pinget	Quelqu'un
1966	Irène Monesi	Nature morte devant la fenêtre
1967	Claire Etcherelli	Élise ou la Vraie vie
1968	M. Yourcenar	L'Oeuvre au noir
1969	Jorge Semprun	La Deuxième mort de Ramon Mercader
1970	François Nourissier	La Crève
1971	Angelo Rinaldi	La Maison des Atlantes
1972	Roger Grenier	Ciné-roman
1973	Michel Dard	Juan Maldonne
1974	René-Victor Pilhes	L'imprécateur
1975	Claude Faraggi	Le Maître d'heure
1976	M. L. Haumont	Le Trajet
1977	Régis Debray	La neige brûle
1978	François Sonkin	Un amour de père
1979	Pierre Moinot	Le Guetteur d'ombres
1980	Jocelyne François	Joue-nous Esparla
1981	C. Hermary-Vieille	Le Grand Vizir de la nuit
1982	Anne Hébert	Les Fous de Bassan
1983	Florence Delay	Riche et légère
1984	Bertrand Visage	Tous les soleils
1985	Hector Bianciotti	Sans la miséricorde du Christ
1986	René Belletto	L'Enfer
1987	Alain Absire	L'Egal de Dieu
1988	Alexandre Jardin	Le Zèbre
1989	Sylvie Germain	Jour de colère
1990	Pierrette Fleutiaux	Nous sommes éternels
1991	Paula Jacques	Déborah et les anges dissipés
1992	Anne-Marie Garat	Aden
1993	Marc Lambron	L'Oeil du silence
1994	Olivier Rolin	Port Soudan

1995	Emmanuel Carrère	La classe de neige
1996	Geneviève Brisac	Week-end de chasse à la mère
1997	Dominique Noguez	Amour noir
1998	François Cheng	Le Dit de Tianyi
1999	Maryline Desbiolles	Anchise
2000	Camille Laurens	Dans ces bras-là
2001	Marie Ndiaye	Rosie Carpe
2002	Chantal Thomas	Les Adieux à la reine
2003	Dai Sijie	Le complexe de Di
2004	Jean-Paul Dubois	Une vie française
2005	Régis Jauffret	Asile de fous
2006	Nancy Huston	Lignes de faille
2007	Eric Fottorino	Baisers de cinéma
2008	Jean-Louis Fournier	Où on va, papa?
2009	Gwenaëlle Aubry	Personne
2010	Patrick Lapeyre	La vie est brève et le désir sans fin
2011	Simon Liberati	Jayne Mansfield 1967
2012	Patrick Deville	Peste e choléra
2013	Léonora Miano	La Saison de l'ombre
2014	Yanick Lahens	Bain de lune
2015	Christophe Boltanski	La Cache

Bagutta

The following list does not include the winners of the 'Bagutta Opera Prima' section.

1927	G. Battista Angioletti	Il giorno del Giudizio
1928	**Giovanni Comisso**	**Gente di mare**
1929	**Vincenzo Cardarelli**	**Il sole a picco**
1930	Gino Rocca	Gli ultimi furono i primi
1931	Giovanni Titta Rosa	Il varco nel muro
1932	**Leonida Répaci**	**I fratelli Rupe**
1933	Raul Radice	Vita comica di Corinna
1934	**Carlo Emilio Gadda**	**Il castello di Udine**
1935	Enrico Sacchetti	Vita di artista
1936	**Silvo Negro**	**Vaticano minore**
1937–1946: *not awarded*		
1947	Dario Ortolani	Il sole bianco
1948	P. A. Quattroni Gambini	L'onda dell'incrociatore
1949	Giulio Confalonieri	Prigionia di un artista
1950	Vitaliano Branati	Il bell'Antonio
1951	Indro Montanelli	Pantheon minore
1952	Francesco Serantini	L'osteria del gatto parlante
1953	Leonardo Borgese	Primo amore
1954	Giuseppe Marotta	Coraggio, guardiamo

1955	Alfonso Gatto	La forza degli occhi
1956	Giuseppe Lanza	Rosso sul lago
1957	Pierre Angelo Soldini	Sole e bandiere
1958	Lorenzo Montano	A passo d'uomo
1959	Italo Calvino	Racconti
1960	Enrico Emanuelli	Uno di New York
1961	Giorgio Vigolo	Le notti romane
1962	Giuseppe Dessì	Il Disertore
1963	Ottieri Ottiero	La linea gotica
1964	Tommaso Landolfi	Rien va
1965	Biagio Marin	Il non tempo del mare
1966	Manlio Cangogni	La linea del Tomori
1967	Primo Levi	Storie naturali
1968	Piero Chiara	Il Balordo
1969	Niccolò Tucci	Gli atlantici
1970	Alberto Vigevani	L'invenzione
1971	Pietro Gadda Conti	La paura
1972	Anna Banti	Je vous écris...
1973	Sergio Solmi	Meditazioni sullo scorpione
1974	Gianni Celati	Le avventure di Guizzardi
1975	Enzo Forcella	Celebrazioni di un trentennio
1976	Mario Soldati	Lo specchio inclinato
1977	Sandro Penna	Stranezze
1978	Carlo Cassola	L'uomo e il cane
1979	Mario Rigoni Stern	Storia di Tönle
1980	Giovanni Macchia	L'Angelo della notte
1981	Pietro Citati	Breve vita di Katherine Mansfield
1982	Vittorio Sereni	Il musicante di Saint-Merry
1983	Giorgio Bassani	In rima e senza
1984	Natalia Ginzburg	La famiglia Manzoni
1985	Francesca Duranti	La casa sul lago della luna
1986	Leonardo Sciascia	Cronachette
1987	Claudio Magris	Danubio
1988	Luciano Erba	Il Tranviere metafisico
1989	Luigi Meneghello	Bau sette!
1990	Fleur Jaeggy	I beati anni del castigo
1991	Livio Garzanti	La fiera navigante
1992	Giogio Bocca	Il Provinciale
1993	Giovanni Giudici	Poesie 1953–1990
1994	Alberto Arbasino	Fratelli d'Italia
1995	Daniele Del Giudice	Staccando l'ombra da terra
1996	Raffaele Baldini	Ad nota
1997	Sergio Ferrero	Gli occhi del padre
1998	Giovanni Raboni	Tutte le poesie 1951–1993

1999	Fabio Carpi	Patchwork
2000	Andrea Zanzotto	Le poesie scelte
2001	Serena Vitale	La casa di ghiaccio
2002	Roberto Calasso	La letteratura e gli dei
	Giorgio Orelli	Il collo dell'anitra
2003	Eva Cantarella	Itaca
	Michele Mari	Tutto il ferro della Tour Eiffel
	Edoardo Sanguineti	Il gatto lupesco
2004	Franco Cordero	Strane regole del S. B.
2005	Rosetta Loy	Nero è l'albero dei ricordi, azzurra l'aria
2006	Filippo Tuena	Le variazioni di Reinach
	Eugenio Borgna	L'attesa e la speranza
2007	Alessandro Spina	I confini dell'ombra
2008	Andrej Longo	Dieci
	Elena Varvello	L'economia delle cose
2009	Melania Mazzucco	La lunga attesa dell'angelo
2010	Corrado Stajano	La città degli untori
2011	Andrea Bajani	Ogni promessa
2012	Gianfranco Calligarich	Privati abissi
	Giovanni Mariotti	Il bene viene dai morti
2013	Antonella Tarpino	Spaesati. Luoghi dell'Italia in abbandono tra memoria e futuro
2014	Maurizio Cucchi	Malaspina
	Valerio Magrelli	Geologia di un padre
2015	Sandro Veronesi	Terre rare

Viareggio

The 'Premio letterario Viareggio-Répaci' is currently awarded in four different categories: 'Opera prima', 'Narrativa', 'Poesia', 'Saggistica'. A further 'Premio Internazionale Viareggio-Versilia' is aimed at the promotion of social progress and international peace. Although no distinctions were made between poetry and prose in the first decades of the prize, in the following list, where relevant, only the winners of the 'Narrativa' section have been included.

1930	Anselmo Bucci	Il pittore volante
	Lorenzo Viani	**Ritorno alla patria**
1931	**Corrado Tumiati**	**I tetti rossi**
1932	Antonio Foschini	Le avventure di Villon
1933	**Achille Campanile**	**Cantilena all'angolo della strada**
1934	Raffaele Calzini	Segantini, romanzo della montagna
1935	Mario Massa	Un uomo solo
	Stefano Landi	Il muro di casa
1936	Riccardo Bacchelli	Il rabdomante
1937	Guelfo Civinini	Trattoria di paese
1938	Vittorio G. Rossi	Oceano

	Enrico Pea	La maremmana
1939	**Maria Bellonci**	**Lucrezia Borgia**
	Arnaldi Frateili	Clara fra i lupi
	Orio Vergani	Passo profondo
1940–1945: *not awarded*		
1946	Silvio Micheli	Pane duro
	Umberto Saba	Il canzoniere
1947	Antonio Gramsci	Lettere dal carcere
1948	Aldo Palazzeschi	I fratelli Cuccoli
	Elsa Morante	Menzogna e sortilegio
1949	Carlo A. Jemolo	Stato e Chiesa in Italia negli ultimi cento anni
1950	Francisco Jovine	Le terre del sacramento
	Carlo Bernari	Speranzella
1951	Domenico Rea	Gesù fate luce
1952	Tommaso Fiore	Un popolo di formiche
1953	Carlo E. Gadda	Novelle dal ducato in fiamme
1954	Rocco Scotellaro	È fatto giorno
1955	Vasco Pratolini	Metello
1956	Carlo Levi	Le parole sono pietre
	Gianna Manzini	La Sparviera
1957	Italo Calvino	Il barone rampante
	Arturo Tofanelli	L'uomo d'oro
	Natalia Ginzburg	Valentino
1958	Ernesto De Martino	Morte e pianto rituale nel mondo antico
1959	Marino Moretti	Tutte le novelle
1960	G. B. Angioletti	I grandi ospiti
1961	Alberto Moravia	La noia
1962	Giorgio Bassani	Il giardino dei Finzi Contini
1963	Antonio Delfini	Racconti
1964	Giuseppe Berto	Il male oscuro
1965	Goffredo Parise	Il Padrone
1966	Alfonso Gatto	La storia delle vittime
1967	Raffaello Brignetti	Il gabbiano azzurro
1968	Libero Bigiaretti	La controfigura
1969	Fulvio Tomizza	L'albero dei sogni
1970	Nello Saito	Dentro e fuori
1971	Ugo Attardi	L'erede selvaggio
1972	Romano Bilenchi	Il bottone di Stalingrado
1973	Achille Campanile	Manuale di conversazione
1974	Clotilde Marghieri	Amati enigmi
1975	Paolo Volponi	Il sipario ducale
1976	Mario Tobino	La bella degli specchi
1977	Davide Lajolo	Veder l'erba dalla parte delle radici

1978	Antonio Altomonte	Dopo il presidente
1979	Giorgio Manganelli	Centuria
1980	Stefano Terra	Le porte di ferro
1981	Enzo Siciliano	La principessa e l'antiquario
1982	Primo Levi	Se non ora, quando?
1983	Giuliana Morandini	Caffè specchi
1984	Gina Lagorio	Tosca dei gatti
1985	Manlio Cancogni	Quella strana felicità
1986	Marisa Volpi	Il maestro della betulla
1987	Mario Spinella	Lettera da Kupjansk
1988	Rosetta Loy	Le strade di polvere
1989	Salvatore Mannuzzu	Procedure
1990	Luisa Adorno	Arco di luminara
1991	A. De Benedetti	Se la vita non è vita
1992	Luigi Malerba	Le pietre volanti
1993	Alessandro Baricco	Oceano mare
1994	Antonio Tabucchi	Sostiene Pereira
1995	Maurizio Maggiani	Il coraggio del pettirosso
1996	Ermanno Rea	Mistero napoletano
1997	Claudio Piersanti	Luisa e il silenzio
1998	Giorgio Pressburger	La neve e la colpa
1999	Ernesto Franco	Vite senza fine
2000	Giorgio Van Straten	Il mio nome a memoria
	Sandro Veronesi	La forza del passato
2001	Nicolò Ammaniti	Io non ho paura
2002	Jaeggy Fleur	Proletarka
2003	Giuseppe Montesano	Di questa vita menzognera
2004	Edoardo Albinati	Svenimenti
2005	Raffaele La Capria	L'estero quotidiano
2006	Gianni Celati	Vite pascolanti
2007	Filippo Tuena	Ultimo parallelo
2008	Francesca Sanvitale	L'inizio è in autunno
2009	Edith Bruck	Quanta stella c'è nel cielo
2010	Nicola Lagioia	Riportando tutto a casa
2011	Alessandro Mari	Troppa umana speranza
2012	Nicola Gardini	Le parole perdute di Amelia Lynd
2013	Paolo Di Stefano	Giallo d'Avola
2014	Francesco Pecoraro	La vita in tempo di pace
2015	Antonio Scurati	Il tempo migliore della nostra vita

Premio Planeta

Since 1974, a prize for second place is awarded. It amounts today to 150,000 euro. The following list only includes first prize winners.

1952	Juan José Mira	En la noche no hay caminos
1953	Santiago Lorén	Una casa con goteras
1954	**Ana María Matute**	**Pequeño teatro**
1955	Antonio Prieto	Tres pisadas de hombre
1956	Carmen Kurtz	El desconocido
1957	Emilio Romero	La paz empieza nunca
1958	F. Bermúdez de Castro	Pasos sin huellas
1959	Andrés Bosch	La noche
1960	Tomás Salvador	El atentado
1961	Torcuato Luca de Tena	La mujer de otro
1962	Angel Vázquez	Se enciende y se apaga una luz
1963	**Luis Romero**	**El cacique**
1964	Concha Alós	Las hogueras
1965	Rodrigo Rubio	Equipaje de amor para la tierra
1966	Marta Portal	A tientas y a ciegas
1967	Angel María de Lera	Las últimas banderas
1968	Manuel Ferrand	Con la noche a cuestas
1969	**Ramón J. Sender**	**En la vida de Ignacio Morel**
1970	Marcos Aguinis	La cruz invertida
1971	Josep María Gironella	Condenados a vivir
1972	Jesús Zarate-póstumo	La cárcel
1973	Carlos Rojas	Azaña
1974	Xavier Benguerel	Icaria, Icaria...
1975	**Mercedes Salisachs**	**La gangrena**
1976	Jesús Torbado	En el día de hoy
1977	**Jorge Semprún**	**Autobiografía de Federico Sánchez**
1978	**Juan Marsé**	**La muchacha de las bragas de oro**
1979	Manuel V. Montalbán	Los mares del sur
1980	Antonio Larreta	Volavérunt
1981	Cristóbal Zaragoza	Y Dios en la última playa
1982	Jesús Fernández Santos	Jaque a la Dama
1983	José Luis Olaizola	La guerra del general Escobar
1984	Francisco G. Ledesma	Crónica sentimental en rojo
1985	Juan A. Vallejo-Nájera	Yo, el rey
1986	Terenci Moix	No digas que fue un sueño
1987	Juan Eslava Galán	En busca del Unicornio
1988	Gonzalo T. Ballester	Filomeno, a mi pesar
1989	Soledad Puértolas	Queda la noche
1990	Antonio Gala	El manuscrito carmesí
1991	Antonio Muñoz Molina	El jinete polaco
1992	Fernando Sánchez Dragó	La prueba del laberinto

1993	Mario Vargas Llosa	Lituma en los Andes
1994	Camilo José Cela	La cruz de San Andrés
1995	Fernando G. Delgado	La mirada del otro
1996	Fernando Schwartz	El desencuentro
1997	Juan Manuel de Prada	La tempestad
1998	Carmen Posadas	Pequeñas infamias
1999	Espido Freire	Melocotones helados
2000	Maruja Torres	Mientras vivimos
2001	Rosa Regás	La canción de Dorotea
2002	Alfredo Bryce Echenique	El huerto de mi amada
2003	Antonio Skármete	El baile de la victoria
2004	Lucía Etxebarria	Un milagro en equilibrio
2005	Maria de la Pau Janer	Pasiones romanas
2006	Álvaro Pombo	La fortuna de Matilda Turpin
2007	Juan José Millás	El mundo
2008	Fernando Savater	La Hermandad de la Buena Suerte
2009	Ángeles Caso	Contra el viento
2010	Eduardo Mendoza	Riña de gatos
2011	Javier Moro	El imperio eres tú
2012	Lorenzo Silva	La marca del meridiano
2013	Clara Sánchez	El cielo ha vuelto
2014	Jorge Zepeda Patterson	Milena o el fémur más bello del mundo
2015	Alicia Giménez Bartlett	Hombres desnudos

Premio Nadal

1944	**Carmen Laforet**	**Nada**
1945	José Félix Tapia	La luna ha entrado en casa
1946	**José María Gironella**	**Un hombre**
1947	**Miguel Delibes**	**La sombra del ciprés es alargada**
1948	Sebastián Juan Arbó	Sobre las piedras grises
1949	Jose Suárez Carreño	Las últimas horas
1950	Elena Quiroga	Viento norte
1951	**Luis Romero**	**La noria**
1952	Dolores Medio Estrada	Nosotros, los Rivero
1953	Luisa Forrellad	Siempre en capilla
1954	Francisco Alcántara	La muerte sienta bien a Villalobos
1955	**Rafael Sánchez Ferlosio**	**El Jarama**
1956	José Luis Martín Descalzo	La frontera de Dios
1957	Carmen Martín Gaite	Entre visillos
1958	José Vidal Cadellans	No era de los nuestros
1959	Ana María Matute	Primera memoria
1960	**Ramiro Pinilla**	**Ciegas hormigas**
1961	Juan Antonio Payno	El curso

1962	José María Mendiola	Muerte por fusilamiento
1963	Manuel Mejía Vallejo	El día señalado
1964	Alfonso Martínez Garrido	El miedo y la esperanza
1965	**Eduardo C. Calderón**	**El buen salvaje**
1966	Vicente Soto	La zancada
1967	José María Sanjuán	Réquiem por todos nosotros
1968	Alvaro Cunqueiro	El hombre que se parecía a Orestes
1969	Francisco García Pavón	Las hermanas coloradas
1970	Jesús Fdez. Santos	Libro de las memorias de las cosas
1971	José María Requena	El cuajarón
1972	José María Carrascal	Groovy
1973	J. A. García Blázquez	El rito
1974	Luis Gasulla	Culminación de Montoya
1975	Francisco Umbral	Las ninfas
1976	Raúl Guerra Garrido	Lectura insólita de El Capital
1977	José Asenjo Sedano	Conversación sobre la guerra
1978	Germán Sánchez Espeso	Narciso
1979	Carlos Rojas	El ingenioso hidalgo Federico García Lorca
1980	Juan Ramón Zaragoza	Concerto grosso
1981	Carmen Gómez Ojea	Cantiga de aguero
1982	Fernando Arrabal	La torre herida por un rayo
1983	Salvador García Aguilar	Regocijo en el hombre
1984	José L. de Tomás García	La otra orilla de la droga
1985	Pau Faner	Flor de sal
1986	Manuel Vicent	Balada de Caín
1987	Juan José Saer	La ocasión
1988	Juan Pedro Aparicio	Retratos de ambigú
1989	*not awarded*	
1990	Juan José Millás	La soledad era esto
1991	Alfredo Conde Cid	Los otros días
1992	Alejandro Gándara	Ciegas esperanzas
1993	Rafael Argullol	La razón del mal
1994	Rosa Regás	Azul
1995	Ignacio C. Hernández	Cruzar el Danubio
1996	Pedro Maestre	Matando dinosaurios con tirachinas
1997	Carlos Cañeque	Quién
1998	Lucía Etxebarría	Beatriz y los cuerpos celestes
1999	Gustavo Martín Garzo	Las historias de Marta y Fernando
2000	Lorenzo Silva	El alquimista
2001	Fernando Marías	El niño de los coroneles
2002	Angela Vallvey	Los estados carenciales
2003	Andrés Trapiello	Los amigos del crimen perfecto
2004	Antonio Soler	El camino de los ingleses
2005	Pedro Zarraluki	Un encargo difícil

2006	Eduardo Lago	Llámame Brooklyn
2007	Felipe Benítez Reyes	Mercado de espejismos
2008	Francisco Casavella	Lo que sé de los vampiros
2009	Maruja Torres	Esperadme en el cielo
2010	Clara Sánchez	Lo que esconde tu nombre
2011	Alicia Giménez Bartlett	Donde nadie te encuentre
2012	Álvaro Pombo	El temblor del héroe
2013	Sergio Vila-Sanjuán Robert	Estaba en el aire
2014	Carmen Amoraga	La vida era eso
2015	José C. Vales	Cabaret Biarritz

INDEX

Académie Goncourt 26
  see also Prix Goncourt
Aguinis, Marcos, *La cruz invertida* 143, 147 n. 140
Agustí Peypoch, Ignacio 116
Albertini, Luigi 76
Aldecoa, Ignacio, *El furor y la sangre* 126
Anderson, Benedict 24 n. 39, 63
Aristeion prize 4, 23 n. 30
Aristotle, *Poetics* 55 n. 98
  Aristotelean philosophy 45
  see also mimesis
art:
  function of 100–102
  references to 83–90
Audoux, Marguerite, *Marie-Claire* 29, 52 n. 19, 22, 29 & 46
author:
  concept of 102–106
  and diegesis 76–83, 90–96, 113, 127–129, 135–141
  function of 18–20, 57–59, 90–102
autobiography, *see* biography

Bachelli, Riccardo 8
Bagutta, *see* Premio Bagutta
Barthes, Roland 100, 122–23, 136
  see also sign
Bell, Clive, *Art* 105, 112 n. 191
Bellonci:
  Bellonci, Goffredo 3, 23 n. 23, 92
  Bellonci, Maria 3, 22 n. 19, 92, 111 n. 144
  Lucrezia Borgia 8, 92, 93
  Il premio Strega 3, 22 n. 19
  see also Premio Strega
Belfond, Pierre, *La deliberation* 23 n. 26
Bergson, Henri Louis 30, 52 n. 34 & 35, 98, 104, 112 n. 187
  Essai sur les données immediates de la conscience 30, 52 n. 35
  Le rire 112 n. 187
biography:
  autobiography, genre 87, 90–95, 111 n. 147 & 153
  and literary prizes criticism 3, 4
  see also Goncourt
Blanchot, Maurice, *The Space of Literature* 111 n. 167 & 173
Bloch, Ernst 25 n. 60 & 61, 41, 48, 50, 54 n. 81 & 86, 55 n. 110, 112, 118 & 123, 98, 105, 106 n. 4, 109 n. 82, 111 n. 171, 112 n. 197, 144 n. 1

A Philosophy of the Future 111 n. 171
The Utopian Function of Art and Literature 25 n. 60
  see also utopia
Boura, Olivier, *Un siècle de Goncourt* 3, 22 n. 16, 23 n. 36
  see also Prix Goncourt
Bourdieu, Pierre 22 n. 6
  Le marché des biens symboliques 22 n. 6
  Les règles de l'art. Genèse et structure du champ littéraire 22 n. 6
Bueno, Gustavo, *El mito de la cultura* 118, 144 n. 16

Caballero Calderón, Eduardo, *El buen salvaje* 117, 123, 127, 145 n. 40, 146 n. 64, 69 & 72
Campanile, Achille, *Cantilena all'angolo della strada* 77, 78, 92, 108 n. 62
Cardarelli, Vincenzo 69, 78, 81, 82, 92, 107–10
  Appendice di prosa 69
  Il sole a picco 65, 67, 68, 80, 64
Carocci, Alberto 65
Cela, Camilo José 126, 131, 144 n. 12
censorship 6, 8, 23 n. 37, 120, 124, 24 n. 43
Champeau, Geneviève, *Les Enjeux du réalisme dans le roman sous le Franquisme* 121, 131–32, 145 n. 27, 146 n. 82
Cicognani, Bruno, *L'età favolosa* 8
Civinini, Guelfo 77
classicism 66–67
cognition:
  sciences of 10–12
  theory of 10–21
Cohen, Anthony Paul, *The Symbolic Construction of Community* 53 n. 62, 73, 96, 106 n. 18, 107 n. 39 & 47, 108 n. 66, 111 n. 165
Colantuoni, Alberto 64
Collingwood, Robin G., *Principles of Art* 55 n. 114, 105, 112 n. 195
colonialism 9, 24 n. 46, 28, 32, 66
  see also Le Bris and Rouaud
Comisso, Giovanni 7, 80, 82, 92, 110 n. 110
  Cina Giappone 80
  Gente di mare 82
community (symbolic) 73
Corradini, Enrico 63

Delibes, Miguel 21 n. 4, 117, 126, 135, 144 n. 12, 146 n. 73, 78, 81, 90, 96 & 103, 147 n. 128
  Cinco horas con Mario 126

La sombra del ciprés es alargada 117, 126, 137, 140, 142, 146 n. 73
Durkheim, Emile 25 n. 58

Edwards, Derek 25 n. 63, 65, 114, 144 n. 2, 145 n. 19
Epicurus, *Letter to Herodotus* 60, 106 n. 9
Estaunié, Edouard, *La Vie secrète* 28, 29, 52 n. 6, 9, 24 & 28

Farrère, Claude, *Les Civilisés* 28, 31, 52 n. 5, 10, 15 & 18, 53 n. 42
Fascism:
   ideology and culture 5–8, 16, 19, 56, 63, 68, 80, 86–87, 118
   resources 23 n. 37, 24 n. 40, 43 & 44, 107 n. 23 & 38, 108 n. 52, 110 n. 122
   see also mental illness
Fernández Santos, Jesús, *Los bravos* 126
Ferres, Antonio, *La piquet* 126
Foschini, Antonio, *L'avventura di Villon* 8
Fracchia, Umberto 64
Franci, Adolfo 64
Franco, Francisco, *see* Francoism
Francoism 7, 16, 21, 25 n. 66, 113–122, 132, 139, 144, 145 n. 27

Gadda, Carlo Emilio 66, 67, 78, 80, 86, 92, 93, 95, 107 n. 44, 109 n. 92, 111 n. 143, 146 & 162
   Il castello di Udine 66, 78, 92, 107 n. 44
   Le meraviglie d'Italia 80
García Hortelano, Juan, *El jarama* 126, 131
genre 58, 79, 93–94, 116
Giron de Velasco, José Antonio, *see* Francoism
Gironella, José María, *Un hombre* 117, 134, 146 n. 89 & 95
Goncourt:
   Goncourt Edmond 26, 34, 39, 40
   Goncourt Jules 26, 39, 40
   see also biography; Prix Goncourt
González Hevia, Leoncio 25 n. 66, 118
González Ruano, César 117
Goodman, Nelson, *Languages of Art* 47, 48, 55 n. 102 & 108
   see also metaphor
Goytisolo, Juan, *Señas de identidad* 121, 124, 126, 131
Grand Prix de Littérature de l'Académie Française 40
Grand Prix du Roman de l'Académie Française 40
Grosso, Alfonso, *La zanza* 126
Guelbenzu, José María, *El Mercurio* 126

Halliwell, Stephen, *The Aesthetics of Mimesis: Ancient Texts and Modern Problems* 45, 55 n. 99
   see also mimesis
Heidegger, Martin 40, 54 n. 78, 61, 105, 106 n. 17, 112 n. 188
Herder, Johann Gottfried 61
Humboldt (von), Alexander 61, 96, 97 106 n. 12 & 13

Jaloux, Edmond, *Le Reste est silence* 30, 52 n. 20 & 31
James Tait Black Memorial Prize 41
journalism:
   Italian journalism 1890–1930: 58, 63, 72, 76–83, 93, 104, 109 n. 105
   literary prizes criticism: 1, 3, 14, 21 n. 4, 124

Lacan, Jacques, *Le Stade du miroir* 10, 17, 18, 44, 50, 51, 55 n. 122, 73, 99
Laforet, Carmen, *Nada* 3, 22 n. 21, 117, 126, 146 n. 66
Lakoff, George and Mark Johnson, *Metaphors We Live By* 48, 48, 55 n. 109 & 117
   see also metaphor
Lara, Manuel José 117
Leach, Edmund, *Culture and Communication: The Logic by which Symbols are Connected* 45, 54 n. 914, 56, 106 n. 1
Leblond, Marius-Ary, *En France* 32
Le Bris, Michel & Rouaud, Jean (eds), *Pour une littérature-monde* 24 n. 46
   see also colonialism
linguistics 1, 24 n. 49, 60
Llera (de), Luis, *La modernización cultural de España 1898–1975* 118, 145 n. 18
López Pacheco, Jésus, *Central eléctrica* 126
López Salinas, Armando, *La mina* 126
Lorenzo (de), Pedro, *La creación como patriotismo* 121

Man Booker Prize 22 n. 12 & 13
Manchester, Martin, *The Philosophical Foundations of Humboldt's Linguistic Doctrines* 60, 106 n. 12 & 13
Marsé, Juan, *La muchacha de las bragas de oro* 135, 146 n. 68, 77, 79, 94, 100, 102, 147 n. 106, 125, 130, 135
Martín Descalzo, José Luis, *La frontera de Dios* 117
Martín Gaite, Carmen, *Entre visillios* 117
Martínez Cachero, José María, *La novela española entre 1936 y el fin de siglo* 115, 122, 125, 144 n. 6 & 13, 145 n. 24, 29, 48 & 53
Masoliver, Juan Ramón 117
Matute, Ana María 117, 146 n. 76, 88, 93 & 104, 147 n. 108, 121, 127 & 137
   Pequeño teatro 117, 132, 133, 137, 140, 142, 146 n. 76
   Primera memoria 117
Mejía Vallejo, Manuel, *El día señalado* 117
mental illness:
   representation of 87–91
   see also Fascism; Tumiati
Merleau-Ponty, Maurice, *Phenomenology of Perception* 45, 55 n. 95, 57, 73–75, 98, 104, 106 n. 2, 107 n. 20, 108 n. 67, 109 n. 77 & 79, 112 n. 185, 134, 146 n. 97
metafiction 21, 113, 115, 126, 131
metaphor:
   exemplificatory metaphor 47–48, 101
   function (of) in literary competitions 15–20, 44–50, 55 n. 109, 56, 101, 106 n. 19

in texts 28–29, 34, 36, 67, 71, 78, 88, 90, 99
see also Goodman; Lakoff and Johnson; utopia
mimesis:
   in Ancient Greece 103
   and structuralism 45–47, 55 n. 99
   see also Aristotle; Halliwell; realism
Mira, Juan José, *En la noche no hay caminos* 117
Monelli, Paolo 64
Moravia, Alberto, *L'amore coniugale* 21 n. 4
Moselly, Emile, *Terres Lorraines* 34
Mussolini, Benito, *see* Fascism

Nadal Gaya, Eugenio, *Ciudades en España* 116
naturalism 47, 125
Nau, John Antoine, *Force Ennemie* 26, 32
Negro, Silvio 80, 109 n. 105

Pea, Enrico 7, 77, 84, 92, 109 n. 88, 110 n. 118
   L'Arca di Noè: racconti, memorie, elzeviri 77, 109 n. 88
   La maremmana 7, 77
Peirce, Charles Sanders 25 n. 59
Perfetti, Francesco, *Il nazionalismo italiano dalle origini alla fusione col Fascismo* 63, 107 n. 23, 25, 29, 31 & 33
Pergaud, Louis, *De Goupil à Margot: histoires de bêtes* 28, 29, 33, 52 n. 3, 7, 11, 16 & 25, 53 n. 51
Pinilla, Ramiro, *Las ciegas hormigas* 125, 126, 143, 145 n. 52 & 54, 147 n. 138
Plato 55 n. 96 & 113, 60
   Cratylus 60
   platonic philosophy 45, 49, 50
   The Republic 55 n. 96
Pombo, Álvaro, *La fortuna de Matilda Turpin* 2, 22 n. 11
portrait 69, 83, 86–87, 91–94, 108 n. 55
Premi de les Lletres Catalanes Ramon Llull 117
Premi Sèrie Negra 117
Premio Azorín 117
Premio Bagutta:
   history of 5, 7, 8, 23 n. 31 & 32, 41, 63–65
   resources on 3, 22 n. 20, 23 n. 32, 107 n. 34
   winners of 7, 66, 78, 80, 82
Premio de novela Fernando Lara 117
Premio Don Quijote 116
Premio Enrique Larreta 116
Premio Eugenio Nadal:
   history of 16, 116, 117, 124
   resources on 3, 22 n. 21
   winners of 117, 125, 126
Premio Fastenrath 116
Premio Femina (Spain) 116
Premio Fundación March 116
Premio Internacional de Primera Novela 116
Premio José Antonio Primo de Rivera 116
Premio Lecturas 116
Premio letterario Viareggio Répaci:
   history of 3, 5, 7, 16, 41, 64, 84

   resources on 23 n. 21, 107 n. 35
   winners of 7, 8, 21 n. 4, 71, 77, 78, 80, 81, 87, 92
Premio Menorca 116
Premio Miguel de Cervantes 116
Premio Miguel de Unamuno 116
Premio Planeta:
   history of 116–17
   resources on 22 n. 11, 144 n. 12
   winners of 2, 21 n. 4
Premio Strega 3, 22 n. 19, 92
   see also Bellonci
Premio Valencia 116
Prezzolini, Giuseppe 62
Prix Femina:
   history of 5, 9, 16, 26, 27, 40
   resources on 52 n. 2
   winners of 27, 28, 30, 31
Prix Goncourt:
   history of 2, 4–6, 9, 16, 26, 27, 30, 33, 34, 37, 39, 40, 43, 46, 63, 150
   resources 3, 6
   winners of 2, 21 n. 4, 22 n. 16, 17 & 18, 27, 28, 31, 33, 34
   see also Boura; Goncourt
Prix Interallié 41
Prix Renaudot 5, 9, 23 n. 34, 38, 39, 41

realism 21, 47, 113, 121–126, 131, 145 n. 27
   see also mimesis
Répaci Leonida 3, 5, 23 n. 31, 64, 107 n. 35
Roccatagliata Ceccardi, Ceccardo 84
Rojas, Carlos 117
Romero, Luis 117, 122, 139, 145 n. 31, 33, 37 & 46, 146 n. 91, 147 n. 105, 110, 115 & 133
   El Cacique 117, 122, 136, 137, 139, 145 n. 31, 147 n. 111
   La noria 117, 133, 137, 138
Rorty, Richard, *Contingency, Irony and Solidarity* 140, 141, 147 n. 129
Rossi, Vittorio, *Oceano* 7

Sacchetti, Enrico, *Vita d'artista* 7
Salisachs, Mercedes, *La gangrena* 117, 147 n. 124 & 126
Salsa, Carlo 64
Salvador, Tomás, *El atentado* 117
Sánchez Ferlosio, Rafael, *El Jarama* 117, 131, 146 n. 71 & 80
Santos, Luis Martín, *Tiempo de silencio* 126
Sartre, Jean-Paul, *Qu'est-ce que la Littérature?* 32, 33, 53 n. 43, 105, 112 n. 198, 124, 125, 145 n. 47
Saussure (de), Ferdinand 14, 35, 44, 45, 60, 61, 100
   see also sign
Savignon, André, *Filles de la pluie: scènes de la vie ouessantine* 28, 29, 34, 52 n. 4, 8, 13 & 27
Savinio, Alberto, *Ascolta il tuo cuore, città* 80
self-consciousness 95, 126, 131

Semprún, Jorge, *Autobiografía de Federico Sánchez* 123, 127, 128, 131, 145 n. 38, 43 & 45, 146 n. 63, 70 & 86
Sender, Jamón José, *En la vida de Ignacio Morel* 117, 128, 146 n. 67
sign 14, 25 n. 59, 35, 48, 61, 96, 100–102
  see also Barthes; Saussure
Soler, Bartolomé 117
Stockwell, Peter, *Cognitive Poetics: An Introduction* 11, 21 n. 2, 24 n. 49 & 56, 55 n. 101, 148, 149, 151 n. 1
Suárez Carreño, José, *Las últimas horas* 117, 126

Talon-Hugon, Carole 54 n. 85, 55 n. 120, 112 n. 182, 120, 145 n. 20
Teixidor, Joan 116
Tena (de), Torcuato Luca, *La mujer de otro* 117
Tharaud, Jean and Jérôme, *Dingley, l'illustre écrivain* 32
travel 19, 56–57, 66, 72, 76–90, 94, 102, 104
Tumiati, Corrado, *Tetti Rossi* 8, 78, 87, 91, 109 n. 93, 110 n. 127–139, 111 n. 141
  see also mental illness; utopia

utopia:
  and culture 48, 51, 104, 113, 119, 122
  ontological function 1, 17–19, 41–44, 48, 97–98, 115, 150
  resources 21 n. 1, 151 n. 2
  and time 18–19, 37, 42–44, 57–59, 97–98
  traditional view of 83, 91
  see also Bloch; metaphor; Tumiati

value:
  artistic 8, 16, 41, 85, 103, 132
  monetary 2, 14
  semiotic, *see* sign
Vellani Marchi, Mario 64
Verga, Giovanni, *I Malavoglia* 125, 126
Vergani, Orio 5, 22 n. 20, 64, 107 n. 34
Viani, Lorenzo 8, 24 n. 41, 81, 84, 86, 87, 88, 92, 107 n. 42
  Ritorno alla patria 8, 87
  Gli ubriachi 87
Viareggio, *see* Premio letterario Viareggio Répaci
Visconti, Luchino, *La terra trema* 125

Weltanschauung 11, 56, 59, 72
Wittgenstein, Ludwig 134, 135, 141, 146 n. 98

www.ingramcontent.com/pod-product-compliance
Lightning Source LLC
LaVergne TN
LVHW061252060426
835507LV00017B/2026